T0372355

Security Officers and Supervisors

Security Officers and Supervisors: 150 Things You Should Know presents an array of relevant topics, including addressing "Tips of the Trade" on how to manage a team of professionals and serve as an effective supervisor. This includes both keeping management informed of decisions, aligning policy, procedure, and training with business objectives and hiring and managing a team of professionals to maintain the continuity of operations and a safe, secure environment. There are many factors involved in managing a department and workforce and the book uses a handy-reference format to present the salient information, both concrete knowledge and the softer skills, required for managers to motivate individuals and lead teams to pull in the same direction.

Short, easy-to-read chapters include lists of relevant definitions, some do's and don'ts, best practices, emerging trends, and well as example case studies based on the authors' professional experience. The primary goal is to provide a foundation for readers to identify, comprehend, and apply management concepts and security principles in their own environments so that readers will be readily prepared to troubleshoot problems and overcome challenges.

Key Features:

- Outlines how best to work with other departments to advocate for your team and create a prosperous, successful environment.
- Identifies the essential components to being a recognized leader and manager, detailing important keys to success.
- Offers tips to remain current on key technologies, emerging challenges, and personal development in order to foster growth and improve management skills.

Building and leading a trusted team that can set and achieve clearly outlined objectives begins with leadership. *Security Officers and Supervisors: 150 Things You Should Know* outlines those principles and traits required for professionals to succeed when promoted (though, more often than not, thrust!) into a security supervisory role.

Lawrence J. Fennelly, CSSM, CPOI is an internationally recognized authority on crime prevention, security planning and analysis, and the study of how environmental factors (Crime Prevention Though Environmental Design, CPTED), physical hardware, alarms, lighting, site design, management practices, litigation consultants, security policies and procedures, and guard management contribute to criminal victimization. Lawrence is a frequent presenter at the annual ASIS International (GSX) Seminar. He was the recipient of the prestigious President's Award by ASIS International in 2015.

Marianna A. Perry, MS, CPP is a Certified Protection Professional (CPP) through ASIS International and has 35+ years of progressive experience in law enforcement, physical security, safety, and loss control. Marianna received her BA degree from Bellarmine University and her Master's degree from Eastern Kentucky University. She is a safety and security consultant and is a frequent presenter at the annual ASIS International (GSX) Seminar. Marianna is a former trooper and detective with the Kentucky State Police and was previously the Director of the National Crime Prevention Institute (NCPI) at the University of Louisville.

Security Officers and Supervisors

150 Things You Should Know

Lawrence J. Fennelly and Marianna A. Perry

CRC Press is an imprint of the
Taylor & Francis Group, an **informa** business

First edition published 2025
by CRC Press
2385 NW Executive Center Drive, Suite 320, Boca Raton FL 33431

and by CRC Press
4 Park Square, Milton Park, Abingdon, Oxon, OX14 4RN

CRC Press is an imprint of Taylor & Francis Group, LLC

ISBN: 978-1-032-51534-2 (hbk)
ISBN: 978-1-032-51526-7 (pbk)
ISBN: 978-1-003-40271-8 (ebk)

DOI: 10.4324/9781003402718

Typeset in Garamond
by SPi Technologies India Pvt Ltd (Straive)

We dedicate this book to Sandi Davies for all of her hard work to raise the level of professionalism for security officers through educational and certification programs.

Sandi became the Executive Director of the International Foundation for Protection Officers (IFPO) in 1991 and the organization has professionally certified over 160,000 security officers in 50 countries.

In September 2023, Sandi received the Outstanding Security Performance Award (OSPA) Career Achievement Award at the ASIS International Annual Global Security Exchange (GSX). Additionally, in 2016, Sandi won the Karen Marquez Award for the book *Women in the Security Profession: A Practical Guide for Career Development.*

Thank you

The authors would also like to thank Rick C. Mathews for his editing expertise.

Contents

PART 2 SECURITY SUPERVISORS AND MANAGERS

Foreword

Security officers play a vital, yet unappreciated role in our society. They protect us everywhere – at work, at play, at school, in the hospital, and while shopping. Security officers protect us almost everywhere we go.

In recognition of their service, International Security Officer Recognition Day is on July 24th every year.

Any initiative that provides recognition to security officers should be seriously considered. Officers are unseen, looked past, and forgotten by the public at large. A recent search of movies which positively depict security officers uncovered a grand total of two. With over 400 films made per year in the United States and Canada, this is an incredibly small number.

There are, however, efforts underway to recognize security officers. ASIS International, the International Foundation for Protection Officers (IFPO) as well as the Anti-Terrorism Accreditation Board (ATAB) have endorsed the "Thin Purple Line" initiated by Tom Conley with the Conley Group, Inc. which is similar to the "Thin Blue Line" in law enforcement. It provides acknowledgment and recognition of the role that security officers play in protecting our society.

Allied Universal® employees established a GoFundMe to assist the family of a fallen team member and other Maui-based coworkers with costs resulting from the 2023 wildfires and devastating aftermath. All security service providers should follow suit.

Security officers need to hone their skills as much as possible to help them more effectively protect the people they serve. It also aids in career advancement because only those who have mastered the skills at their current position will be promoted. It's up to security managers to supervise to motivate and coach their subordinates.

Professional investigative skills are integral and will enhance relations with law enforcement and other government entities.

Skill development is also a necessity for the safety of the officer as well as those he/she protects.

Poor tactics lead to tragedy. Unfortunately, assaults upon and murders of security officers are widespread. In the United Kingdom, there are efforts underway to compile data regarding assaults. In the United States, the firm, *Private Officer*, has collected information on security officers murdered on-duty. The data is staggering.

Within a few months, there were two days in which three security officers were murdered while on-duty in the United States.

Always be safe. Before knowing how to protect, security officers need to know **WHY** to protect. They need to understand protective concepts so they can apply them. The *WAECUP Theory* developed by Bottom and Kostanoski is foundational. It postulates that loss is caused by waste, accident, error, crime, and unethical/unprofessional practices. The enterprise security risk management model championed by ASIS International builds upon WAECUP. It also parallels the all-hazards approach used in emergency management.

The old boxing saying, "You get hit with the punches you don't see" is spot-on in the business of protection. As risks become more dynamic, it will become even more so in the future.

Professional organizations are important to security officers and supervisors. Organizations provide networking opportunities, professional development, certification, and often discounts. ASIS International and the International Foundation for Protection Officers (IFPO) offer memberships worldwide. In the United Kingdom, there is the Guild of Security Industry Professionals as well as the Security Industry Federation. Networking is important to keep abreast of new laws, industry trends, etc. Being in a professional organization provides this opportunity. Membership also enables security officers to have a unified voice which may be the most important reason to belong to a security organization.

Chris A. Hertig, CPP, CPOI

Chris Hertig has been an advocate of security education and training for over 40 years. Widely published and an active member of professional organizations, he is both a Certified Protection Professional (CPP) and Certified Protection Officer Instructor (CPOI).

1

SECURITY OFFICERS

Chapter 1

Being a Security Officer Is NOT an Easy Job

A security officer is responsible for protecting property and individuals and deterring theft, vandalism, and terrorism. Terrorism? Yes, the security officer must constantly be vigilant. They are watching for suspicious people or activities, and when something does happen, the security officer is usually the first on the scene. Security officers often have to confront individuals who are criminals, whether they are armed with a weapon or not. By doing this, they are placing themselves in danger for the job they are paid to do. Some security officers are responsible for operating the technology at their work site. This means they are watching the property using cameras and responding to alarms. Security officers are responsible for enforcing their employer's property rules and procedures. Unfortunately, many times, this is not an easy task.

Another troubling issue for security officers is that the wages are low, and many contracts are awarded to the "lowest bidder" without considering the job the security officer is expected to do. According to the Bureau of Labor Statistics, in 2019, the median salary for a security officer was $29,710 per year. The median hourly wage for a security officer in 2019 was $14.29 per hour.[1] This brings us to the issue of training. It is critical that training be ongoing so officers can maintain their skills. They have to be well versed in criminal law, search and seizure, unlawful detention, and de-escalation techniques. At each location where a security officer works, they have to be knowledgeable of the "post orders" of the location and any specific duties their employer expects. Security officers must be adequately supervised and have access to help when they need it. Security officers have to know the proper procedures to follow for the employees, visitors, contractors, and vendors of the employer. Training that includes professionalism, good personal hygiene, and grooming is also sometimes necessary. The uniform of a security officer should be the appropriate size and should

DOI: 10.4324/9781003402718-2

be clean and pressed. Shoes or boots should be appropriate for working conditions and should be clean and in good repair. The employer should furnish any personal protective equipment (PPE) required for the security officer to wear. Security officers have to interact with the public courteously and professionally, but have to be prepared to address any dangerous or emergency situation that may arise. Specific training is required if the security officer is issued lethal or nonlethal weapons. The minimum educational requirement for an officer is generally high school or the equivalent. At this level, unfortunately, many security officers may not have the maturity level, communication skills, or adequate training to effectively perform the duties their position requires. The security officer's employer should encourage and facilitate professional certifications in the security industry, such as the Certified Protection Officer (CPO) through the International Foundation for Protection Officers (IFPO) or the CPP (Certified Protection Professional) through ASIS International. These certifications and other industry certification programs will ensure the security officer has a certain degree of knowledge, will make them more of an asset to their employer, and, at the same time, move the security industry to a more professional level. A physical fitness program is a must for the security officer that is serious about their job. Officers need to look sharp in their uniform to be a security professional.

Security officers have to be available 24/7. The employer's people and property must be protected nights, weekends, and holidays – sometimes when others are not working. Officers must maintain either paper or electronic activity logs of all activity that occurred during their shift. This information will be passed on to the security officer on the incoming shift. A security officer must be able to communicate professionally verbally and in writing professionally professionally. They may be called on to testify in court for criminal activity that they witnessed. Unfortunately, security officers have to deal with mentally ill, angry, aggressive, or dangerous individuals. All in all, it's a risky job. Security officers often have to escort terminated employees or trespassers off the property and deal with unruly individuals while, at the same time, keeping themselves and others around them safe.

Licensing and training requirements for security officers vary from country to country and across different states in the United States. There is no standardization of requirements.

The COVID-19 pandemic changed the duties that may be required of/security officers. Some security officers were required to enforce "social distancing," the wearing of face masks, and taking the temperature of each individual before they were allowed access to the property.

Note

1 Occupational Outlook Handbook – Security Guards and Gaming Surveillance Officers. Retrieved on June 23, 2020 from: https://www.bls.gov/ooh/protective-service/security-guards.htm

Chapter 2

Professionalism

What Does Being "Professional" Mean?

Professionalism is defined by the *Merriam-Webster Dictionary* as "the skill, good judgment, and polite behavior that is expected from a person who is trained to do a job well."[1]

Below, the acronym **PROFESSIONAL** outlines the attributes of a professional[2]:

P – Precise, exact, and detailed
R – Responsive to clients and the public
O – Objective in thought, and free of prejudice and preconceived notions
F – Factual in all reporting processes and honest
E – Ethical
S – Sincere about doing the best job possible
S – Striving for perfection by constantly trying to improve one's job performance
I – Informed about events and trends within one's profession
O – Observant of people and the work environment
N – Neat and orderly in dress and work
A – Accommodating and helpful to others
L – Loyal to one's employer, clients, and profession

This topic begins with the word **"Professional"** for a reason. At a recent ASIS International GSX (Global Security Exchange) Annual Security Conference, we heard quite a few discussions about professional dress and the fact that the bar has slipped or, in some cases, has completely fallen. Right or wrong, others often make decisions about our capabilities and knowledge by the "way we look" or, in other words, the way we dress. Look at "N" in the above acronym: **N – neat and orderly in dress and work.** Why is this important? The answer is simple: because you're a "security professional." The author of the acronym above goes on to say,

DOI: 10.4324/9781003402718-3

"Deportment: How one carries oneself, bearing, outward manifestation of attitude, and image."

Let's talk more about appearance. When we took over one particular account, we had a security officer with holes in both elbows of his black sweater and his pants were too long. We had a supervisor immediately obtain a new uniform for him – from head to toe.

At another account, the security officer working the midnight shift was wearing a "doo-rag" on his head. Another officer at a different location didn't have his uniform shirt tucked in his pants.

Most people will bend or break the rules if they can get away with it. As a security manager or supervisor, it is your job to see that your staff are properly wearing the assigned uniform. They will respect you for it. If someone "looks" professional, it is likely that they will also "act" professional. This is the way to change organizational culture.

A few things to bear in mind about deportment are

- Dress should be neat, precise, and conservative.
- Shoes should match belt.
- No purses or large bags for women.
- Socks should always match the pants and cover the calf.
- Conservative ties, properly tied; silk is a good choice of material.
- Jewelry worn judiciously.
- "Less is more," with makeup and cologne.
- Uniforms should be worn "uniformly." All officers should have the same placement of insignia and equipment.

If the information above doesn't apply to you, then you're already a PROFESSIONAL.

Congratulations and possibly you need to mentor others about appropriate dress.

Notes

1 http://www.merriam-webster.com/dictionary/professionalism

2 The Professional Protection Officer, IFPO, Elsevier Publishers, 2010, p. 571.

Chapter 3

The Mission of a Security Officer

The mission of a security officer is to protect company assets – people, property, and information – and to limit the opportunity for a crime to occur by being proactive, visible, and consistent. Even though many times the job may be routine, be aware that complacency may lead to a loss to the company.

Regardless of the specific, routine, day-to-day duties listed in the post orders, the primary task is protecting life and property. This includes not only the client and their employees, but also visitors, contractors, and vendors that may be on site.

DOI: 10.4324/9781003402718-4

Chapter 4

The Role of the Security Officer

Uniforms demonstrate consistency and authority within an organization. Security officers are often the first people visitors to a facility or organization encounter; therefore, employers see the need for their officers to be professionally attired. However, security officers should not rely only on their uniforms to maintain a professional image; they must also ensure that every facet of their being projects a positive public image, including their demeanor and how they interact with people.

Uniforms not only allow a protection officer to obtain the community's respect but also provide a foundation for a protection/security officer's self-respect. According to Sennewald (1985, p. 66), "Issuing or permitting the use of shabby uniforms.... takes away from a man's sense of pride. High standards for uniforms, on the other hand, automatically instill self-pride, and hence, self-respect" (Bupp & Bietsch 2008).

 DOI: 10.4324/9781003402718-5

Chapter 5

Post Orders

All personnel must read, understand, adhere to, and perform their duties to these standards. All forms of direction must be consistent with the written policy and procedures. Specific post orders shall be adhered to when the post orders conflict with the general orders.

Arrival/Departure of Post

1. Inspect all post equipment to ensure it is operational.
2. Inspect the post for damage to equipment and property.
3. Test the walk-through magnetometer and hand-held magnetometer (if applicable).
4. Check the post for cleanliness and perform any post maintenance required to maintain a safe and presentable work area.
5. Account for all post keys.
6. Ask the officer you are relieving if there is any important information to pass on.
7. Ensure all necessary post paperwork and forms are available.
8. Locate and review the post orders.
9. Report any post discrepancies to a supervisor immediately; do not wait until a break or shift change.
10. Upon completing post checks and assuming duties, report to your immediate supervisor that you have assumed your post and its conditions.

The following are NOT allowed on any post for either use or storage:

- Televisions, except those installed by the client, which are part of the security information network.

DOI: 10.4324/9781003402718-6

- Personal computers, radios, digital music devices, compact disc/tape players (with or without earphones or earbuds).
- Cell phones/pagers/personal data assistants (PDAs, i.e., palm pilots and organizers): While personal cell phones may be carried on your person, they are not to be used on post! If you do not have access to a two-way radio or client-provided telephone on your post, notify a supervisor as soon as you are able to. Using personal cell phones for nonsecurity/nonemergency-related matters is prohibited.
- Hand-carried bags of all types (purses, backpacks, etc.) are to be kept out of the sight of the general public;
- Reading material (only work-related material is allowed), religious materials, newspapers, magazines, schoolbooks, etc., are not authorized unless approved by the client or employer.
- Food items and beverages (exception: water in clear bottles or cups). Eating on post is prohibited unless the post orders for that specific post state otherwise.
- If you do not report unauthorized items to your supervisor, you will be held accountable for them being on the post you assumed.
- Security personnel will not tamper with telephones, office equipment, or any personal effects in client offices, common areas, or other designated workspaces.
- Equipment or items that present a safety hazard may be handled when safe to do so.

Post Safety Hazards

Any safety hazard must be reported to your supervisor immediately. Safety hazards include but are not limited to exposed equipment wires, blocked exits or other life safety concerns, damaged fans/heaters, wet surfaces, or anything that could potentially harm you or the public.

Duty Log (Pass-On Log)

A daily duty log for each post will contain a record of ALL activities, special events, unusual occurrences, and specific instructions/alerts. The log will be maintained in an electronic format on the post computer or device or in paper/pen format. The log will be kept and updated by the officer assigned to the individual post. The duty supervisor will monitor and authenticate the log. The logbook (either digital or paper) will be turned over at 2400 hours each day, and a new page/entry will commence at 0001. All entries must be complete and legible. In the absence of unusual circumstances, log entries shall be made at least once every hour to indicate post status. Officers must **indicate in the security log when they assume a post and when they are relieved or close a post.**

Preparing for Duty

- Personnel shall be physically rested before reporting to duty to ensure both mental and physical alertness during their assigned tour.
- Security officers should refrain from consuming alcoholic beverages a minimum of eight hours before scheduled duty to eliminate any residual odor or effect.
- Security officers should be cognizant that certain prescribed medications may adversely affect their ability to perform their job duties safely and effectively. Officers taking a prescribed medication must carry it in a container labeled by a licensed pharmacist or be prepared to produce the container if asked.
- Security officers should report for scheduled duty on time and in the proper uniform. Personnel are required to be on post at the assigned start time of their shift.
- The security officer will remain at their post unless instructed otherwise by a direct supervisor or until properly relieved by the authority of their security manager. If an emergency occurs, notify your direct supervisor immediately using your radio or post phone. The radio is the primary means of communication (where applicable); post telephones are secondary.

Breaks

Security officers must be aware of the time allowed for breaks and not exceed the allotted time. Once relieved for the break, the officer must report back from that break within the allotted time. Smoking and eating are allowed in designated areas only.

Officers are reminded that all policies and procedures still apply to officers on break. Security officers are to conduct themselves professionally at all times, whether actively performing security functions or while on break.

Post Protocol

If you are working at an access control post, anytime someone approaches your post location, you must stand while conducting your duties.

During peak times, all security personnel may be stationed out of their security desk (if applicable), and all personnel at access control locations will be required to stand and station themselves in a position best to carry out the specific duties of their post.

There is to be no loitering at posts by security officer personnel not currently assigned to that post. Security officers should not allow any other individuals to loiter at their post.

At no time will a security officer depart from or secure a post without being properly relieved as prescribed (exceptions for situations where an officer is placed in imminent danger, i.e., fire or building collapse).

Telephone Bomb Threat

Follow these procedures in the event a telephone bomb threat is received or reported:

- If possible, place the bomb threat information before you and refer to it when speaking with the caller. (The bomb threat information should be in the post-order book or in an electronic file; if it is not, notify your supervisor.)
- Keep the caller on the line as long as possible. Ask him/her to repeat the message. Document every word spoken by the caller.
- If the caller does not indicate the location of the bomb or the location of the possible detonation, ***ask for this information***.
- Inform the caller that the building is occupied and that the detonation of a bomb could result in death or serious injury to many innocent people.
- Pay particular attention to background noise, such as music playing, motors running, and any other noise that may provide valuable information in identifying the caller's location.
- Listen closely to the caller's voice for accents, speech impediments, male/female, or any other condition that could help identify the caller.
- After the caller hangs up, proceed with the following steps depending on the time of the call:
  - Immediately report the call to the client representative.
  - Notify local authorities (police and fire) via 911.
  - Notify your supervisor and manager immediately.

Medical Emergencies

- Ensure the medical emergency is not a diversionary tactic.
- For access control posts, access control is the primary responsibility; maintain security and control at all times.
- Immediately notify local authorities and request medical assistance.
- Administer first aid, perform CPR, and use an automated external defibrillator (AED) as necessary.
- Keep people away from the victim (crowd control).
- Assist medical personnel as necessary.
- Obtain all pertinent information for an incident report.

Fire Alarm

- Assume there is a fire until advised otherwise by an authorized official (fire personnel, police, or building facility manager).
- Call the client representative and give the location of the fire, if known.
- Access control posted officers will not require persons with "visitor only" or "temporary" badges to surrender them during evacuation. Upon returning to the building, those persons with visitor and temporary passes will be rescreened.
- Officers assigned to exterior patrols will move evacuating personnel away from the building where possible.
- All posts and patrols will stand by for special instructions.

If a security officer has any questions concerning the content of post orders or is unsure of the required duties, a supervisor or manager should be contacted immediately.

Chapter 6

Ethics and Standards of Conduct

The following standards of conduct apply to all team members. As a security officer, you are held to a higher standard of conduct and should be an example to others. Since you enforce rules and policies, it is imperative that security officers demonstrate high ethical standards. Anytime a security officer demonstrates dishonest or unethical behavior, he/she is not just harming the company, but discrediting the entire security profession.

Any member team who fails to maintain proper standards of conduct and violates any provision of the handbook interferes with orderly and efficient operations or harms the company reputation and may be subject to disciplinary action, up to and including termination.

By providing this list, it in no way restricts legal discretion to terminate the employment relationship. An employer reserves the right to determine what type of disciplinary action, including warning, suspension, or termination, may result from violating standards of conduct.

The following list is not all-inclusive but merely indicative of the types of actions considered subject to disciplinary action:

1. Theft, attempted theft, removal without proper approval, or unauthorized possession of any property, such as goods or beverages, employer property, or property of another team member or guest
2. Offensive or disruptive behavior, including fighting with or threatening team members or guests, interfering with others in the performance of their duties, or acting in an immoral or indecent manner on employer property

DOI: 10.4324/9781003402718-7

3. Harassing, threatening, intimidating, coercing, or unlawfully discriminating against others
4. Violation of the Harassment-Free Workplace Policy and/or failure to report any such incident
5. Using abusive language or profanity
6. Discourtesy or inappropriate conduct with guests or team members
7. Possessing, consuming, distributing, or being under the influence of alcohol or any controlled substance on the premises
8. Unauthorized possession of weapons, firearms, explosives, or other dangerous devices on employer premises
9. Willful or negligent failure to abide by employer safety rules and practices or conduct that creates a safety hazard
10. Horseplay or other actions that endanger others – employer, guest, contractor, or vendor property or work
11. Intentional or negligent conduct resulting in destruction of or damage to employer property or supplies or the property of another team member, customer, visitor, or guest
12. Causing general dissension and unrest among team members, including malicious gossip or false accusations
13. Defamation of the character of another team member or guest, including a false, malicious statement
14. Disloyalty to employer, including but not limited to slandering your employer or acting in such a manner that could damage the reputation or result in a loss of trust in the employer
15. Sleeping, loafing, loitering on the job, or leaving assigned work area without authorization
16. Solicitation of gratuities
17. Dishonesty regarding any aspect of employment with the employer
18. Misappropriation of employer funds: failure to handle funds as per employer guidelines
19. Criminal acts
20. Breach of security
21. Vandalism
22. Unauthorized distribution or solicitation during working time.
23. Falsifying, altering, or making material omissions in any employer document or record, including but not limited to employment application, timecards, guest checks, and tip reports
24. Unauthorized discussion or removal of employer confidential information (including payroll information or information contained in personnel records)
25. Unauthorized disclosure, discussion, or removal of employer trade secrets or other confidential or proprietary information.
26. Insubordination (refusal to carry out reasonable instructions)

27. Failure to follow instructions
28. Refusal to work a reasonable amount of overtime when required
29. Unexcused absence on scheduled workdays without an approved reason and/or without proper notification
30. Excessive absenteeism
31. Excessive tardiness
32. Excessive break time
33. Loss of a controlled key
34. Unauthorized duplication of employer keys
35. Poor job performance, including unsatisfactory attitude that detracts from job performance or the efficient operation of the employer
36. Willful or negligent neglect of duty causing waste or defective work
37. Gambling on premises
38. Soliciting or collecting funds on property without written permission of your supervisor
39. Smoking, vaping, or chewing gum in restricted areas
40. Being in an unauthorized or non-designated work or guest area during scheduled work period or on your days off, without your supervisor's specific authorization
41. Receiving visitors or conducting personal business during working time
42. Failure to abide by meal/break periods
43. Taking meal/break periods in an unauthorized area
44. Failure to report on the job accident or injury
45. Falsely stating or making claims or injury
46. Failure to meet performance standards
47. Failure to follow grooming and appearance standards
48. Violation of employer rules or procedures, including those outlined in the handbook and elsewhere, or violation of departmental policies and procedures
49. Patronizing the guest facilities without the permission of your supervisor
50. Release of operational information of any type or scope to the media or other individuals without direct authorization from your supervisor

If a security officer is discharged in violation of any of the above items, they may not be permitted on employer property for a period of one year from the date of termination.

Chapter 7

What Authority or Power Do I Have as a Security Officer?

One of the leading questions asked by security professionals nationwide is "What power do I really have?"

In all fairness, this is a legitimate question and the answer to that question is not always simplistic! Typically, a security officer is hired to do one thing: protect people, assets, and information.

> We deter, observe, and report. Sounds simple enough, right? In most cases, the answer is 'Yes!' But what happens when it's not that simple? What happens when someone is not cooperative with us? What happens when a crime is committed in our presence? What can we legally do about it?

What power do I have as a security officer? The answer is none. Dial 911 for the police.

Yes, your presence is a deterrent. Yes, you observe and report to your supervisor, the facilities manager, and the police if necessary. Yes, you get involved in issues, medical assistance, fires, assaults, thefts, slips and falls, alarms going off, and bomb threats, and you observe and report. When a crime is committed in your presence, you call the police! Dial 911. You may be a material witness to the incident.

These are all legitimate procedures that all security/protection officers must discuss with their supervisors. Everyone needs to be on the same page. For example,

DOI: 10.4324/9781003402718-8

if there is a breach of peace in the parking lot, be courteous and professionally tell them to leave. Suppose they don't, call the police.

Keep in mind that if you use a cellphone to call for law enforcement assistance, you may not reach the closest law enforcement agency. If this happens, request to be transferred to the local police for a faster response. Why do we address this issue? It's simple. We don't want you to be sued in civil court for a mistake that could have been prevented.

> Question what is considered a 'public offense or breach of peace.' Take the time to talk to a local attorney and your local sheriff/police departments. In the military, everything was done with the motto of 'CYA' (Cover your …)! Most police departments are more than willing (and even eager) to assist security officers in a quest of gaining expertise. Plus, it helps you gain rapport with your local department.

Security/protection officers should be well–trained about powers of arrest, how to de-escalate situations, and what kind of force can be used in different situations. When it comes to the use of force, "*the security officer is no different from a private citizen – they are confined to using only the force that is necessary to repel an attack or to protect their life or someone else's life.*"

Eddie Sorrells, CPP, PCI, PSP, chief operating officer and general counsel for DSI Security Services, states in an article in *Security Management* magazine.[1] He goes on to say, "*responding to nonlethal situations with lethal force can be a problem, and of course security officers can be criminally liable for that and even civilly liable.*"[2]

Security/protection officers should be trained about the legal ramifications of detaining someone they believe has committed an offense. There is a legal risk when a security officer detains or attempts to detain someone without having the authority of a police officer. It's important to remember that, in most situations, security/protection officers have the same authority as private citizens to detain someone for a crime they believe has been committed.

The bottom line is, as a security officer, you need to do your research! Find out what your state/local law allows/prohibits and follow it. Even if your state law grants you a specific amount of leniency, that doesn't mean that there aren't city/town/county laws that restrict your authority. Security licensing agencies may be able to provide more information on this topic. You must ensure that you comply with the laws of the specific jurisdiction where you are working.

Security companies that provide contract security and those that employ proprietary security need to ensure that their security/protection officers are well–trained and that they understand their job duties, their limitations, and their rights. Security/protection officers must be well trained, understand how to effectively respond to different situations, and know the scope of their authority. Be diligent, be safe, and be a *security professional*!

In conclusion, here is a simple question. "What two things are required to make a legal arrest?" The answer to that question is "generally" ***probable cause*** **and the** ***authority*** **to make the arrest.**

Notes

1 Legal Challenges Limit Security Officers' Authority. Retrieved on March 3, 2020 from: https://www.asisonline.org/security-management-magazine/articles/2019/09/legal-challenges-limit-security-officers-authority/

2 Ibid

Chapter 8

Public Relations and the Art of Service: 10 Points

The Art of Service

What is your favorite restaurant, and why? Last week, we went to a restaurant in the neighborhood and were greeted at the door by the owner. We introduced everyone who was with us. The meal was great! The service was good, and the owner stopped by the table to confirm we all were happy with the service and the meal. We know all of us have had bad experiences at restaurants. But, if it's a bad experience, do you go back? NO! Think about this as you perform your job duties.

A security officer may work at the front desk. He/she answers the phone and greets people as they enter and exit the building. Everyone – employees, customers, clients, vendors, visitors, and contractors – judge the appearance and professionalism of the officer at the desk. They make a mental note of how they have been treated, whether it is good or bad, even though they may never comment. Consider the following points:

1. **Command presence**:
   You are the authority figure. If someone has a question or a problem, they come to you for the solution. Was the response handled appropriately and promptly?
2. **Communicating with angry people**:
   Ensure that you reply in a clear but soft tone of voice. If an individual is upset or angry, your objective is first to help and understand why they are upset and then to calm them down and find a solution to the problem.

DOI: 10.4324/9781003402718-9

3. **Communication**:
   Listen very closely when someone speaks to you. Listen especially closely to pleas for help and assistance and give clear directions on how you will handle the situation and solve the problem. Remember that you communicate not only verbally but also with your body language, expressions, and tone of voice.
4. **Dealing with mentally ill persons**:
   Seek to understand the situation. Express your concern and offer support. Be protective of the person and others in the area. Everyone's safety is your number one concern. Control the situation with clear decisions and empathy. Communicate clearly with authorities when necessary.
5. **Defusing conflict and crisis**:
   Approach and assess the situation before taking action. Ask questions if you don't understand something, but don't accuse the individual. Offer alternatives to diffuse the altercation. Listen with empathy, but be mindful of your own emotions. Sometimes, dealing with the conflicts of others can trigger your own anxiety level. Use active listening techniques and keep your tone and body language neutral. Be supportive of the individual, but understand the difference between aggressive and assertive language.
6. **Engaging the customer**:
   Always respond both verbally and with body language in a professional manner. Greet people and respond when they speak to you, even if only to smile and nod. If you work at a location with regular customers or employees, greet them by name.
7. **Lobby or reception area security**:
   The public's safety in the lobby or reception area is your primary responsibility. Practice situational awareness and know your post orders to respond quickly and appropriately. Pay attention to what is going on around you. Sometimes, you may hold doors open, pick up dropped items, help visitors find an office in a building directory, or give directions. This is all part of providing good customer service. If part of your job responsibility includes inspecting identification or personal items, do this respectfully.
8. **Lost children**:
   Treat a lost child as directed in the emergency procedures of the post orders. Communicate clearly with the parent/guardian as well as the law enforcement.
9. **Tactical communications**:
   Be professional when communicating, whether by phone, intercom, radio, or in person. This means following protocol – no profanity and no slang words. Don't dismiss anyone's complaint or concern. Be a problem solver!
10. **Public relations**:
    A large part of the job of a security officer is customer service or public relations. You can be polite and friendly while still keeping people and property safe. You must have good verbal and interpersonal communication skills and be able to communicate clearly to avoid misunderstandings.

Chapter 9

Productivity: Six Reports

Security officers are a significant investment for the management of any organization – for either contract or proprietary security. The following reports will help optimize the effectiveness of security/protection officers, enhance the facility's security, and protect the overall security investment.

We are proposing six monthly reports that will show that all physical security components have been checked and are working properly or that they have been reported as nonoperational and have been or are being repaired.

Report #1: Check every light indoors and outdoors – including stairwells, garages, and parking lots. Be observant for nonoperational lighting and lights that are "on" during the daytime. Determine if sensors or timers for lighting need to be replaced or repaired. Additionally, identify dark areas where additional lighting may be needed. Use a digital light meter to determine appropriate lighting levels for different areas of the property. Ensure that all emergency lighting is operational.

Report #2: Check and test all emergency notification alerts, elevator emergency call buttons, mass notification systems, intercoms, and door entry security systems to ensure all are working properly.

Report #3: Check to ensure that every fire extinguisher and automated external defibrillator (AED) is in place. Ensure all fire extinguishers are fully charged and in the "green" position and that the vendor has inspected each fire extinguisher within the last year. Check each AED to ensure that it is showing in the green "ready" position and that AED pads are not expired.

Report #4: Check each camera in the video surveillance system to ensure each is positioned correctly and is recording and that the network video recorder/server is working properly. Ensure that picture quality is adequate. Cameras

DOI: 10.4324/9781003402718-10

in outdoor environments may need a regular cleaning schedule to ensure the lenses are clear for high-quality images.

Report #5: Check and test all sensors of the intrusion detection system – magnetic switches on doors/windows, glass-break sensors, passive infrared (PIR) sensors, interior microwave sensors, and video motion detectors, including dual technology devices. This may require two individuals with radio or cell phone contact.

Report #6: Battery-operated door alarms may need to be physically tested (opened) to ensure they are operational. Some door hardware/software may have low-battery indicators. Notification alarms, such as those for doors propped open and annunciation alarms controlling access to vulnerable areas, need to be checked.

Tim Crowe stated in *Analysis of Space*, "How well does the space support its current or intended use? Is there physiological support for the intended function? Is there physiological control of the property, especially problem areas?"[1]

Make these six steps part of your security master plan.

Note

1 Crime Prevention through Environmental Design Training Manual; Tim Crowe, NCPI, 1994.

Chapter 10

Respect

When security officers treat employees, visitors, vendors, and contractors with respect, they not only improve morale but also help everyone treat one another with respect. Managers and supervisors often set the entire tone for the workplace with their behavior, but a security officer may be the first contact someone has with a company. When they respect those individuals they interact with, the entire company can change. Employees, visitors, vendors, and contractors feel appreciated and apply themselves to their jobs.

DOI: 10.4324/9781003402718-11

Chapter 11

How to Be Successful

Be friendly, yet polite and professional. Acknowledge people. Arrive on time and ready to work. Be a sharp dresser and wear your clean, pressed uniform correctly and proudly. Greet the client's/employer's employees and visitors as they enter and exit the building or area. Follow established policies and procedures and perform security duties effectively and efficiently.

If there is a complaint or a request, listen carefully. Acknowledge the issue, assess the situation, affirm understanding, and discuss solutions. While a security officer will not be able to satisfy everyone, remember it is how a situation is handled and how the individual "felt" about the way it was handled that will be remembered.

Many companies in the United States today are overmanaged and under-led and need to develop their capacity to exercise leadership. Successful corporations don't wait for leaders to come along. They actively seek out people with leadership potential and expose them to career experiences designed to develop that potential. With careful selection, nurturing, and encouragement, many people can play important leadership roles in an organization. Strong leadership with weak management is not a good situation and, in many cases, is much worse than strong management with weak leadership. The challenge is to combine strong leadership and strong management and use each to balance the other.

DOI: 10.4324/9781003402718-12

Chapter 12

Are You Feeling Overwhelmed?*

Are you feeling overwhelmed by your obligations at work and home? If so, you are in good company. The majority of US employees complain that they feel overwhelmed, according to surveys. As supervisors and managers focus on security officer productivity, we have heard this complaint hundreds of times from managers and leaders.

Productivity has many aspects. When thinking about your productivity, you need first to understand your priorities. Then, you can plan your schedule to focus on your top priorities and downplay your routine functions. Daily, you need to reduce the amount of time you spend on getting through the small stuff that clutters up your life and hone your skills at more effectively dealing with your colleagues. Both will go a long way toward helping you achieve your goals.

* Assessment: How Productive Are You? Retrieved on January 15, 2019 from: https://hbr.org/2018/08/assessment-how-productive-are-you

DOI: 10.4324/9781003402718-13

Chapter 13

Stress and Burnout

> Stress is defined as a state of mental or emotional strain caused by adverse circumstances. At one point or another, most people deal with feelings of stress.
>
> In fact, one study found that 33% of adults reported experiencing high levels of perceived stress.[1]

Stress is a fact of life in the workplace and is a normal part of every job. What makes the difference is how you choose to deal with stress. People react differently to stress because everyone has a different personality and a different set of coping skills.

Stress and burnout are possibly the biggest threats to the security industry. Long hours, "alert overload," and a perceived unfavorable opinion of business value are taking a toll on the industry. One of the reasons for this is that since security does not produce revenue, it is considered a "cost center." Security operations may negatively affect profitability and, throughout the years, have been considered a "necessary expense" of doing business. One of the ways security was explained in the retail industry years ago is that good security is defined as what you *don't* see on the monthly profit and loss (P&L) statement. Organizations tend to "forget" about security until something "bad" happens, and many times, "bad" things happen because of security officer's stress and/or burnout. It doesn't matter whether security is in-house or outsourced; burnout remains the same. Security is a profession that requires strict attention to detail and focused attention at all times. Many times, complacency will cause those working in the industry to miss important indicators or clues that there is a security issue. Accountability is a key factor. It doesn't matter whether or not security personnel have limited security experience or are seasoned veterans; accountability in the security industry remains the same.

DOI: 10.4324/9781003402718-14

Stress is the bodily response to pressure from a situation, and there are three different types of stress[2]:

Acute stress – The most common type of stress, resulting in a "fight or flight" response where symptoms disappear after the stressor is gone.
Episodic stress – When acute stress occurs regularly and a person does not have time to recover from the stressor, this can result in a lower overall tolerance of stress and increased sensitivity to stressors.
Chronic stress – Long-term stress from situations where a person feels he/she does not have control over the outcome, potentially causing serious effects to mental and physical health.

Stress is common in the security industry. When a person encounters stress, the body produces a stress hormone to initiate a "fight or flight" response. Everyone experiences stress, but chronic stress can affect a person's mental health—especially if that person has an underlying health condition, such as anxiety, depression, or another serious health issue. Chronic stress can also have a detrimental effect on problem-solving, a skill that is critical for those working in the security industry.

Three job factors lead to stress:

1. Design of tasks
2. Management style
3. Relationships

What does stress do to your body?

- It can lead to poor health and injuries.
- More and more people are reporting high levels of stress.
- As high as 25% of people say that their job is their number one source of stress.

Burnout

- Work overload leads to burnout.
- Some people see burnout as a sign of accomplishment.
- Burnout leads to a decline in productivity.

How can you recognize the signs of stress?

- Change in moods or behavior
- Sleep disturbances or lack of sleep
- Upset stomach
- Headaches
- Trouble with relationships
- COVID-19 stress issues

What is the best way to deal with workplace stress?

- Prioritize your tasks and your stress issues.
- Take several quick mental breaks during the day.
- Watch what you eat; consider eating two or three small meals a day.
- Recognize factors that trigger a stressful situation.
- Recognize what you can and can't change.
- Monitor your reaction to stressful situations.
- Talk to someone about it.
- Consider your doctor as a first step.
- Relax and do nothing on your days off.

Look for ways to reduce the intensity of your emotional and physical reactions. Usually, stress cannot be eliminated, so you have to find a way to manage it. There is not one right or wrong way to manage stress. Only you know the best way to relieve your stress.

How to Reduce Stress in Your Life

- Determine what causes your stress.
- Recognize what you can change.
- Moderate your physical and emotional reactions to stress.
- Don't let stress force you to call in sick.

Two quick and easy ways to deal with stress are to limit your caffeine intake and steer clear of gossip at work.

It's up to you to make changes to decrease the impact of stress in your life. Sometimes, we can't change things right away. Stress has an adverse effect on your body and mind. When you're feeling stressed, take a step back and look at the big picture. Only you can take care of your health and wellness.

Suggestions for Stress Management[3]

Some suggestions to help control the stress in your life:

- Don't be afraid to take a risk.
- Turn every obstacle or problem into a creative growth experience.
- Make conscious decisions.
- Don't be afraid to make mistakes.
- Set priorities.
- If you find yourself in a rut, change your routine.
- Form a mental picture of "you" – who you would like to be and work on becoming that "you."

- Evaluate your present work or job.
- Keep the balance between too little and too much stress.
- Learn to relax.
- Don't allow criticism to stop you.
- Work toward your dream.
- Don't let things drift.
- Acknowledge your fears.
- Don't blame others.
- Don't compromise who you are.
- Do something for others.
- Arrange for privacy.
- Don't overdo a problem.
- Make timely decisions.
- Don't insist on winning.
- Be yourself.
- Don't judge yourself too sternly.
- Respect yourself.
- Don't do wrong.
- Don't wait for the sword to fall.
- Find security inside yourself.
- Be healthy.
- Take one thing at a time.
- Handle your anger before it handles you.
- Find a confidant.
- Choose your associates carefully.
- Get involved.
- Balance your work and your leisure.
- Seek the humor.
- Make your desires clear.
- Analyze your pet peeves.
- Know your stress level.
- Correct your mistakes.
- Be realistic.

Burnout in the Security Industry

Many times, security policies and procedures are unclear, not specific enough, or there is very limited training, so when security personnel complete a task or activity believing that they are operating within the scope of their job responsibilities, they find out later that they are being held accountable for a situation they were not trained to handle or a situation where they had no control over the outcome. This results in stress.

"Burnout," a term that has been frequently used as a word for this stress, anxiety, and depression, was officially recognized by the World Health Organization (WHO) in 2019 as an "occupational phenomenon," not a medical condition.[4] It is a syndrome that results from chronic workplace stress that is not successfully managed and is characterized by

- Feeling drained of energy
- Distancing oneself mentally from his/her job and/or feeling negative or cynical toward one's job
- Experiencing a reduction in one's ability to do his/her job[5]

In a research study, both managers and front-line workers stated that they felt stress from:

- Unmanageable workload
- Career stagnation
- Constant interruptions
- Toxic culture
- Dated technology

Managers felt that the primary cause of burnout was stress from an unmanageable workload, and front-line workers felt it was constant interruptions.[6]

Stress and fatigue can affect a security officer's mental and physical performance, especially if the security officers or security professionals are assigned 12-hour instead of 8-hour shifts. There is a labor shortage in the security industry – for skilled security officers as well as IT security professionals. One research study found that there are approximately 300,000 cybersecurity positions in the United States alone that are vacant.[7] This means additional work – and pressure – for those covering these positions. A global survey of 343 cybersecurity executives published in November 2017 by the Enterprise Strategy Group and the Information Systems Security Association found that almost 40% of those surveyed stated that the skills shortage was causing high rates of burnout and staff turnover.[8] The *New York Times* reported that Cybersecurity Ventures' predicted that there will be 3.5 million unfilled cybersecurity jobs globally by 2021, up from 1 million positions that were unfilled in 2014.[9]

Many times, security officers and other security professionals work double shifts because of poor scheduling or inadequate staffing. This leads to serious safety and security concerns because security officers who are tired, stressed, or generally burned out

- React more slowly than usual
- Fail to notice things going on around them
- Respond incorrectly
- Show poor logic and impaired judgment

- Are unable to concentrate
- Are less motivated
- Are more forgetful
- Have a greater tendency for taking risks
- Have reduced motor coordination
- Have slower reaction time
- Have impaired or reduced alertness
- Lose cognitive and logical reasoning skills
- Are unable to process communications[10]

Sometimes, to offset fatigue and stress, officers may rely on caffeine from energy drinks or coffee to increase their level of alertness, but these effects are short-lived and lead to accidents and possibly dangerous security situations. There is no substitute for adequate rest and time away from the job. Poor job performance is often more apparent when tasks are repetitive, such as checking IDs or logging trucks in a vehicle gate, which are common security functions.[11] If a security breach occurs because of any of these reasons, the implications could be a life-and-death situation.

If stress becomes excessive or if a person feels he/she has no control over the stressor, there can be lasting repercussions. Sometimes, stress or pressure can be beneficial and help us get through difficult situations without negative effects, but only if that stress is short term and we can return to a resting state. If the stress response persists over time, the effect can cause a permanent state of "fight or flight" and can impact both physical and mental health. Security is not the only industry that is experiencing stress and burnout. First responders such as the military, law enforcement, and healthcare providers are also facing increased pressure during their work.

One of the reasons that there is increased pressure for IT and cybersecurity professionals is that the stakes have risen dramatically. Hackers aren't just taking an individual's credit card info but are targeting power grids, hospitals, manufacturing facilities, and other critical infrastructure – all of which could have devastating repercussions. There are several reasons that IT and cybersecurity have escalating job stress – the systems are always under attack, and there is no downtime. There is no specific start time or finish time. It is a constant nonstop situation that requires a hyper-alert state for extended periods. In the cybersecurity world, the stress never ends.[12]

Chronic stress can have a negative impact on the immune, digestive, and cardiovascular systems, according to the National Institute of Mental Health (NIMH). "Some people may experience mainly digestive symptoms, while others may have headaches, sleeplessness, sadness, anger, or irritability," the NIMH said.[13] "Over time, continued strain on your body from stress may contribute to serious health problems, such as heart disease, high blood pressure, diabetes, and other illnesses, including mental disorders such as depression and anxiety."[14]

Professionals today feel the pressure of an "always on" work culture, causing stress and which may lead to burnout. In January 2020, Deloitte's Marketplace Survey of 1,000 full-time US professionals found that[15]

- 77 percent of respondents say they have experienced employee burnout at their current job.
- 91 percent of respondents stated that having an unmanageable amount of stress or frustration negatively impacts the quality of their work.
- 83 percent of respondents say burnout from work can negatively impact their personal relationships.
- 87 percent of professionals surveyed say they have passion for their current job, but 64 percent say they are frequently stressed, which goes against the myth that passionate employees are immune to stress or burnout.
- Nearly 70 percent of professionals feel their employers are not doing enough to prevent or alleviate burnout within their organization.
- 21 percent of respondents say their company offers no programs or initiatives to prevent or alleviate burnout.

Security operations professionals have an exceptionally high stress level because of ransomware, phishing and social engineering, web skimming malware, supply chain attacks, and brute-forcing and credential stuffing.[16] Unfortunately, the security industry is measured most of the time by failure – in other words, when something goes wrong. When that is coupled with an industry that has to "keep secrets" to keep the information confidential, it leads to a toxic situation that leads to higher-than-normal levels of stress and job burnout.[17]

One security incident may occur because of a simple oversight or a vulnerability that was overlooked or enabled by a failure to promptly detect malicious activity in progress. In many cases, inexperienced, stressed, or fatigued security officers make these mistakes, but the results take a toll on the entire industry. An unfortunate security incident can harm the reputation of the organization, affect customer attrition, and cost exorbitant legal fees. The Ponemon Institute for Data Center Security estimates the average cost of a breach is now close to $4 million, so the decisions being made in a security operations center may have the most effect on the organization's bottom line.[18]

The bottom line is that companies need to put emphasis on workplace culture. It's interesting to note that one in four professionals say they never or rarely take all of their vacation days. We need to consider why this is happening. Leaders set the tone for the organization, and a healthy workplace culture must exist to have competent, productive employees who can effectively combat stress so that it doesn't result in burnout. To do this, people should be at the organization's center, and communication should be a two-way street. Workers in the security industry need to feel valued for their contributions to the organization. If positive changes are to happen within an organization, change has to happen *with* the people, not *to* them.

Security is a critical industry that requires people to be "present" and in control of forces that lead to burnout and cause people to leave the industry.

Notes

1 Signs and Symptoms of Too Much Stress. Retrieved on February 11, 2022 from: https://www.healthline.com/nutrition/symptoms-of-stress
2 How to Help Prevent Employee Burnout. Retrieved on August 30, 2020 from: https://www.asisonline.org/security-management-magazine/articles/2020/06/how-to-help-prevent-employee-burnout/
3 Controlling Stress. Retrieved on February 11, 2022 from: https://www.linkedin.com/pulse/controlling-stress-richard-flint/
4 Burn-out an "Occupational Phenomenon." Retrieved on November 19, 2023 from: https://www.who.int/standards/classifications/frequently-asked-questions/burn-out-an-occupational-phenomenon
5 Study Warns Burnout Is a Major Problem for Virtually Everyone. Retrieved on August 30, 2020 from: https://totalsecurityadvisor.blr.com/emerging-issues-in-security/study-warns-burnout-is-a-major-problem-for-virtually-everyone/
6 Ibid.
7 Cybersecurity's insidious new threat: workforce stress. Retrieved on November 05, 2020 from: https://www.technologyreview.com/2018/08/07/141139/cybersecuritys-insidious-new-threat-workforce-stress/
8 Ibid.
9 Cybersecurity Talent Crunch To Create 3.5 Million Unfilled Jobs Globally By 2021. Retrieved on November 05, 2020 from: https://cybersecurityventures.com/jobs/
10 Safety Smart! Fatigue and Safety, May 2014.
11 Ibid.
12 Cybersecurity's insidious new threat: workforce stress. Retrieved on November 05, 2020 from: https://www.technologyreview.com/2018/08/07/141139/cybersecuritys-insidious-new-threat-workforce-stress/
13 I'm so Stressed Out? Retrieved on November 19, 2023 from: www.nimh.nih.gov/sites/default/files/documents/health/publications/so-stressed-out-fact-sheet/im-so-stressed-out.pdf
14 How to Help Prevent Employee Burnout. Retrieved on August 30, 2020 from: https://www.asisonline.org/security-management-magazine/articles/2020/06/how-to-help-prevent-employee-burnout/
15 Workplace Burnout Survey. Retrieved on August 31, 2020 from: https://www2.deloitte.com/us/en/pages/about-deloitte/articles/burnout-survey.html
16 5 of the Spookiest Threats Entering Your Security Operations Center. Retrieved on November 05, 2020 from: https://www.siemplify.co/blog/5-of-the-spookiest-threats-entering-your-security-operations-center/
17 Security Operations Center Burnout: A Guide for SOC Professionals. Retrieved on November 05, 2020 from: https://www.siemplify.co/burnout/
18 Ibid.

Chapter 14

The Importance of Effective Report Writing

A Brief Guide of the Dos and Don'ts

Suppose you ask any security officer. In that case, you will find most have completed a daily activity report (DAR), an incident report (IR), or an accident report (AR) in the course of conducting their duties. These reports may be submitted hand-written or in an electronic format. This is a vital responsibility of the position, yet the types of reports produced can go beyond these three examples and may vary depending on the site location. This then establishes the need to create some standard policies and procedures to help ensure uniformity.

Using strong observation skills will allow you to draft a detailed record of security, safety, and procedural issues at your site. Strong observation skills will help you collect more information in a shorter period. Better attention to detail will result in a more accurate and complete report.

Effective Writing Dos

When writing and filing any report, it is important to focus on what makes a report effective. Here are some tips that DO make a final hand-written report effective:

- DO print clearly and legibly.
- DO use dark ink, preferably black.
- DO cross out mistakes and initial them.
- DO use professional language.
- DO proofread for accuracy, especially names, dates, and times.
- DO check spelling, punctuation, and capitalization.

DOI: 10.4324/9781003402718-15

Effective Writing Don'ts

When hand-writing reports, officers should take note that there are some specific items that they should avoid:

- DON'T use sloppy handwriting – print if your cursive is illegible.
- DON'T use a pencil when writing a report.
- DON'T use liquid paper or correction tape to cover over writing mistakes.
- DON'T use slang, incomplete sentences, jargon, humor, texting language, or sarcasm.

The 4 Ws in Report Writing

As you conduct your duties, it is important when you encounter an incident that you take notes, which will aid you in completing your reports. To produce an accurate, in-depth, and proper report, you must know and understand the types of questions to ask when presented with a situation. They are called the 4 Ws. The 4 Ws are who, what, when, and where. It is important to understand that they go beyond the basic form and can change depending upon the incident or crime. To know what is best, we have provided some example questions for an incident or crime. This list is not intended to be complete, nor is every question required to be asked doing your duties.

When asking the WHO for an INCIDENT:

- WHO was involved?
- WHO are the witnesses?
- WHO reported the incident?
- WHO may have seen something before or after the incident?

When asked the WHO for a CRIME:

- WHO is the victim?
- WHO called the police?
- WHO responded to the call?
- WHO was questioned?

When asking the WHAT for an INCIDENT or CRIME:

- WHAT happened?
- WHAT was the response to what happened?
- WHAT evidence was found?

- WHAT was damaged?
- WHAT vehicles were involved (traffic crashes)?
- WHAT was stolen (robbery or theft)?

When asking the WHEN for an INCIDENT or CRIME:

- WHEN did you report it?
- WHEN did the incident occur?
- WHEN did you arrive at the scene?
- WHEN did you notify the police/emergency services? The company?

When asking the WHERE for an INCIDENT or CRIME:

- WHERE did it happen?
- WHERE was the location of the incident or crime?
- WHERE was the evidence found?
- WHERE were the items stored?

The 5 Cs in Report Writing

To further create a well-documented and thorough report, it is important to also follow the 5 Cs. They are correct, clear, concise, cohesive, and complete. The 5 Cs of writing are important and go hand-in-hand with the 4 Ws.

- **Correct** – Review the accuracy of details, plus proper spelling, grammar, and punctuation.
- **Clear** – Choose your words carefully and write legibly so that any reader can easily understand the written message.
- **Concise** – Use the fewest words to say what you need to; do not divert off-topic and avoid repetition and long, extraneous reports.
- **Cohesive** – Event should logically and chronologically flow from one point to the next and in a direct line of thought.
- **Complete** – Include all relevant information and important details to help ensure the report provides an accurate picture of events.

Opinions vs. Facts

When writing any report, strive to keep your opinions to yourself and focus on the events of the incident. It is up to law enforcement and the courts to determine the guilt or innocence of an individual in a situation and take appropriate action. When writing a report, opinions may arise from answering "how" and "why." The evidence may not support opinions, so do not draw conclusions in your reports. Factual items like names, addresses, phone numbers, or a business name are far more important than establishing fault or guilt.

When examining facts, it is fine to add in a report the relationship of one person to another, such as friends, relatives, a supervisor, or a third party. Finally, actual items, such as physical descriptions of a person, vehicle, or objects involved in the incident, are perfectly acceptable as long as you do not include opinions.

Conclusion

So, as you conduct your daily duties, remember that reports reflect you. Reports protect people, property, and officers. Accurate observations are a crucial component in writing an effective report. Keep a notebook with you at all times to help ensure your reports are detailed and accurate. Be sure that you have included and answered the 4 Ws using the 5 Cs. This is achieved through professional language, proper spelling and grammar, and legibility. Finally, report only the facts of the incident.

Chapter 15

Security Officers Who Give Life-Saving Care and Good Samaritan Laws

Introduction

Until recently, the majority of security officer positions did not require much security industry knowledge or life-saving skills. There was a lack of industry training standards, but that trend is quickly changing. Standard training for security officers includes crime prevention, situational awareness, company rules and regulations, their general duties, public relations, customer service, terrorism awareness, criminal law, search and seizure, report writing, fire prevention and suppression, etc., along with CPR cardiopulmonary resuscitation/automated external defibrillator (CPR/AED) and first aid.

With that in mind, approximately 610,000 people die of heart disease in the United States every year – that's one in every four deaths, and heart disease is the leading cause of death for both men and women.[1] About 47% of all sudden cardiac deaths occur outside a hospital.[2]

These statistics must be recognized as important arguments for the required industry training for security officers in first aid, CPR, and AED as many times security officers are the first responders on the scene. Even though their primary duties are security related, responding to *any* emergency situation is an ancillary function of security officers.

The first step any security officer should take when responding to a medical emergency is to call 911, and while he/she is waiting for EMS to arrive with advanced medical training, the security professional could be performing life-saving CPR or giving first aid and/or other industry standard life-saving techniques. In

DOI: 10.4324/9781003402718-16

certain situations, the security officer may be the only individual on site who knows how to perform CPR and operate an AED. It is critical, especially in a cardiac emergency, that someone acts quickly and decides to help save lives.

There are also ethical, legal, and cultural factors to consider that may influence decisions about when to provide CPR for someone experiencing a cardiac incident, and this is when it becomes critical for security officers to have the proper industry training.

There are sometimes early warning signs that may alert others when someone is experiencing a cardiac emergency:

- Chest pain or discomfort.
- Upper body pain or discomfort in the arms, back, neck, jaw, or upper stomach.
- Shortness of breath.
- Nausea, lightheadedness, or cold sweats.

In many of these situations, the person experiencing a cardiac emergency doesn't react to their symptoms and seek medical care. So, the cardiac emergency does not occur in a hospital setting. This is evident since almost half of cardiac deaths occur outside the hospital. An observant security officer may recognize this behavior and be prepared to intervene – by calling 911 and performing CPR. Without quick intervention, many times from a security officer performing life-saving CPR and defibrillation, death from sudden cardiac arrest is certain.

Chain of Survival[3]

The Cardiac Chain of Survival was developed in 1990 by the American Heart Association and has become the standard of care for cardiac victims. When there is a cardiac emergency, first responders are encouraged to follow the six-step sequence shown in Figure 15.1.

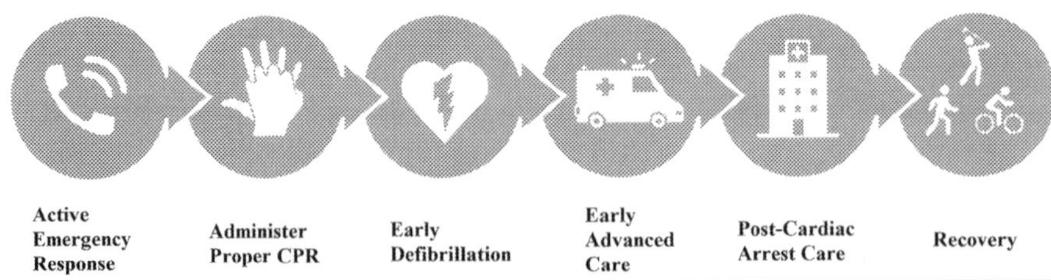

Figure 15.1 Immediate life-saving measures and responses have been shown to markedly improve outcomes and save lives.

Image used with permission and courtesy of Shutterstock.com.

First Aid

To complement CPR/AED training, first aid training will help non-medical professionals such as security officers to provide emergency care before professional first responders, such as EMS arrive. Topics covered in first aid training include:

- Asthma emergencies
- Anaphylaxis
- Burns
- Choking
- Diabetic emergencies
- External bleeding
- Environmental emergencies
- Poisoning
- Neck, head, and spinal injuries
- Stroke
- Seizure[4]

In addition to traditional first aid training, the DHS (Department of Homeland Security) endorses a national awareness campaign called, *Stop the Bleed*.[5] The goal of the *Stop the Bleed* initiative is to encourage bystanders to become trained to help in a bleeding emergency until medical responders arrive. This training is critical in an active shooter situation, a terrorist attack, or in other incidents involving mass casualties. *Stop the Bleed* is an excellent training program for security officers and it can be incorporated into existing training curricula.

Good Samaritan Laws originate from the biblical parable that provides the definition as an individual who intervenes to assist another individual without prior notion or responsibility or promise of compensation.[6] If the victim is unconscious or unresponsive, a good samaritan can help them on the grounds of implied consent. If the person is conscious and can reasonably respond, a rescuer should ask permission first.[7] The premise of the Good Samaritan Laws is to provide protection from claims of negligence for those individuals who provide care without expectation of payment. Each state in the United States has its version(s) of the Law, and federal laws also exist. Even though most Good Samaritan Laws in the United States are state laws, there is one applicable federal law involving physicians and other health-care providers – the 1998 Aviation Medical Assistance Act (AMAA). This law provides protection for good samaritans while on a flight.[8] On airplanes, the AMAA protects physicians and other health care providers who act as good samaritans on airlines registered in the United States.[9]

Other countries besides the United States have differing laws, opinions, and regulations regarding the good samaritan scenarios. Most have no legal obligation to treat. Many western countries recognize the moral duty to stop and render treatment rather than a legal requirement.[10] In the United States, all 50 states have Good

Samaritan Laws and the provisions of these laws have minor variations from state to state.[11] The concept of liability is different from country to country.

Most Good Samaritan Laws do not apply to medical professionals or career emergency responders during *on-the-job conduct*, but some extend protection to professional rescuers when they are acting in a volunteer capacity.[12]

The recent Good Samaritan Legislation addresses the current opioid crisis. Drug overdose is the leading cause of accidental death in the United States.[13] The most common drugs associated with these overdoses are opioids. Because of this, 40 states and the District of Columbia have enacted Good Samaritan Laws specific to opioid overdoses. These laws encourage both victims and witnesses to call 911 and grant them some immunity under the law. The general idea is that this targeted immunity will lead to more lives saved from opioid overdoses.

It doesn't matter whether it is a security breach, a safety issue, or a medical emergency as the public relies on security officers to be able to handle any of these situations, and those who employ security officers have a moral and ethical responsibility to ensure that they are providing well-trained first responders. Security is a proactive discipline and having security officers who are trained in CPR/AED and first aid is a part of being proactive by being prepared to respond – regardless of the emergency situation. Well-trained security officers are able to provide the best value to their employers as well as the people they protect – especially in the most critical, life and death situations.

Notes

1 Heart Disease in the United States. Retrieved on January 20, 2019 from: https://www.cdc.gov/heartdisease/facts.htm

2 CDC. State Specific Mortality from Sudden Cardiac Death: United States, 1999. *MMWR.* 2002;51(6):123–126.

3 Out-of-Hospital Chain of Survival, Retrieved on January 25, 2019 from: https://cpr.heart.org/en/resources/cpr-facts-and-stats/out-of-hospital-chain-of-survival

4 What is First Aid? Retrieved on January 18, 2019 from: https://www.redcross.org/take-a-class/first-aid/performing-first-aid/what-is-first-aid

5 Stop the Bleed. Retrieved on January 19, 2019 from: https://stopthebleed.usuhs.edu/

6 Arneau WM, Harris DM, Viera AJ. Cross-Sectional Survey of Good Samaritan Behaviour by Physicians in North Carolina. *BMJ Open.* 2016 Mar 10;6(3):e010720.

7 Good Samaritan Laws. Retrieved on March 8, 2020 from: https://www.ncbi.nlm.nih.gov/books/NBK542176/

8 Martin-Gill C, Doyle TJ, Yealy DM. In-Flight Medical Emergencies: A Review. *JAMA.* 2018 Dec 25;320(24):2580–2590.

9 Stewart PH, Agin WS, Douglas SP. What does the law say to Good Samaritans?: A review of Good Samaritan statutes in 50 states and on US airlines. *Chest.* 2013 Jun;143(6):1774–1783.

10 McQuoid-Mason DJ. When are doctors legally obliged to stop and render assistance to injured persons at road accidents? *S. Afr. Med. J.* 2016 May 08;106(6). doi: 10.7196/SAMJ.2016.v106i6.10503.
11 Adusumalli J, Benkhadra K, Murad MH. Good Samaritan Laws and Graduate Medical Education: A Tristate Survey. *Mayo Clin Proc Innov Qual Outcomes.* 2018 Dec;2(4):336–341.
12 Stewart PH, Agin WS, Douglas SP. What Does the Law Say to Good Samaritans?: A Review of Good Samaritan Statutes in 50 States and on US Airlines. Chest. 2013 Jun;143(6):1774-1783.
13 Nguyen H, Parker BR. Assessing the Effectiveness of New York's 911 Good Samaritan Law-Evidence from a Natural Experiment. *Int. J. Drug Policy.* 2018 Aug;58:149–156.

Chapter 16

"If You See Something, Say Something™"

> The US Department of Homeland Security (DHS), "If You See Something, Say Something™" Campaign, and the US Department of Justice, Nationwide Suspicious Activity Reporting (SAR) Initiative (NSI)
>
> In July 2010, the US Department of Homeland Security (DHS) launched the national 'If You See Something, Say Something™' campaign to raise public awareness of the indicators of terrorism and terrorism-related crime, as well as the importance of reporting suspicious activity to law enforcement. The campaign was originally implemented by New York City's Metropolitan Transportation Authority (MTA), which licensed the slogan's use to DHS for anti-terrorism and anti-terrorism crime efforts. DHS launched the campaign in conjunction with the US Department of Justice's Nationwide Suspicious Activity Reporting Initiative (NSI), with the goal of training state and local law enforcement to recognize behaviors and indicators of terrorism and terrorism-related crime.[1]

The goal of the DHS is to strengthen "homeland security" by increasing "hometown security." DHS encourages citizens in the private sector to form partnerships with state, local, tribal, and territorial governments to understand the importance of reporting suspicious activity to state and local law enforcement.

Partnership programs increase awareness by displaying and distributing outreach materials. Partners may include

- States, cities, and counties
- Airports and mass transit entities

DOI: 10.4324/9781003402718-17

- Sports leagues and teams
- Major sports events and entertainment venues
- Colleges and universities
- Fairs and festivals
- Private sector businesses
- Media outlets[2]

The DHS encourages everyone to work together to build a strong, secure nation. We all have a part to play in keeping ourselves and our country safe. Through collaborative partnerships, we're building a stronger "homeland" by building stronger "hometowns." Each of us is a part of a different community, and if you see something that doesn't seem right to you, say something. Informed and alert individuals and communities are essential to keep the homeland safe. "If You See Something, Say Something™" engages the public to protect our homeland through awareness, building partnerships, and outreach. For more information or to obtain outreach materials and public service announcements (PSAs) for educational purposes, visit www.dhs.gov/See-Something-Say-Something

DHS encourages businesses to be proactive, so if there is an incident or an attack, everyone will be better prepared[3]:

- Reach out and develop relationships in your community, especially with local law enforcement, and if you have a business, invite them for a tour of your facility. Establishing these relationships before an incident can help speed up the response when something happens.
- Connect with community security and preparedness organizations such as InfraGard, an FBI public–private partnership program.
- Contact the local DHS protective security advisor available to support your efforts.
- Communicate with your customers and inform them about the security measures you are taking to ensure a positive experience and maintain public safety.
- Be aware of current threats related to your geographic region.
- Develop plans, including security, emergency response, emergency communications, and business continuity plans, while considering the protection of your employees and customers, access control, video surveillance, signage, suspicious activity reporting, and parking security.
- Evaluate your security requirements and design a monitoring, surveillance, and inspection program consistent with your business operations.
- Develop evacuation and shelter-in-place plans and ensure that multiple evacuation routes are marked with appropriate signage and that rallying points are available.
- Develop and implement a security plan for computer and information systems hardware and software.

- Engage local first responders (police, fire, and medical) in all of the above efforts to ensure your efforts are in synergy with theirs.
- Provide your employees with training resources and exercise your plans often. The best-laid plans must be exercised to be effective.
- Train employees on identifying and reporting suspicious activities, active shooter scenarios, and what to do if they suspect an improvised explosive device (IED). Ensure they understand security basics, emergency response, business continuity plans, and increased awareness of potential threats.
- Test and evaluate your emergency communications plan.
- "If You See Something, Say Something™" is more than just a slogan. Call local law enforcement.
- Post details on reporting suspicious activity and encourage employees, tenants, and visitors to report suspicious behavior to property management security or local law enforcement. Things to consider include unattended vehicles; repeat visitors or outsiders who have no apparent business in nonpublic areas; abandoned parcels, suitcases, backpacks, and packages; and other unusual activities.
- Get involved with the department's "If You See Something, Say Something™" campaign.

Suspicious Behavior

Some behaviors that could be viewed as suspicious are

- Someone taking unusual interest in a particular building, parking lot, or surrounding area
- Unusual requests for information
- Suspicious activity by unauthorized persons
- Suspicious activities regarding documents
- Someone running from a car or building

Suspicious activity, such as photography, videotaping, sketching, drawing, pacing off distances from entrances, or continuously observing persons entering and exiting the facility, should be brought to the attention of the client representative and a security supervisor or manager immediately. If the person(s) leaves the area, observe the direction and means of departure. If the individual departs via motor vehicle, a complete description including color, make, model, and tag number must be recorded and given to the supervisor. If the individual departs via metro bus or subway, try to get as detailed a description as possible, even the bus number, if possible.

Contact your local law enforcement agency to report suspicious activity, but if there is an emergency situation, call 911. You will need to tell law enforcement exactly what you saw and describe any individual(s) involved, including[4]

Who or what you saw
When you saw it
Where it occurred
Why you think it's suspicious

New Jersey Bomber 2016

On September 26, 2016, Lee Parker was homeless and digging through trash with Ivan White. They are being hailed as heroes after they found a bag full of pipe bombs at the Elizabeth Train Station, moved the bag away from people, and alerted authorities. By their actions, the two men may have saved lives. Their discovery was made on the same weekend bombs went off in Manhattan's Chelsea neighborhood and Seaside Heights, New Jersey. Ahmad Khan Rahami, 28, was later arrested for those attacks following a gun battle with police.[5]

The goal of the US Department of Justice's NSI is to train state and local law enforcement to recognize suspicious behaviors and indicators of terrorism and terrorism-related crime. The NSI is a joint partnership effort of the DHS, the Federal Bureau of Investigation (FBI), and state, local, tribal, and territorial law enforcement partners to help prevent terrorism and terrorism-related crime through the gathering, documenting, processing, analyzing, and sharing of SAR information.

The "If You See Something, Say Something™" campaign works to coordinate its efforts with the NSI through the DHS Office of Intelligence and Analysis, which leads the interagency coordination for support to both the NSI and the National Network of Fusion Centers.[6] For additional information about the NSI, visit http://nsi.ncirc.gov.

A goal of the DHS mission is to ensure that the civil rights and civil liberties of individuals are not violated during security efforts, activities, and programs. The "If You See Something, Say Something™" campaign respects privacy, civil rights, and civil liberties and emphasizes behavior, not appearance, in identifying suspicious activity. Factors such as race, ethnicity, gender, national origin, religion, sexual orientation, or gender identity are not suspicious in themselves; and only suspicious behavior and situations should be reported, such as an unattended backpack/package or someone breaking into a secure area. Only reports that document behavior reasonably indicative of criminal activity associated with terrorism will be shared with federal partners.[7]

The Following Websites have Information on DHS Programs and Resources[8]

Protective security advisors proactively engage with government partners and the private sector to protect critical infrastructure. For more information or to contact your local PSA, e-mail NICC@hq.dhs.gov.

The Ready Campaign provides help with planning for businesses at http://www.ready.gov/business.

DHS active shooter resources are available at http://www.dhs.gov/active-shooter-preparedness.

"If You See Something, Say Something™" information is available at http://www.dhs.gov/see-something-say-something.

NSI information is available at https://nsi.ncirc.gov/.

AR training for private sector partners is located at https://nsi.ncirc.gov/hsptregistration/private_sector/.

Counter-IED information and resources are available at www.dhs.gov/tripwire.

Information on DHS cybersecurity programs is available at www.dhs.gov/cyber.

To find out more about the Cybersecurity Awareness Campaign, go to http://www.dhs.gov/stopthinkconnect.

For tips from the US Computer Emergency Response Team, go to https://www.us-cert.gov/ncas/tips.

InfraGard is a public–private partnership between the FBI and the private sector that represents individuals from businesses, academic institutions, state and local law enforcement, and fire and EMS agencies, as well as other participants dedicated to sharing information, education, and intelligence. For additional information, please go to

http://www.heritageemergency.org/homeland-security-starts-with-hometown-security/.

Notes

1 If You See Something, Say Something™ Partnership Guide. Retrieved on 12-30-16 from: https://www.dhs.gov/sites/default/files/publications/SeeSay-Overview508.pdf
2 Become a Partner. Retrieved 12-30-16 from: https://www.dhs.gov/see-something-say-something/become-partner
3 Tools and Resources to Help Businesses Plan, Prepare, and Protect from Attack. Retrieved 12-30-16 from: http://www.heritageemergency.org/wp-content/uploads/2016/06/Hometown-Security-Fact-Sheet-04062016-508.pdf
4 If You See Something, Say Something™. Retrieved on 12-30-16 from: https://www.dhs.gov/see-something-say-something
If You See Something, Say Something Campaign Partnership Guide. https://www.dhs.gov/sites/default/files/publications/SeeSay-Overview508.pdf
5 Homeless 'Hero' Who Found Bombs at New Jersey Train Station Gets a Home, Money. Retrieved on 01-01-17 from: http://www.insideedition.com/headlines/18892-homeless-hero-who-found-bombs-at-new-jersey-train-station-gets-a-home-money
6 The Nationwide SAR Initiative. Accessed on 01-01-17 at: http://nsi.ncirc.gov
7 If You See Something, Say Something Campaign Partnership Guide. https://www.dhs.gov/sites/default/files/publications/SeeSay-Overview508.pdf
8 DHS Tools and Resources to Help Businesses Plan, Prepare, and Protect from an Attack. Retrieved on 12-30-16 at: http://www.heritageemergency.org/wp-content/uploads/2016/06/Hometown-Security-Fact-Sheet-04062016-508.pdf

Chapter 17

Physical Security: Ten Things You Should Know

> Experts agree that technology is useless unless properly implemented with a comprehensive security strategy[1]
>
> Tim Kridel, 2022

1. There are different metal fences, but the four main types are chain link, barbed tape, barbed wire, and concertina.
2. Depending on the security application, a chain-link fence should be 9-gauge wire or heavier and 6–8 ft inches in height. The openings in the mesh should be no larger than 2 inches.
3. The two kinds of protective barriers are structural and natural.
4. Barriers are psychological deterrents geared to deter, delay, and supplement security officers.
5. Fences and/or barriers control pedestrian traffic and vehicular traffic.
6. Categories of burglary-resistant glass are Plexiglas, plastic glazing, and safety glass.
7. There are six types of basic protection available for window openings: two-track storm windows, double-locks on sash windows, double-locks on sliding glass windows and doors (charley bar and secondary lock), steel bars, mesh wire, and burglary-resistant glass.
8. The weakest point in the window is the glass. Beware that the glazing compound (putty) may be removed on Monday, and the glass may be removed and/or broken on Tuesday.

DOI: 10.4324/9781003402718-18

9. Doors come in different shapes and sizes, ranging from solid core and metal to hollow core. Some have hinges on the inside, whereas some may have hinges on the outside. Some hinges may have nonremovable hinge pins.
10. The most common door locks are double-cylinder/double-keyed deadbolt, single-cylinder/single-keyed deadbolt, and thumb latch deadbolt. Door viewers (peepholes) with a 360-degree field of view also enhance security because whoever is outside of the door can be identified before the door is opened or unlocked.

Note

1 School security & safety insert, November/December 2022, p. 6 Tim Kridel.

Chapter 18

Twenty-Five Reasons Why You Need to Obtain a Security Certification

1. Credibility.
2. Knowledge.
3. Professionalism.
4. Opportunity.
5. Increase your earning potential.
6. Long-term financial gain.
7. Acceptance in the security industry.
8. Pathway to a career in security.
9. Job security.
10. Career advancement.
11. Gives you a broader range of skills.
12. Job satisfaction.
13. Self-satisfaction.
14. Personal development.
15. An example to others.
16. Makes you more desirable to employers.
17. Enhances your communication skills.
18. Enhances your critical thinking skills.
19. Enhances your problem-solving skills.
20. Networking opportunities.
21. Makes you less likely to face unemployment.

DOI: 10.4324/9781003402718-19

22. More self-confidence.
23. Greater economic stability.
24. Helps make you a contributor to the security industry.
25. An investment in your future.

Contact ASIS International[1] and the International Foundation for Protection Officers[2] (IFPO) for certification information.

Notes

1 About Certification. Retrieved on 12-10-22 from: https://www.asisonline.org/certification/asis-board-certifications2/?utm_medium=cpc&utm_source=google&utm_campaign=asisfy22&utm_content=cert&gclid=EAIaIQobChMI-cXSjYTw-wIV9RplCh3PtQBbEAAYASAAEgK2pfD_BwE

2 Certification Programs. Retrieved on 12-10-22 from: https://ifpo.org/about-certificates-certification/

Chapter 19

Analyzing Risks

Risks for facilities can arise from the geographic location and industry-specific issues; the specific nature of the business or some incidents may be a crime of opportunity. A comprehensive risk assessment should include recommendations for addressing vulnerabilities.

Once vulnerabilities are identified, if they are not corrected, it could result in liability exposure for the company if an incident does occur.

DOI: 10.4324/9781003402718-20

Chapter 20

Master Planning of Physical Systems for Security Officers: Six Points

The phrase "master plan" is more than just an expression. It also applies to your physical security systems.

1. **Intrusion alarms**
   - What is it you intend to alarm and protect?
   - Who will monitor the system?
   - What components/sensors will be used?
   - How will this alarm fit into your overall master plan?
2. **Access control**
   - Is it needed or is it a requirement?
   - It should be a part of the property's perimeter, entry to building(s), and entry to sensitive areas.
   - Will it be standalone or part of a bigger package?
   - Consider the overall design; will it include biometrics?
   - Badge/fob/electronic control must be a part of your plan.
3. **Security surveillance systems**
   - Consider the latest technology and equipment because, in five years, it will no longer be state of the art.
   - Consider the monitoring and response and how it will be administered.

DOI: 10.4324/9781003402718-21

- High-definition, multiscreen, digital recording, interior, pan, and tilt, video analytics, – consider what this system will achieve and how it will do so and whether AI (artificial intelligence) will eventually become part of your security surveillance system.
- Plan in advance for expansion of the surveillance system.

4. **Lighting**
   - Is energy-efficient lighting (such as LED bulbs) being used?
   - Who will monitor lighting for nonoperational fixtures/bulbs?
   - How will nonoperational lighting be reported?
   - Nonoperational lights should be repaired/replaced within 24 hours.
5. **Control/server/digital storage room**
   - Consider how it is to be laid out.
   - Define the space and its usage.
   - Will the security surveillance system be monitored from this area? (insert new bullet point here) What physical security components will be used to ensure the security of the room?
6. **Customer service/security front desk**
   - Will there be screening for all employees, visitors, contractors, and vendors?
   - Is a visitor management system needed, and will temporary badges be issued?
   - Will magnetometers be used?
   - Are procedures in place if a weapon is found?
   - Will monitoring be done for contagious/infectious individuals?

Chapter 21

Security Officers and Penguins (Yes, Penguins)

Not a lot has been written about the success of penguins, but we think they have great work habits and an incredible work ethic. Penguins believe in providing excellent customer service which is based on their training. We also know they like a healthy work environment with fresh fish for lunch. Penguins prioritize their duties to achieve their goals, and they are focused on their work.

Humans can learn a lot from penguins. Have you ever watched how penguins all work together as a unit? Penguins teach their young the value of hard work and find warmth among friends. They appreciate a good snow day and always go the extra mile. This is part of what leadership is all about. Penguins also set goals, make plans for the future, and stick to the job until goals are achieved. They also tackle the hardest goals first because then the rest becomes easy.

Have you ever heard a penguin say, "NO way, that is not in my job description?" They will, however, say to other penguins, "No problem. I will take care of it now." They don't hate each other nor are they jealous of the status of others or their achievements. We have never heard a penguin use profanity or speak ill of another penguin.

Penguins like to be prepared for the workload of the next day before they go home. This way, they get a jump or a "waddle" on things. Finally, penguins don't overthink their assignments. They know what has to be done and work together because they all know they are part of the team.

How can security officers be more like penguins? For starters, security officers need to learn the proper way to communicate and understand the goals of the security department before they can provide superior service to ensure a memorable experience for their clients as well as guests. To achieve daily goals, each and every

DOI: 10.4324/9781003402718-22

security officer should be called upon to achieve excellence by the following nine points, which are the core of excellent customer service standards:

1. Maintain eye contact at all times.
2. Use and remember the guest's name.
3. Provide timely service.
4. Ask the visitor/guest about any additional needs.
5. Always give guests a prompt, friendly, and cheerful greeting.
6. Be knowledgeable and informative.
7. Be well-groomed and wear a sharp-looking uniform.
8. Take responsibility for the guest inquiries and problems.
9. Finally, thank the guest at the right moment.

Chapter 22

The Importance of Effective Communication

Communication is the virtual foundation of everything security officers do. Since security officers work so closely with the general public, they must communicate effectively and professionally.

Consider this, only 7% of a message is received through the actual words. Around 38% of the impact of a message comes through tone of voice, and 55% of the impact of a message comes through body language, so security officers need to maintain approachable body language. The following are examples of acceptable body language:

- An open posture by having your hands at your sides or clasped in front of you
- Facing the individual
- Having a pleasant facial expression
- Having a professional image

To be an effective communicator, we must understand that communication is a process and a skill that involves certain techniques to be utilized by both the sender and the receiver. Do not let your emotions speak for you. The communication process requires that you stay in control.

Three Steps to Effectively Communicate

1. Organize your message by thinking before you speak.
2. Deliver your message by using the proper tone of your voice. This will have a significant impact on communication.
3. Check that you understand the inquiry by asking the listener to make sure that you heard the correct message.

DOI: 10.4324/9781003402718-23

Three Steps to Active Listening

1. Pay full attention to the speaker by establishing and maintaining eye contact and focusing fully on the speaker.
2. Paraphrase and repeat the message in your own words to ensure you heard him or her correctly.
3. Respond to the speaker or guest about what you will do as a result of their message.

A few years ago, we were in Washington, DC, at the Ritz Hotel and overheard the desk clerk state, "Excuse me, Mr. Cole (Lesley Cole, CPP). I have a message for you." Lesley accepted it and thanked him. We were impressed that this clerk, who had spoken with hundreds of guests, remembered Lesley's name. Did the desk clerk communicate effectively? Absolutely!

It's a Process to Be Successful

A security officer should anticipate the visitor's needs as a part of their daily responsibilities. It all starts with a smile; nothing communicates more to an individual than a friendly smile. Remember the process we have discussed. Greet the visitors, listen carefully and acknowledge the complaint or request, always assess the situation, affirm understanding, and then discuss solutions. While a security officer will not be able to satisfy every visitor, remember it is how a situation is handled that will be remembered.

Chapter 23

Ten Key Communication Points for Security Officers

1. **Command presence** – A security officer is an authority figure, and if someone has a question or a problem, they will expect the protection officer to have the solution. The question is, was the issue handled swiftly and appropriately?
2. **Angry people** – When communicating with angry people, a security officer should reply in a clear but soft tone. If an individual is upset or angry, the first objective should be to help them and calm them down.
3. **Communication** – A security officer should listen very closely to the requests being made, to pleas for help and assistance, and also listen closely to instructions.
4. **Dealing with mentally ill persons** – A security officer should remember not always to assume the worst of conditions. Instead, be protective, understanding, and helpful.
5. **Defusing conflict and crisis** – A security officer should ask questions if they don't understand something.
6. **Engaging the customer** – A security officer should always act in a professional manner.
7. **Lobby or reception area** – A security officer should always remember that many times, they are working in a public space, and their professionalism is always on display.
8. **Lost children** – Security officers should treat this as an emergency procedure that needs to be practiced and followed.

DOI: 10.4324/9781003402718-24

9. **Tactical communications** – A security officer should be professional and direct when transmitting on the radio or cell phone.
10. **Public relations** – A security officer should remember that professionalism is 100% of their job.

Chapter 24

Ten Things That Require Zero Talent*

1. Being on Time
2. Having a Good Work Ethic
3. Effort
4. Energy
5. Body Language
6. Passion
7. Doing Extra
8. Being Prepared
9. Being Coach-able
10. Having a Good Attitude

---

* Prepared by George Guilfoy, 7/16/2019 on LinkedIn site.

DOI: 10.4324/9781003402718-25

Chapter 25

Six-Point Checklist for Intrusion Detection Systems

A security officer will see the good, the bad, and the ugly as they inspect intrusion detection systems (alarms). Sometimes, they will be told, "Yes, it's working because when I turn the key, it goes from red to green, so I know it's okay."

1. Check every component and make sure it's working. Turn the system on and walk around the coverage area to test the sensors.
2. If a door is alarmed, test it by opening it. If a door has a portable alarm, use quality lithium batteries, not cheap batteries, or you will end up paying for a service call when you have a malfunction.
3. Service calls make alarm companies money. See if you can reset the alarm yourself. If it won't reset, learn as much as you can about the system so possibly, the next time, you can reset it yourself.
4. Depending on the level of risk and the protection required, alarm systems should be tested from daily to once a month.
5. If false alarms are an issue, fix the system ASAP to reduce false alarms in your system. Many law enforcement agencies now send an invoice if there is a false alarm.
6. User error is a cause of many false alarms. Educate personnel on entrance/exit procedures and protocols. Be Proactive.

DOI: 10.4324/9781003402718-26

Chapter 26

Six-Point Checklist for Access Control Credentials (Keys/Fobs/Cards/ Mobile/Biometric)

Check with Human Resources and ask them for the total number of employees in the company. For example, if there are 1,055 and there are 1,575 access control credentials issued, what does this tell you? Obviously, someone is not adding and deleting individuals as required nor is the system being audited.

1. Access control fobs/cards are like mechanical and master keys. In the situation above, no one was deleting the credentials of those employees who left the company. Ensure there is a procedure in place.
2. Ask, "Are badges and access control credentials or keys collected from those employees who have left the company?" Have electronic/biometric access control for those employees that have left the company been disabled? Unfortunately, in many cases, the answer is NO!
3. There should be a list of those employees with master access and/or master keys. Find out how many there are and compare them to the authorized employee list.
4. If records are poorly kept or not at all, note it. However, the computer to the access system can tell you in minutes exactly who has master access credentials.

DOI: 10.4324/9781003402718-27

5. Are specific areas off-limits to those with master access? For example, IT areas, payroll records, and communications areas? Review, review, and review and reduce the risk by following established procedures. If there is no procedure, implement one.
6. Office keys or electronic access should not be given to everyone. Only those staff members whose job duties require office keys should be given access. Individuals in charge of access control distribution should be responsible and keep records of all issued credentials. Mechanical office keys should also read "do not duplicate" and be collected from all employees upon termination or resignation.[1]

Note

1 Crime Prevention. Retrieved on 02-11-19 from: https://www.police.ufl.edu/programs/classes/safety-crime-prevention-class-list/

Chapter 27

Six-Point Checklist for Security Surveillance Systems

Over the years, we have all seen our share of issues with security surveillance systems (CCTV) or network video systems that don't work well, are not properly installed, or don't work in conjunction with other security components. Security cameras are just one component in an overall security process or holistic security program. A reputable, experienced installer with integration experience is critical for a fully functional system.

1. Ensure you know the total number of cameras that are installed on the property and the number that is actively monitored as opposed to the number of cameras that may be "record only" for forensic purposes. Unmonitored cameras may provide a false sense of security and may be a liability issue.
2. Too often, after an incident we hear the comment, … "I don't know why it didn't record." To help ensure this doesn't happen, test the system to ensure all cameras are operational. Regular service is critical to troubleshoot problems within the system. If you experience an issue while monitoring cameras, report it to a supervisor immediately to ensure the problem can be identified and corrected as soon as possible.
3. Check to make sure that cameras are positioned properly or that pan/tilt/zoom or moveable cameras are fully operational. Report any "blind" areas where you cannot monitor activity. Ask about the backup power source for cameras in case of a power outage and ensure you know how it operates.

DOI: 10.4324/9781003402718-28

4. The old expression, "Dummy cameras are installed by dummies." Don't do it. Take them down. We've seen them advertised in popular magazines and even facility managers promote non-operational cameras.
5. Every aspect of the network video operation needs to be checked and working properly. Audit results should be documented and verified for accuracy.
6. Security surveillance systems are transitioning away from outdated analog systems and moving toward artificial intelligence (AI) integrated cameras and cameras with analytics that can be programmed to "record" or "follow" in specific predesignated circumstances. Cameras are also integrated with other security components, such as intrusion detection systems, lighting, and perimeter controls. Training on how to operate these systems is critical.

Chapter 28

Six-Point Checklist for Lights and Lighting

Quite a bit of information has been written about interior and exterior lighting. For example, some locations may use interior or exterior lighting that is motion controlled. As a pedestrian or vehicle approaches the area, the light becomes brighter and then dims as the pedestrian or vehicle exits the area. What a great energy-saving idea!

1. A company may save thousands of dollars in annual energy costs by installing cost-effective LED lighting. When we conduct assessments, we always tell management how to save money as well as how they should spend it.
2. Exterior lighting should be placed in weatherproof, tamper-resistant fixtures. Fixtures damaged by weather and vandalism can increase lighting costs and cause havoc to the lighting budget.
3. Lights ON during the daytime should be replaced or repaired. Check the timers and consider installing dusk-to-dawn sensors.
4. Non-operational lights should be reported on the daily activity report and repaired/replaced within 24 hours. Non-operational lighting that poses imminent danger should be reported immediately and corrected as soon as possible.
5. Illumination levels should meet local and national organizational recommendations.
6. Interior and exterior emergency lighting must be checked daily on routine patrols as part of the lighting inspection process. Lighting should be uniform and designed in such a way as to avoid shadowy areas and ensure an average luminance level that is sufficient for the risk level of the particular location.

DOI: 10.4324/9781003402718-29

Chapter 29

Six-Point Checklist for Fences and Walls*

1. Consider a continuous barrier around the entire property or high-risk areas. The fence height should be 8 feet high, with 2-inch-square-mesh and 11 gauge or heavier wire. You don't want a potential offender to be able to climb onto your property.
2. Fences can be topped with three barbed wire strands and securely fastened to rigidly set posts. If bushes or hedges are in the area, they shouldn't exceed 3 ft to ensure clear, natural surveillance.
3. There should be at least 10 ft of clear space on both sides of the fence.
4. Walls around high-risk areas should be monitored by video surveillance.
5. Ensure identification credentials are issued to all employees and they are checked at gates or doors by a security officer or monitored security system.
6. Fences and their gates and walls and their doors or openings should be strong enough to resist attack and be considered one concentric layer of protection.

* Risk Analysis and the Security Survey, Third edition, James F. Broder, CPP, Elsevier, 2006, p. 14 & 15.

DOI: 10.4324/9781003402718-30

Chapter 30

Six-Point Checklist for Policies and Procedures

Policies and procedures are intended to ensure that security measures are followed and people, property, and other assets are kept safe. Enforcement should be monitored and audited to ensure compliance.

1. Policies are rules and guidelines adopted by an organization to reach its long-term goals.
2. Procedures are the specific methods employed to express policies in action in the organization's day-to-day operations.[1]
3. Procedures change more often than policies. For example, access control for a small company may be at the discretion of a security officer. Still, then as the company grows, access control credentials (card or fob) are issued. Controlling access is the policy, but the procedure for accomplishing that has changed.
4. All employees should be trained on company policies and procedures.
5. Emergency procedures are vital to a company's security plan.
6. If new procedures are implemented, employees must receive training in the new procedures in order to comply with the existing policy.

Note

1 Policies and Procedures. Retrieved on 02-11-19 from: http://www.businessdictionary.com/definition/policies-and-procedures.html

DOI: 10.4324/9781003402718-31

Chapter 31

Six-Point Checklist for Security officers

Security officers are employed by a public or private entity to protect an organization's assets – people and property from harm or damage.

1. Security officers receive basic orientation training that includes security officer authority and law enforcement interaction, ethics, deportment and professional conduct, human and public relations, effective enforcement techniques, and report writing.
2. Security officers must be trained in the customer's/employer's site-specific policies and procedures of the organization.
3. Security officers are trained in asset protection, security management, physical security, and crime prevention.
4. Security officers work either a fixed, stationary post vehicle/foot patrol or a combination of the these.
5. Security officers learn about emergency procedures, fire protection, life safety, and how to perform cardiopulmonary resuscitation (CPR) and use an automated external. Defibrillator (AED).
6. Some security officers receive specialized training, such as weapons training, crisis prevention intervention, or safe driving.

DOI: 10.4324/9781003402718-32

Chapter 32

Six-Point Checklist for Crime Prevention through Environmental Design (CPTED)

CPTED is a short form for the proactive crime-fighting technique known as Crime Prevention Through Environmental Design. CPTED is based on the theory that: "The proper design and effective use of the built environment can lead to a reduction in the incidence and fear of crime, and an improvement in the quality of life." There are seven basic principles of CPTED[1]:

1. Natural surveillance is a design strategy directed primarily at keeping intruders under observation.
2. Natural access control is a design strategy directed at decreasing crime opportunities.
3. Territorial reinforcement is a design strategy that realizes that physical design can create or extend a sphere of influence so that users develop a sense of proprietorship or territoriality.
4. Environmental maintenance/image is related to territorial reinforcement. A well-maintained area sends the message that people notice and care about what happens in an area.
5. Environmental maintenance/checklist:
   - Graffiti should be removed or painted over.
   - Weeds should be removed.

DOI: 10.4324/9781003402718-33

- Debris should be removed from the grounds.
- All lighted signs should be in working order.
- All light fixtures should be in working order.

6. Activity support is the fifth strategy, and target hardening is the sixth, followed by geographical juxtaposition (wider environment).
7. There are currently three generations of CPTED, and security officers need to remember that CPTED works in conjunction with traditional physical security countermeasures.

Note

1 Fennelly, Lawrence J. & Perry, Marianna A. Traditional Physical Security Countermeasures (Crime Prevention) vs. Crime Prevention Through Environmental Design (CPTED), 2018.

Chapter 33

Ten Security Books Every Security Officer Should Have on Their Bookshelf

1. *Women in Security*, Elsevier Publishers, 2016.
2. *CPTED and Traditional Security Countermeasures: 150 Things You Should Know*, CRC Publishers, 2018.
3. *Handbook of Loss Prevention & Crime Prevention*, Sixth Edition, Elsevier Publishers, 2020.
4. *Investigations: 150 Things You Should Know*, Second Edition, 2018.
5. *Effective Physical Security*, Fifth Edition, Elsevier Publishers, 2018.
6. *Principles of Emergency Management and Emergency Operations Centers* (ASIS International Book of the Year), CRC Press, 2022.
7. *Soft Target Hardening: Protecting People from Attack* (ASIS International Book of the Year), CRC Press, 2018.
8. *Hospital and Healthcare Security*, Sixth Edition, CRC Press, 2015.
9. *Security Supervision and Management: Theory and Practice of Asset Protection*, CRC Press, 2015.
10. *Antiterrorism and Threat Response: Planning and Implementation*, Second Edition, CRC Press, 2024.

DOI: 10.4324/9781003402718-34

Chapter 34

Vulnerability Assessment

Needs and deficiencies must be determined to have an effective security program.

- A vulnerability assessment is a critical (and well thought out) on-site examination that is used to observe security that is currently in place, identify security deficiencies or excesses, determine what level of security is needed, and, finally, suggest options for consideration to assist in the mitigation of identified areas for improvement that may assist in lowering the overall risk profile. If implemented, these recommendations will effectively control the identified risks.
- After the vulnerability assessment, the client and the assessor will conduct a cost/benefit analysis to determine what the prioritization should be for the presented findings and options for considerations and implementation while being cognizant of budgetary and other factors that may affect timelines and implementation. It will be determined if the recommendations are affordable, feasible, and practical. They will be budgeted as short-term or long-term projects.
- The assessor will utilize and gather statistical data from law enforcement, such as Uniform Crime Reporting (UCR), National Incident-Based Reporting System (NIBRS), National Crime Victim Victimization Survey (NCVS), and Department of Homeland Security (DHS), to examine the frequency and severity of events in your area to determine what can be done to remove or reduce the threat to your campus.
- A vulnerability assessment should be completed annually (or more often if there are issues or significant changes to the building or campus environment).

DOI: 10.4324/9781003402718-35

Chapter 35

Crime Prevention Strategies That Will Help You with an Assessment

Ensure that you are objective when determining needs for a particular location. Each resource you utilize should be particular to that specific risk. Don't get trapped into the mindset that every location is the same and make general recommendations.

Obtain crime statistics for the area of your assessment, as well as incident reports for on-site issues that have occurred. It is best to look for year-over-year changes in crime and incidents. When you make recommendations to address vulnerabilities, ensure patterns of issues are considered so your recommended countermeasures will be effective.

You should develop a relationship with the law enforcement officers in the area where you are conducting an assessment. If the department has a crime prevention officer, they will help you better understand neighborhood issues. You will find that these strategic partnerships will benefit you and your customer customers.

Study the crime patterns, on-site incidents, and risk levels for similar businesses to determine if you are facing issues that are particular to that specific industry or if the issues are specific to that geographical area. This way, you can work with law enforcement networks to effectively deal with the issues you are facing.

Conduct crime awareness and personal safety/security training programs for your customers. This training will raise their level of awareness and their general safety and also help curb on-site incidents as well as crime in the area. Examples include opening and closing procedures, safety in parking lots and off-site parking, robbery prevention, and reporting suspicious behavior.

DOI: 10.4324/9781003402718-36

Help your customer establish a culture of safety and security by developing a safety and security program. Your goals include increasing the safety of customers and employees, protecting the company "brand," and protecting other company assets. Upper management should not just support the safety and security program but should instead be an active part of it.

You must understand the issues of a particular industry, the issues of a particular area, and the customer's business operations to develop effective countermeasures to address vulnerabilities.

Chapter 36

Thirty Things Most Books Don't Tell You to Look for When Doing Vulnerability Assessments

Security design and access control are more than bars on windows, a security guard booth, a camera, or a wall. Crime prevention involves systematically integrating design, technology, and operation to protect three critical assets – people, information, and property. Protection of these assets is a concern and should be considered throughout the design and construction process.

The most efficient, least expensive way to provide security is during process design. Designers who are called on to address security and crime concerns must be able to determine security requirements, know security technology, and understand the architectural implications of security needs.[1]

1. Lighting: When a light is on during the daytime, you burn energy and need to discover why it is "ON" and shut it "OFF." We suggest that you upgrade to light sensors, but if you're still using timers, adjust them, considering daylight savings time – every spring and fall, if necessary. Every light must be checked and operational. Ensure there is lighting overlap so light is evenly distributed and there are no dark spaces. A good rule of thumb for parking lot lighting is that poles should be spaced as far apart as they are tall – for example, if you use 20-ft light poles, the poles should be spaced 20 ft apart. Consider highly efficient LED lighting for an return on investment (ROI).

DOI: 10.4324/9781003402718-37

2. Key card/fob/digital control is always an issue ... When was the master system put in place? If beyond five years, start to re-key by the development of a second master key system, or if you have a removal core system, start removing the cylinders. Many facilities, especially those in healthcare, have gotten away from keypads and are using motion-detected door switches for entry/exit. Mechanical keys should be a backup to keyless entry. Check if your keyless entry systems are fail-safe or fail-secure if there is a power failure.
3. For surveillance systems, count the cameras on the property and then the cameras on the monitors. Is every camera operating properly and positioned correctly? Do high-value/high-security areas have overlapping coverage? Are cameras integrated/interfaced with access control if there is a breach?
4. Video surveillance may:
   - Increase protection
   - Work with other components in the security process – layered security
   - Reduce personnel costs
   - Improve access control procedures
   - Provide surveillance of remote areas
   - Provide surveillance of critical locations
   - Monitor traffic through perimeter gates and interior areas
   - Work in conjunction with emergency procedures

5. Cameras

   Pan/tilt/zoom camera – Capable of movement and may include a built-in motion detection feature that can trigger alarms and follow activity in the field of view.

   Fixed focus camera – Capable of monitoring activity from one distance and in one area.

   Integrated positioning camera – 360 degrees of continuous rotation.

   Vandal-proof camera – Capable of withstanding attack.

   Weather-resistant camera – May be water-resistant, has a built-in heater, defroster, or defogger, and may also be equipped with a wiper blade for the lens.

   Covert cameras – Can be disguised to monitor activity so personnel can respond to suspicious behavior to prevent a crime from occurring.

   Dummy or decoy camera – Do not film images or send signals. The camera shells are mounted in a conspicuous location and are intended to be a visual deterrent, but may also create a false sense of security and possible liability. Do not use them.

   Video surveillance signage should be visible.

   Camera domes – Can be pressurized with dry nitrogen to protect the camera against moisture, corrosive gases, and airborne contaminates; may be made of polycarbonate for bullet resistance for use in high crime areas; or may be used to conceal the direction the camera is pointed simply or if there is a camera in the dome.

6. Heavy doors like doors on houses of worship may need heavy-duty locking systems.
7. Padlocks must be quality products, not junk padlocks, and no numbers should be engraved on the bottom of the padlock. Replace often.
8. Are combination padlocks the same as above # 7?
9. Bushes and shrubbery shouldn't be over 3 ft tall, and the first tree branch must be 7–8 ft off the ground.
10. Ask, "What is the overall value of contents in the building?" Use layered security measures, but don't let the cost of your security measures exceed the cost of what you're protecting. No value can be placed on human life – use what it takes for maximum protection.
11. Fire extinguishers must be identified and inspected regularly. Security should be checking them, and there should be an annual inspection by a fire extinguisher professional – check the date on the tag.
12. Check garages for proper signage. Ensure that intercoms and phone systems are operational. Pay close attention to ensure adequate lighting in stairwells and elevator lobbies.
13. Is no trespassing signage posted? (if applicable)
14. Is crime a concern on the property? If so, get crime statistics and determine vulnerable areas needing extra security measures.
15. Are there infection-control issues? Security may enforce the wearing of masks, do temperature checks, and keep a log of entry for contact tracing if problems arise.
16. Is the location of parked company vehicles secure? Keys should be secured with sign-in/sign-out procedures.
17. Is the loading dock secured and is the area well-lit? Cameras should be monitored, and all deliveries in and shipments out should be logged and documented.
18. Check the lighting levels in the warmer months when deciduous trees have leaves to ensure that the leaves are not obstructing the lighting.
19. Are cameras in elevators working properly, and are they vandal-proof? Security officers should check the lighting to ensure it is operational. If lighting is not operational and it is a high-risk area, additional security measures should be in place.
20. Open exterior doors to ensure the alarm system works properly. Cameras should alert if the door is opened, and an alarm should sound in the security operations center.
21. Check all door latches for jimmy marks made by someone attempting access.
22. Is the lighting in the parking lots adequate? Use a light meter and IESNA guidelines.

23. Is there any vandalism or graffiti on the property? Remove within 24 hours and report to local police or gang unit so they can track gang-related activity and tagging.
24. Are doors and windows on ground level secured, as well as those that can be accessed from the fire escape? Doors and windows on the first floors should have releases on the inside if there are bars so anyone inside can escape if there is a fire or another emergency.
25. Is the property properly maintained? Does the property look like someone cares and is taking care of it?
26. Access control credentials - what is the total number of employees versus the total number of people who have access?
27. Exposed hinges. If the door opens outward, you must make sure that exposed hinges are secured.
    If exposed hinge pins can be removed, an intruder can gain entry by swinging the door on the lock after prying open the single hinge. To ensure that the door is equipped with non-removable hinge pins, drill a matching hole in each hinge leaf or remove a matching screw from each. In one hole, insert a screw that is 1/2 inches longer than the hole is deep. Cut off the screw head with a hacksaw so that when the door closes, the headless screws will fit into the hole on the opposite leaf and hold the door to the frame even with the hinge pins removed.
28. Problem Doors
    Sliding patio doors – Place a locking mechanism that vertically secures the top and the bottom of the door to the track. These locks can be key-operated or hand-tightened. A wooden dowel placed in the track to block the door from being opened can be defeated. Sliding patio doors should have anti-lift devices and locks fitted to the top and bottom to stop them from being removed from outside unless they already have a multi-locking system. Get specialist advice. If you are getting new or replacement patio doors, ask the system supplier for their high-security specification.

Patio doors present several security problems:

- The glass panels of many doors can be lifted out of their tracks and removed.
- The locking mechanism can easily be pried open and provides little security.
- The fixed panel is sometimes held in place by brackets with screws exposed to the exterior.

To stop the door from being lifted out of its frame, the "jimmy-plates" or screws should be mounted at the top of the track to reduce any vertical play in the door.

A "Charlie Bar" folds horizontally and blocks movement of the sliding portion of the door. This type of locking device has the advantage of high visibility, which may deter a potential intruder, and is also easy to install. A metal rod, a cut-down hockey stick, or a length of wooden doweling fitted snugly along the bottom of the door track is an easy do-it-yourself method of preventing a patio door from being forced open.

29. How to secure doors that have glass panels:
    - Install a clear, unbreakable polycarbonate panel over the glass inside the door or use the pane to replace the existing glass. Fasten the panel securely on the inside of the door.
    - Install grated wire mesh, a wrought iron grille, or decorative wire grate over the glass. Make sure there is no access through the grate.
    - Install a clear anti-penetration film over the glass.
30. Area/space protection

    Photoelectric eyes or beams – Use a pulsed, infrared beam and transmit a beam across a protected area.

    Ultrasonic detectors – Use low-frequency sound waves projected from the sensor to detect a change in frequency.

    Microwave detector – Sensors detect intruders using a radiated radio frequency (RF). Movement will cause a disturbance in the generated RF field, which will cause a change in this frequency. Any motion will activate the alarm.

    Infrared detectors – Passive infrared detectors sense radiation from a human body moving through the optical field of view.

    Pressure mat sensors – Can be hidden under a carpet of any protected area to detect the presence of the weight of the intruder.

    Sound sensors – A microwave and an electronic amplifier detect sounds exceeding the normal limit.

    Chemical sensors – A system that can detect human vapors.

    Vapor trace sensors – Use a chemical detector for explosives or in-flammables.
31. Locks[2]

    1 inch Minimum throw on deadbolt – The throw of the deadbolt is the length that the deadbolt extends out of the door edge. A minimum throw of 1" is recommended. Longer throws make it more difficult to gain entry by spreading the door frame.

    Saw-resistant bolts – Some deadbolts come with internal anti-saw pins. The pins spin freely inside the bolt. If someone tries to break in by sawing off the deadbolt, the pin will make this difficult because it spins back and forth with every movement of the saw blade.

    Captured key deadbolt – Burglars can gain entry through a locked door by breaking the glass in the door light or sidelight, reaching in, and simply unlocking the door. Many homeowners, to prevent this, install double-cylinder deadbolt locks with keyholes on both sides of the door. Don't let double-cylinder deadbolts create a fire safety danger to your family. In the case of a fire, when the family needs to get out of the house quickly, you don't want to be wasting time looking for the key to unlock the door. Most building codes do not allow this type of lock on doors used to exit the house for this very reason. To solve this conflict between family safety and security, one manufacturer developed a deadbolt lock with a captured key feature. On the interior side of the door, the deadbolt lock has a thumb-turn that can be removed from the lock, leaving a keyhole. The idea is that when no one is home, there is no need for the thumb-turn. The last person to leave removes the thumb-turn and creates a double-cylinder deadbolt condition.

Captured key thumb-turn – The thumb-turn cannot be removed without a lock key. Therefore, small children cannot remove the thumb-turn from the lock. Also, the thumb-turn can be used as a house key. It is important that whenever anyone is in the home, the thumb-turn is left in the lock at all times.

Hardened cased steel and beveled casings – On a typical deadbolt lock, the outside housing of the lock is called the "casing" or "case." Many lock manufacturers make their casings out of hardened steel, and many make the casing beveled. The hardened cased steel makes the casing more resilient against blows from a hammer. Beveling the casing makes it difficult to get pliers or pipe wrenches to stay on the lock when trying to twist it loose.

Anti-drill feature – Some intruders know how to drill out a lock. Some manufacturers combat this by installing hardened steel chips within the lock housing. When the drill bit hits these steel chips, it tears up the drill bit.

Notes

1 *Building Resilience: Crime Prevention Through Environmental Design* by the National Institute of Building Sciences Excerpted from the 12th Edition of *Architectural Graphic Standards Randall I. Atlas, PhD, AIA, CPP, Atlas Safety & Security Design, Inc., Miami, FL.*

2 Appendix X4 of ASTM F476-84 (Reapproved 1991) Standard Test Methods for Security of Swinging Door Assemblies; American Society for Testing and Materials/State Farm.

Chapter 37

The Changing Face of the Security Industry

Times have changed! Baby boomers are retiring, and younger professionals bring different skill sets to the security industry. Security professionals are better educated and better prepared to deal with new challenges. The face of traditional security is changing, and information security (IT) is now required in most security applications. The names of the ASIS Councils are now committees of subject matter experts. Research is being done to advance the security profession to provide the highest level of protection while increasing the bottom-line profitability of organizations at the same time. The combination of business and security is now a major field of study, along with information technology. (IT). This has become the new norm. This change has come about to better prepare security professionals to protect people, assets, property, and information effectively.

The new security "buzzwords" in 2022 and beyond are:

- What kind of ***skill set*** does the candidate/officer have?
- What ***certifications and specialization*** does the candidate/officer have?
- Both ***physical and informational security*** will be merging with the move toward certifications.
- ***Career pathways*** will be used by way of ***internships.***
- Your ***certification*** will be the bar for testing qualifications.
- Education for a career in security is being ***redesigned.***

Are you ready? You need to plan for the future now! Education and training provided must meet new and changing threats.

 DOI: 10.4324/9781003402718-38

Supervisors and managers must be well-versed in these topics and inspire their subordinates to acquire more education, training, and experience. They must continually emphasize professional growth and the development of the individual officer, agent, or investigator. Organizational development occurs when substantial numbers of the protection organization have undergone professional development experiences. The supervisor is the conduit for professional growth. He or she must embrace professional and organizational development opportunities and lead by example.

What Is a Security Supervisor?

- The person who represents higher authority.
- The person who assesses situations and conditions to make on-the-spot judgments without favor, prejudice, or fear.
- The person who is a responder to any and all situations.
- The person who must galvanize the efforts of many to attain stated goals.
- The person who must assign tasks and ensure compliance and constant quality performance.
- The accountable person and, therefore, first in line to shoulder reaction, both good and bad.
- Finally, the person who must make decisions for management based on his or her own professional development.

What does it mean to be a supervisor? First, a security supervisor may be called on to handle different types of conflicts in a myriad of circumstances. Second, a security supervisor will be required to meet the expectations of management and/or the client in the daily routine of security operations.

The supervisor is the backbone of the organization. His/her scope of responsibility is rather unique.

What Is a Security Manager?

- A manager designs and develops security, safety, and investigative programs.
- A manager works with budgets and other resources (equipment, uniforms, technology, software, etc.) to achieve the protective mission.
- A manager oversees processes (procedures) accomplishing organizational goals and objectives.
- A manager is responsible for staff functions if there is no supervisory span of control over line employees. This includes training, technical support, and auditing.

- A manager coordinates activities rather than supervises them.
- A manager is charged with policy formulation.
- A manager oversees line supervisors such as shift leaders, sergeants, and lead officers.
- A manager interacts with department heads and upper management (president, vice president, chief financial officer, chief, director, etc.)
- Professional development is a critical concept. It is the pathway for supervisors to become managers. By professional development, we are referring to:
- Leadership and networking skills are critical, and the supervisor in transition knows the value of industry certifications and career development,
- Communicative abilities include oral, written, and computer skills.
- Reasoning and logical thinking are must-have abilities.
- Formal training, accreditation, or certification is needed for professional growth and personal satisfaction.
- A personal and professional code of ethics must be developed along with high standards to guide oneself.
- Never underestimate the value of mentoring and coaching through on-the-job.
- Knowledge of risk assessment and security countermeasures are important.
- Turnover and job rotation can create overall improvement and present a learning environment.
- Stay current on industry events by reviewing news sources, trade publications, and web sources such as ASIS International and the International Foundation for Protection Officers (IFPO).

As the job changes, so must the training and skill level within the department increase. Professionals develop a "discipline of training" and continuously seek to improve their knowledge and abilities.

The Transition to Supervisor or Manager

The most demanding problem for supervisors within the security profession will be the transition from the position of security officer to supervisor. Supervisors must take responsibility for corporate regulations and the moral and ethical tone of the department, and provide the required level of security and customer service. The supervisor's role should be to assist in enabling the manager to provide support within the organization.

Similarly, new managers have some adjusting to do. We feel it is important to advise readers that as a new manager, one has to learn how to develop and exercise (not abuse) their newly acquired authority, power, and influence effectively. This can be done by establishing one's credibility – the earning of a subordinate's commitment and support.

Management is an art and a science; it is, perhaps, more art than science. New managers are at a crossroads, looking to make the right turns. Consider the following:

- A new manager is the person in charge. His/her elevation to the manager status through promotion has given him/her authority.
- A new manager is a person with a level of power and is a decision-maker.
- A new manager is knowledgeable in his/her field.
- A new manager uses his developed skills, ideas, education, certifications, and experience.
- A new manager supervises his subordinates and passes information down the line and up the chain of command.
- A new manager is responsible for being aware of employer policy as well as client requirements and the level of security required within the organization.
- A new manager develops his/her on-the-job experience as a new manager and starts to understand and accept the new responsibilities and what it means to be a manager.

A newly promoted supervisor or manager should:

- Learn how to supervise and adjust to the new role.
- Develop leadership skills and training of others.
- Develop interpersonal skills and become a mentor to others.
- Develop knowledge of who they are. Know thyself.
- Learn how to cope and deal with stress and emotions associated with management concerns.

As one progresses in his/her career, these learning points become ingrained. They become second nature. They become part of oneself.

Chapter 38

Crime Displacement

Crime displacement is defined as the relocation of crime from one place, time, target, offense, or tactic to another due to some crime prevention initiative, such as countermeasures resulting from a security assessment.

The different types of displacement are:

- Temporal offenders change the time at which they commit a crime.
- Spatial offenders switch from targets in one location to targets in another location.
- Target offenders change from one type of target to another.
- Tactical offenders alter the methods used to carry out crime.
- Offense offenders switch from one form of crime to another.[1]

Basically, crime displacement is a change in crime due to some preventive actions, and many people believe that crime prevention measures simply "move crime around." Still, the displacement of crime does not just involve geographical displacement.

Is Displacement Benign or Malign?[2]

Malign displacement means that there was an undesirable outcome from the displacement. For example, if crime prevention efforts are concentrated on reducing burglaries, the result may be more robberies.

Benign displacement means that society benefits from the changes caused by the displacement. For example, new crimes or new tactics to commit crimes may be less serious and not as dangerous for victims as the previous tactics.

Numerous cases from veteran law enforcement officers and criminologists will tell you that crime can be displaced, but for different reasons and in different

DOI: 10.4324/9781003402718-39

situations. Security countermeasures may act as deterrents and cause different types of displacement. A crime is committed when an opportunity exists. Our goal as crime prevention practitioners is to reduce criminal opportunity to reduce crime and ensure that these changes involve benign displacement so that quality of life is improved.

Notes

1 Analyzing Crime Displacement and Diffusion. Retrieved on 12-18-21 from: https://popcenter.asu.edu/content/tool-guides-analyzing-crime-displacement-and-diffusion-print-full-guide
2 A Review of Research on Crime Displacement Theory. Retrieved on 12-18-21 from: Ching Eng Leong. A Review of Research on Crime Displacement Theory. International Journal of Business and Economics Research. Special Issue: *Supply Chain Management: Its Theory and Applications*. Vol. 3, No. 6–1, 2014, pp. 22–30.

Chapter 39

Using Environmental Design to Increase Security

Target Hardening

The emphasis on design and use deviates from the traditional target-hardening approach to crime prevention. Traditional target-hardening focuses on denying access to a crime target through physical or artificial barrier techniques (such as locks, alarms, fences, and gates). Target-hardening often leads to constraints on the hardened environment's use, access, and enjoyment. Moreover, the traditional approach overlooks opportunities for natural access control and surveillance. The term *natural* refers to deriving access control and surveillance results as a by-product of the normal and routine use of the environment. It is possible to adapt normal and natural uses of the environment to accomplish the effects of artificial or mechanical hardening and surveillance. Nevertheless, crime prevention through environmental design (CPTED) employs pure target-hardening strategies, either to test their effectiveness as compared to natural strategies or when they appear to be justified as not unduly impairing the effective use of the environment.

As an example, a design strategy of improved street lighting must be planned, efficient, and evaluated in terms of the behavior it promotes or deters and the use impact of the lighted (and related) areas in terms of all users of the area (offenders, victims, other permanent, or casual users). Any strategies related to the lighting strategy (e.g., block-watch or neighborhood watch, 911 emergency service, and police patrol) must be evaluated in the same regard. This reflects the comprehensiveness of the CPTED design approach in focusing on both the proper design and

 DOI: 10.4324/9781003402718-40

effective use of the physical environment. Additionally, the concept of proper design and effective use emphasizes the designed relationship among strategies to ensure the desired results are achieved. It has been observed that improved street lighting alone (a design strategy) is ineffective against crime without the conscious and active support of citizens (in reporting what they see) and of police (in responding and conducting surveillance). CPTED involves integrating design, citizen and community action, and law enforcement strategies to accomplish surveillance consistent with the design and use of the environment.

CPTED Strategies

There are seven overlapping strategies in CPTED:

1. Natural Access Control
2. Natural Surveillance
3. Territorial Reinforcement
4. Image and/or Maintenance
5. Activity Program Support
6. Target Hardening
7. Geographical Juxtaposition (Wider Environment)

Access control and surveillance have been the primary design concepts of physical design programs. At the outset of the CPTED program, access control and surveillance systems – preexisting as conspicuous concepts in crime prevention through environmental design – received major attention. Access control and surveillance are not mutually exclusive classifications since certain strategies achieve both, and strategies in one classification typically mutually support each other. However, the operational thrust of each is distinctly different, and the differences must be recognized in performing crime analysis, research, design, implementation, and evaluation.

Access control is a design concept directed primarily at decreasing crime opportunity. Access control strategies are typically classified as organized (e.g., security officers), mechanical (e.g., locks, lighting, and alarms), and natural (e.g., spatial definition). The primary thrust of an access control strategy is to deny access to a crime target and to create a perception of risk in offenders.

Surveillance is a design concept directed primarily at keeping intruders under observation. Therefore, the primary thrust of a surveillance strategy is to facilitate observation. However, it may have the effect of an access control strategy by effectively keeping intruders out because of an increased perception of risk. Surveillance strategies are typically classified as organized (e.g., police patrol), mechanical (e.g., lighting, locks, and alarms), and natural (e.g., windows).

Finally, care and maintenance will allow for the continued use of a space for its intended purpose and contributing to territorial reinforcement. Deterioration and blight indicate less concern and control by a site's intended users and a greater tolerance of disorder. Proper maintenance protects the public health, safety, and welfare in all existing structures, residential and nonresidential, and on all existing premises by establishing minimum standards, best practices, and a master plan. Maintenance is the responsibility of the facilities manager, owners, and occupants.

We recently conducted a physical security assessment of several US Dept of Housing and Urban Development (HUD) properties in the Northeast area. Some of the properties were in fairly good condition and some were simply deplorable. We will discuss the worst of the properties below:

- We estimated that there were over 2000 pieces of paper and/or litter on the ground.
- The complex had 250 units and supplied only two small dumpsters on each side of the complex for trash. Trash was everywhere.
- Four sets of old mattresses and box springs were leaning against the fence in the dumpster area, and it appeared they had been there for some time.
- We counted six broken-down, damaged vehicles with flat tires in the parking area. Two of these cars appeared to have work done to them and were on car jacks in precarious positions.
- Drug dealers were openly selling drugs at 3:30 pm, and individuals who appeared "high" and/or under the influence were sitting on steps at building entrances.
- Homeless individuals who congregated at the far end of the street from the complex were given cell phones and would call the drug dealers and warn them if they saw law enforcement approaching the complex.

Here's a question for you … what do you think about the **Image and Maintenance** of the complex we have described? You can't get to the next level of security until you fix this mess.

The effort to balance design for crime prevention and design for effective use of environments contributed to the shift in focus from organized and mechanical strategies per se to natural strategies. This was because natural strategies exploited the opportunities of the given environment both to naturally and routinely facilitate access control and surveillance and to reinforce positive behavior in the use of the environment. The concept reflects a preference, where feasible, to reinforce existing or new activities or to reinforce the behavior of environment users otherwise so that crime prevention flows naturally and routinely from the activity being promoted.

The conceptual shift from organized and mechanical to natural strategies has oriented the CPTED program to develop plans that emphasize natural access control and surveillance and territorial reinforcement.

Although conceptually distinct, it is important to realize that these strategy categories tend to overlap in practice. It is perhaps most useful to think of territorial reinforcement as the umbrella concept, comprising all-natural surveillance principles, which in turn comprises all access control principles. It is not practical to think of territorial reinforcement, natural surveillance, and access control as independent strategies because, for example, access control operates to denote transitional zones, not necessarily impenetrable barriers. If these symbolic or psychological barriers are to succeed in controlling access by demarcating specific spaces for specific individuals, potential offenders must perceive that unwarranted intrusion will elicit protective territorial responses from those who have legitimate access. Similarly, natural surveillance operates to increase the likelihood that intrusion will be observed by individuals who care but are not officially responsible for regulating the use and treatment of spaces. If people observe inappropriate behavior but do nothing about it, then the most carefully planned natural surveillance tactics are useless in terms of stopping crime and vandalism.

Be Proactive and Think of Solutions.

Chapter 40

Ten Steps to Reduce Risk

1. Conduct a vulnerability assessment or risk survey, including an IT assessment.
2. Conduct a review of your crime stats and incident reports to determine if there are particular areas, days of the week, times of the day, or particular types of issues that are occurring.
3. Review all threats and vulnerabilities and determine risk mitigation options.
4. The definition of crime prevention is broken down as:
   - Anticipation.
   - Recognition.
   - Appraisal of a crime risk.
   - The initiation of an action to remove or reduce a crime risk.
5. Consider risk avoidance, risk reduction, risk spreading, risk transfer, and risk acceptance.
6. Forecast future risks with security countermeasures.
7. Develop a master plan organization followed by updated policies and procedures that align with organization mission statement.
8. ROI – return on investment – remember that decision-makers will buy into most projects with an ROI.
9. Develop a five-year plan. Why? For example, consider converting all exterior lighting to LED fixtures/bulbs and installing energy-efficient lighting inside. You may save enough money on energy costs in the first year to offset the cost of new projects.
10. The process is not as complicated as it seems. After all, your objective is the protection of all assets.

DOI: 10.4324/9781003402718-41

Chapter 41

Different Types of Risks*

Static risks – Result from the destruction of an asset due to dishonesty or human failure – more suitable to insurance than dynamic risks.

Dynamic risks – Result from changes in external factors – the economy, the industry, competitors, and consumers – over which there is no control.

Pure risks – The only possible outcomes are loss or no loss. Usually, only pure risks are insurable.

Speculative risk – A possibility of either loss or gain, and risk is voluntarily accepted because of the possibility of gain.

Fundamental risks – Caused by conditions that are beyond the control of the individuals who suffered the losses, such as unemployment, war, and inflation.

Particular risks – May be static or dynamic but are losses due to individual events and are felt by individuals rather than the entire group. Normally dealt with through insurance or loss prevention.

Classifications of Pure Risk[1]

Personal risk – The possibility of loss of either income or assets due to the loss of the ability to earn income. Four things affect earning power – premature death, dependent old age, sickness or disability, or unemployment.

Property risks – Losses are either direct or indirect and involve two types – loss of the property and loss of the use of property that results in lost income or further expenses.

---

* Perry, MA, National Crime Prevention Institute (NCPI), Introduction to Crime Prevention and Introduction to Physical Security; 1999.

DOI: 10.4324/9781003402718-42

Liability risk – The unintentional injury of other persons or damage to their property through negligence or carelessness.

Risk arising from the failure of others – When another person agrees to perform a service for you and fails to meet this obligation resulting in your financial loss, risk exists.

Note

1 Perry, MA, National Crime Prevention Institute (NCPI), Introduction to Crime Prevention and Introduction to Physical Security; 1999.

Chapter 42

Techniques for Dealing with Risk*

Risk avoidance – The risk exposure does not exist because the organization or individual does not engage in the activity that gives rise to the risk. This is a negative rather than a positive approach to dealing with risk.

Risk reduction – There are two ways to reduce risk – through loss prevention and control. Some techniques are intended to prevent the loss and some are intended to control the severity of the loss if it does occur.

Risk retention – This is the most common method of dealing with risk. Risk retention can be either conscious – the risk is perceived and is not transferred or reduced – or unconscious – when the risk is not recognized. Risk retention may be voluntary – risk is recognized and there is an agreement to assume the losses if they occur – or involuntary – when risks are unconsciously retained or they cannot be avoided, transferred, or reduced.

Risk transfer – May be used for either speculative or pure risks and risks are transferred to someone more willing to bear the risk, such as through insurance or by a contract.

Risk sharing – The possibility of loss is transferred from the individual to the group.

* Perry, MA, National Crime Prevention Institute (NCPI), Introduction to Crime Prevention and Introduction to Physical Security; 1999.

DOI: 10.4324/9781003402718-43

Chapter 43

Strategies to Reduce Risk

1. *Natural access control, entry/exit screening*: Increase the risk of detection for those not in conformity with entry or exit requirements (e.g., border searches and merchandise tags). Many retail stores use greeters that acknowledge patrons as they enter and thank them when they exit. This may help increase a culture of security within your organization.
2. *Formal surveillance*: Deterrence through official in-person law enforcement or security officers in conjunction with a network surveillance system.
3. *Surveillance by employees*: Use employees to increase deterrence, such as hotel doormen, groundskeepers, housekeepers, and janitors. Conduct training in situational awareness and suspicious behavior/actions and how to report potential issues.[1]
4. *Natural surveillance*: Capitalize on natural surveillance provided by people going about their everyday business. To increase visibility to the property, keep hedges/bushes trimmed to a height of 3 ft or less and tree canopies trimmed to 8 ft.
5. Consider organizing a neighborhood/business watch group.[2]

Notes

1 Situational awareness: What it is and why it matters as a management tool. Retrieved on 01-22-23 from: https://www.ckju.net/en/dossier/situational-awareness-what-it-and-why-it-matters-management-tool

2 What is Neighborhood Watch? Retrieved on 01-22-23 from: https://www.nnw.org/what-neighborhood-watch

DOI: 10.4324/9781003402718-44

Chapter 44

The Importance of Signage

There are four basic types of signage:[1]

Informational signs – For example, a sign pole may locate a destination and/or orientate the individual in the built environment.

Directional signs – Where information is displayed to find destinations that may be located at several strategic points in the built environment.

Identification signs – Where information about individual locations, such as buildings, locations, and public facilities, is displayed.

Warning signs – To indicate safety procedures such as emergency exits, no smoking areas, loading zones, and pedestrian crossings.

Signs should be displayed and be legible from a reasonable distance. The size and coloring of the signs, the lettering, and the posting interval must be appropriate to the situation.

Signage: Security Applications and Crime Prevention through Environmental Design

Well-designed, strategically located signs and maps contribute to a feeling of security. Signs should be standardized to give clear, consistent, concise, and readable messages from the street. Having addresses lit up at night will make them even more visible. Where it isn't easy to find one's way around, signs with maps may help. Signs must be visible, easily understood, and well maintained. Graffiti and other

DOI: 10.4324/9781003402718-45

vandalism can make signs unreadable. If signs are in disrepair or vandalized, it gives an impression of a lack of ownership and thus adds to a sense of fear.

Signs should be large, legible, and identifiable. Strong colors, standard symbols, simple shapes, and graphics are recommended for signs for restrooms, telephones, information, and help.

Signs should convey the message with adequate information. For example, the signage should indicate where to go for assistance or help, where the telephones and restrooms are, or their hours of operation.

The message should be conveyed in the appropriate language(s) or pictographs.

Signs should be strategically located at entrances and near activity areas (e.g., intersections of corridors or paths) and placed for visibility at an appropriate height.

Signs should be maintained on a regular basis to ensure that they are visible. This may involve trimming any landscaping growth or cleaning the sign.

In large parks and buildings, maps or leaflets containing information appropriate to the different needs of various groups of users should be available.

The hours of operation and when exits are closed should be indicated at all perimeter entrances.

Control Signs

Signage should be posted where necessary to assist in the control of authorized entry, to deter unauthorized entry, and to preclude accidental entry, for example, traffic signs and STOP signs.

Warning Signs

There must be a system in place to warn intruders that the area is restricted. Warning signs should be installed along physical barriers of an area and at each entry point so they can be seen readily and understood by anyone approaching the perimeter. In areas where English is one of two or more languages commonly spoken, warning signs must contain the local language in addition to English. Warning signs must be positioned on or outside the physical barrier area and should be at intervals of no more than 100 ft.

Signs must not be mounted on fences equipped with intrusion detection alarm equipment because nuisance alarms could be caused by environmental movement of the signs. Additionally, the restricted area warning signs must be posted at all entrances to limited and exclusion areas.

Other Signs

Signs setting forth the conditions of entry to an installation or area should be posted at all principal entrances. They should be legible under normal conditions at a distance not less than 50 ft from the point of entry. Such signs should inform the entrant of the provisions of search of the person, vehicle, packages, etc., or prohibitions (such as against cameras, matches, lighters, and entry for reasons other than official business).[2]

Conclusion

We wish to add one more important item. **No Trespassing** signs should be placed at the entrance to buildings and garages so a legal arrest may occur.

Notes

1 *Army Field Manual, No. 3–19.30.* Headquarters Department of the Army, Washington, DC; 8 January, 2001. p. 9.
2 Ibid.

Chapter 45

Safety on the Job

Safety Rules

The following safety rules and regulations are intended to direct and guide the behavior of security officers while on duty. When the words "shall" or "must" appear in the regulation, compliance with the regulation is mandatory. Failure to comply with such regulations can result in disciplinary action up to and including termination. The severity of the disciplinary action will be determined according to the seriousness of the infraction.

Protective Equipment

- Personnel should wear proper clothing to protect them from the typical conditions of their work area (i.e., security officers assigned to an outside post should wear appropriate additional clothing in winter).
- Personnel shall wear footwear considered safe and appropriate for the site or required by the client:
  - The wearing of canvas shoes or sneakers is strictly prohibited.
  - All security personnel are encouraged to wear approved safety shoes while on duty.
- Personnel shall wear approved hard hats when and where required at the site. Hard hats will be provided by company/client management.
- Personnel shall wear protective safety glasses, as specified, when and where required at the site.
- Protective safety glasses will be provided by company/client management.
- Personnel shall not wear any headphones/earphones except those designed for ear and hearing protection, and only when required at the work site.

DOI: 10.4324/9781003402718-46

- Personnel are required to wear safety vests when working under the following conditions on an assigned site/facility:
  - Roadway areas.
  - Areas with above-average accident rate intersections on the work site roads with bi-directional flows (vehicle/truck gates) when in an area where heavy equipment is in use when an existing traffic control device is out of service and in any construction area.

Motor Vehicles

- All motor vehicles, whether client or company owned, assigned to personnel for the performance of their duty shall be inspected before use with a vehicle inspection report completed signifying the same.
- Vehicle inspections shall be conducted per company policy to ensure that brakes, steering mechanisms, horn, windshield wipers, tires, mirrors, lights, and reflectors are intact and/or operating properly.
- The windshield, lights, mirrors, and rear and side view windows shall be kept clean throughout the day.
- The vehicle's dashboard and floor shall be kept clean and debris-free.
- Mechanical defects shall be reported immediately. Vehicles shall not be operated unless in a safe condition.
- Only authorized individuals shall operate motor vehicles – approved by the supervisor.
- Personnel must wear seatbelts and shoulder harnesses when operating the vehicle.
- Personnel operating the vehicle shall obey posted speed limits and traffic regulations.
- Personnel shall operate the vehicle at a reduced speed with lights on during inclement weather (i.e., snow and rain).
- Pedestrians shall always be given the right of way.
- The engine must be turned off when refueling the vehicle.
- Motor vehicles must never be left running while unattended.
- Vehicles shall not be used for the pursuit of or to create roadblocks to prevent the escape of fleeing suspects.
- Unauthorized passengers are not permitted in motor vehicles.
- Personnel shall not stand directly in front of or behind a stationary, running motor vehicle.
- Personnel shall not step in front of or behind a moving vehicle in an attempt to stop it or otherwise cause the vehicle's driver to alter the vehicle's course.

Golf Carts or Electric Carts

- Personnel are to be trained in using the golf cart based on manufacturer recommendations.

- Manufacturer's instructions on use and operation must be followed.
- The golf cart is always to be operated safely under all conditions. Slow down when necessary, and care should be taken when turning corners.
- Riders must remain seated and hold on when the vehicle moves.
- When not in use, the vehicle should be in park, neutral, or turned off, and if equipped with a parking brake, it should be engaged.
- Seat belts are required on all low-speed vehicles that go faster than 20 mph.

Stairways

- Personnel should use handrails when ascending or descending stairways.
- Personnel should ascend or descend stairways one stair at a time.
- Personnel shall not run up or down stairways.

Office Safety

- Defective office equipment shall be reported to the appropriate manager and taken out of use until repairs have been made.
- Personnel shall not open multiple file cabinet drawers at a time.
- Desk and/or file cabinet drawers shall be closed when not used.
- Scissors shall be closed and stored when not in immediate use.
- Running or jumping is strictly prohibited.
- Aisles and doorways shall be kept clear to ensure safe access.
- Personnel shall not stand on boxes or chairs.
- Flammable materials shall not be stored in mechanical or finance rooms.
- Boxes and other items shall not be stored in hallways or passageways.
- Electrical outlets shall not be adapted to power more equipment than for which they were initially intended.
- Electrical outlets shall have the proper receptacle cover installed on them.
- Sidewalks and entrances shall be kept clear of ice and snow.

Kitchen Safety

- Personnel shall only use water in the coffee maker.
- Only microwave-safe containers will be placed in the microwave oven.
- Personnel shall use the microwave oven to heat food or beverages only.

Handling Materials

- Personnel shall appropriately lift boxes or other equipment as instructed by the manager.
- Materials shall be stored only in authorized areas.
- Stacked materials shall be arranged in an orderly manner.
- Materials to be transported shall be loaded on hand-trucks in a safe/orderly manner.

Fire Protection

- Personnel shall maintain a high standard of housekeeping in areas under their control.
- Managers and supervisors shall ensure personnel know the location of fire alarm boxes and extinguishers and how to operate them.
- Personal portable heating devices are prohibited *unless* approved by the client and/or branch management.
- Smoking is prohibited except in designated areas.
- Access to firefighting equipment must remain unobstructed.
- Access to and through exits must remain unobstructed.

Safety Hazards

This list describes some easily identifiable safety hazards that apply to all client sites. These should be pointed out to security officers working at the site:

- Pipes protruding from walls or low-hanging pipes.
- Uneven floors or pavement.
- Speed bumps in parking areas.
- Ramps and loading docks.
- Cracks, open holes, or ruts in pavement.
- Areas where ice forms or becomes rain-slick, creating a walking hazard.
- Broken, uneven, or missing stairs in stairways.
- Loose handrails on stairways.
- Slippery surfaces caused by improper application of wax, oil, water leaks, etc.
- Poorly lighted areas.
- Sharp edges on fences or gates.
- Heavy objects, such as chains and gates, that an officer must move.
- Hard to open doors.
- Doors with fully automatic closure devices.
- Blind spots by corners, doorways, etc.

Chapter 46

The Art of Training

Training the trainers is not a new idea. Regardless of your area of expertise, trainers want to make a meaningful contribution to the professional and/or personal lives of others. Training requires material and the knowledge of how to teach to make it work and be effective. Whether you are teaching, lecturing, or giving a talk, each requires a different approach.

Teaching requires that you exert influence on the students' minds and take them into areas they have never been before. It's also about selling them a product that they will remember.

Teaching is said to be based on three principles:

1. I hear – **I forget**.
2. I see – **I remember**.
3. I do – **I never forget**.

Visual Aids

When training, consider using some of the following visual aids:

- Overlays (rarely used anymore)
- Dry-erase board
- Flip charts
- Projector for PowerPoint presentations
- Slide projector (rarely used anymore)
- Digital recording
- Go-Pro camera with playback and display

DOI: 10.4324/9781003402718-47

There are many rules for using visual aids; two key ones are

1. Don't have too many.
2. They must be well presented and professionally prepared.

Equipment

Rules for use of any equipment during training:

1. Test it before class and make sure it is working.
2. Use multicolored chalk or pens (except for the color "red" in a PowerPoint presentation).
3. Use a laser pointer. Don't walk in front of a picture. Stand at the side of the screen or board when talking.
4. Check the microphone, podium, and your notes before class.

Introduction

Each person who is to give a presentation should be introduced as if he/she is someone special. Their qualifications and expertise should be identified, and the subject matter should be stated. Emphasize their expertise.

Controlling the Class

1. Controlling the class starts when you start the program on time. For example, 8:00 am vs. 8:20 am. If the class starts 20 minutes late because two students are late, the students control the class and not the instructor.
2. Request that the class take notes utilizing common note-taking methods (laptops, cellular devices, pens/pencils, and paper). Emphasize the key points during the class.
3. Encourage an exchange of questions. You can ask the class questions, but don't ask difficult questions because that may turn off the class.

   If you are asked a question and don't know the answer, don't fake it. Admit you don't know the answer, and ask if anyone in the class knows the answer.

   Here are some tricks of the trade in answering questions:

- "Will you ask that again? I don't think everyone in the class heard you?" Having a question repeated does two things: It gives you time to collect your thoughts, and the second time around, the question may be worded differently *and* to your advantage.

- Praise the student who asked the question. It's like a pat on the head. "This was a very good question. I hope I answered it properly."
- Don't fake an answer you don't know.
- Phrases like these can save you: "Correct me if I'm wrong"; "In my opinion ..." (and answer the question).

Handouts

Almost everyone gives handouts, and it is expected. Handouts should relate to the subject being discussed and, as a general rule, handouts should be distributed after the presentation because they will be a distraction. Consider giving handout material digitally – through e-mail, on a thumb drive, or download passcode. Review the handout material very carefully.

Planning

Teaching and lecturing not just require a degree of knowledge on a specific subject but also require you to know your audience.

Sessions should be planned, e.g., a 50-minute program with 10-minute breaks. Have one 20-minute break in the morning and one in the afternoon, and decide when lunchtime will be. Your program must fit around the above or similar time frames.

If your program is planned and advertised from 9:00 am to 5:00 pm, you should start at 9:00 am sharp and finish at 4:50 pm to 5:00 pm.

Voice Control

In *My Fair Lady* (1964), Eliza Doolittle is transformed from a Cockney flower girl to a lady of gentility. Her voice quality and her diction were the focal points of the movie. Remember to speak clearly and raise and lower your voice as you speak. Don't also forget to make eye contact.

Below are some helpful hints:

- Speak as if you're speaking to this end of the room.
- Look at the person you are speaking to.
- Pay attention to questions being asked.
- Never interrupt.
- Use the proper volume in voice control.

Nervousness

Depending upon the type of program and the presenter's experience, nervousness comes in degrees. If you are drinking coffee or water, the class should be allowed to, too. Everyone is nervous at the beginning of a presentation until they get started. (Think about doing the 7:00 pm news on NBC, and you must wait in a chair, under strong lights, from 6:30 pm to 7:00 pm.) This will make your presentation easier.

Recording Devices

I have read the following for a specific seminar recently: "Recording devices will not be allowed." Depending on the subject matter and why the person wants to record the presentation will aid in your decision as to whether or not to allow recordings.

Ending Your Presentation

In every book or story, there is a golden rule: a strong beginning and a strong ending. This rule will make you become creative and force you to provide a strong finish to your presentation.

Chapter 47

Parking Garages and Parking Lot Security: Using CPTED Principles

The theory of Crime Prevention Through Environmental Design is based on one simple idea: that crime results partly from the opportunities presented by physical environment. This being the case, it should be possible to alter the physical environment so that crime is less likely to occur. – Ronald V. Clarke[1]

It pays to be proactive when determining what security components are needed in a parking garage or parking lot (or any other facility). Consider what would be a "reasonable" level of security and base your security program on the recommendations from the vulnerability/physical security assessment recommendations of a security professional.

Additionally, take into consideration any previous criminal activity in the area, the neighborhood where the parking garage/parking lot is located, the design of the structure or layout of the lot, whether there is an attendant or security officers on duty 24/7, and the initial and ongoing operational costs of security. Active and passive security measures should be used for an effective security program and don't forget to practice target hardening.

It is often a challenge for planners to pick the right combination of security measures to provide the highest level of safety and security possible. An assessment conducted by a security professional can help with this process. It is more difficult and costly to retrofit security into an existing environment than to "build" security into the design of the parking garage or parking lot.

 DOI: 10.4324/9781003402718-48

Many elements can go into a successful parking safety/security program, including upgraded access controls with auditing capabilities so access can be tracked or locked down, if necessary. Adequate lighting must be a part of any security program. Ensure that the type and placement of lighting in parking garages and parking lots are assessed so there are no dark shadows between cars where someone could hide. Lighting in elevator lobbies and stairwells of parking garages should be bright enough to provide facial recognition.

Painting the white walls and ceilings in parking garages can increase lighting because the light will be reflected and the area will appear better lit.

Security officers or law enforcement patrols with varied routes can be a visual deterrent. Landscaping and engineering adjustments utilizing Crime Prevention through Environmental Design (CPTED) concepts can be "built" into the design of the parking garage or parking lot. Parking garages and/or parking lots that are unkempt or rundown invite criminal activity. Sometimes, security equipment will need to be added or upgraded, but something as simple as upgrading maintenance can add to safety and security.

Note

1 Introduction to CPTED. Retrieved on Dec. 12, 2022 from: https://shop.elsevier.com/books/crime-prevention-through-environmental-design/crowe/978-0-12-411635-1

Chapter 48

Fifty Things to Consider When Designing Out Crime

To take a proactive stance, the time to think about potential crime and security issues is at the beginning of a project when these strategies can be developed along with the plans.

Design Out Crime, which is parallel to Sustainable Design, seeks to lessen the impact of products and services on the environment. This same philosophy can be applied to architecture, urban planning, engineering, landscape architecture, and interiors because both philosophies take a "holistic" approach to assess the total environmental impact of a building or area. If crime and security issues are considered at the beginning of a project, the cost will be considerably less than retrofitting them into the design at a later time.

1. Working knowledge of Crime Prevention through Environmental Design (CPTED) concepts and strategies.
2. Fences and walls – size, style, and height.
3. Knowledge about doors, door hardware, non-removable hinges, locks, and door viewers.
4. Knowledge of NFPA 101, Life Safety Code.
5. How to best use windows and the use of natural light.
6. Shatterproof glass, ultra violet A (UVA) resistant, and window film.
7. Building intrusion alarms and fire alarm systems.
8. Knowledge of intrusion alarm sensors for different applications.

 DOI: 10.4324/9781003402718-49

9. Effective access control with anti-prop alarms.
10. Emergency notification systems.
11. Provisions and designated areas for shelter-in-place.
12. Emergency phones and intercoms for the parking garage and parking lots.
13. Mass notification systems for all areas of the property and building(s).
14. Duress (panic) buttons and recommended locations.
15. Heating, Ventiliation and Air Conditioning (HVAC) system controls.
16. Knowledge of protected ventilation systems.
17. Emergency generator location and fuel storage.
18. Lighting budget for the project.
19. Exterior lighting on the building facade and around the buildings of the complex.
20. Appropriate lighting and type for the parking garage or parking lots.
21. Solar-powered lights, LED lighting, and return on investment (ROI).
22. Color rendition of lighting, recommended lighting levels without glare, and light trespass.
23. Dark-Sky Association concerns.
24. Environmental, activist, or "watchdog" groups in the area.
25. Knowledge of Environmental Protection Agency (EPA) regulations.
26. Radio communication for police, fire, and Emergency Medical Services (EMS) with on-site repeater.
27. Obtain or contract for Leadership in Energy and Environmental Design (LEED) professional credentials.
28. Working knowledge of the ROI of "green" buildings to efficiently use water and energy and reduce greenhouse gas emissions.
29. Available surfaces that can be used for parking lots and roofs.
30. Signage – appropriate design, location, letters, or pictographs.
31. Landscape security concepts.
32. Maintenance budget for physical security devices.
33. Landscaping budget for grounds (all vegetation – flowers, bushes, and trees).
34. Security surveillance systems – monitors and control stations.
35. IT security, cybersecurity, and Internet of Things (IoT) issues.
36. Physical security needed for the IT room or area.
37. Knowledge of security countermeasures needed for various levels of security.
38. Knowledge of prime locations in buildings for executive offices.
39. Designing secure shipping and receiving areas for various industries.
40. Access control – electronic and biometrics vs. key control.
41. Security issues specific to the site or industry.
42. Vestibule or foyer security concerns.
43. Pedestrian traffic control – crosswalks, pathways, and skyways.
44. Vehicular traffic controls – traffic humps and bumps to calm traffic.
45. Knowledge to ensure compliance with the Americans with Disabilities Act (ADA).

46. ADA-compliant ingress, egress, pathways, and designated handicapped parking.
47. Knowledge of video surveillance, cameras, and integration of all systems.
48. Specific crime issues in the area – crime patterns and incidents.
49. Creation of a healthy space – types of gym equipment, recreational equipment, etc.
50. Place outdoor seating areas with appropriate bench types.

Conclusion

Consider a proactive approach. It's better to be ahead of the curve than behind it.

Chapter 49

Incident Report Writing

Professional report writing is difficult, and developing this skill requires practice. Many people have never been taught how to write a report properly; some lack the literacy skills necessary and others don't want to write one. All of these obstruct the process and create problems for supervisors. The report must be completed by the end of the shift, and it's important that the new officer understands this.

Six Important Points of the Security Incident Report

Above all, the report should be clear and concise. A good report must answer and address these six basic questions:

1. **What?**	What happened?
2. **Where?**	Where is the exact location of the occurrence?
3. **Who?**	The security officer here must address as many as possible: who made the call, who was notified and when, who was the cause of the incident, etc.
4. **When?**	When were you notified? When did it happen?
5. **Why?**	This involves judgment and opinion and may not be easily proven, but it may be very important in the judgment of guilt or liability.
6. **How?**	How did it happen? Detail of the chain of events.

Security must understand that their report is like a book; everyone may be reading it. Stress the importance of accurate security reports.

DOI: 10.4324/9781003402718-50

Chapter 50

General Safety Rules for Security Officers

The following safety rules and regulations are intended to direct and guide the behavior of security/protection officers while on duty. When the words "shall" or "must" appear in the regulation, compliance with the regulation is mandatory. Failure to comply with these regulations can result in disciplinary action, including termination. The severity of the disciplinary action will be determined according to the seriousness of the infraction.

- Fighting or engaging in horseplay and practical jokes in any form will not be tolerated.
- To avoid injury, strict attention must be paid to your work.
- Drinking intoxicated beverages, being under the influence of liquor, or having the odor of alcohol on one's breath while on duty or in uniform shall be cause for immediate removal from the site and disciplinary action.
- Using narcotics or marijuana while on or off duty or reporting for duty under the influence of narcotics or marijuana may be cause for immediate termination. Security officers may be asked to produce documentation from a physician for any medication or substance that may affect job performance.
- Bringing any firearm and/or ammunition or other weapon on duty unless authorized in writing to do so is strictly prohibited. It shall be cause for immediate disciplinary action and removal from the site.
- Personnel shall obey all warning signs and signals posted at the work site.
- Personnel shall obey the client and company smoking/tobacco regulations. Smoking or vaping is allowed only in designated areas.

DOI: 10.4324/9781003402718-51

- Running is permitted only in extreme emergencies.
- Personnel shall not jump from one level to another (i.e., from a loading dock to ground level).
- Personnel shall keep their work area clean and free of trash and other debris to ensure safe access.
- Personnel should be aware that becoming involved in certain situations during their duties may jeopardize their personal safety.
- When responding to these situations, officers must take appropriate actions to ensure their personal safety while fulfilling their obligation to protect life and property.

Chapter 51

Communications Device Usage

General Use – Radios

1. Make sure the radio is on the proper channel.
2. Turn the radio on and check the volume.
3. When talking on radio, place it 2–4 inches from your face. Key the mic (press-to-talk-button), then speak in a calm and clear voice (do not shout). Hold the button until you have finished speaking. Release the button to hear a response.
4. Keep radio communications to a minimum. The radio is a tool. It cannot be effective if it is cluttered with nonessential transmissions. Operating instructions and post orders will dictate which events must be relayed to higher authority.
5. Realize what you say over the radio could be monitored by other sources and keep radio traffic professional.
6. Make sure the radio is at a location where you can listen to all traffic.
7. The radio must always be secured and/or in your possession to prevent theft or loss.
8. At the end of your shift, make sure the radio is passed on to the next person in charge or turn off the radio and place it in the appropriate charging device if applicable. If necessary, the radio should be secured under lock and key.

Status Check Procedure – Radios or Phones

Some posts may require a mandatory status check. This is to ensure the safety of all employees as well as to ensure communication lines are operating appropriately.

DOI: 10.4324/9781003402718-52

1. All communications will be initiated using your call sign first and the party you are calling. If you are Sierra 7 and are contacting Sierra 4, then you would state, "Sierra 4, this is Sierra 7."
2. The preferred responses when you are contacted are as follows. Example: Sierra 4 tries to contact you (Sierra 7).
   a. Go ahead, Sierra 4.
   b. Sierra 4. This is Sierra 7.
   c. This is Sierra 7. Go ahead.

Unauthorized Transmissions – All Devices

By security company policies and those set forth by the Federal Communications Commission (FCC) Regulation (95.183), the following are listed as unacceptable and forbidden acts while using a security company/client portable hand-held radio or other communication device. The security company/client has expanded upon FCC regulations to include the use of phones or other communication devices that are the security company's or its client's properties.

It is forbidden to use these items (1) in connection with any activity which is against federal, state, or local law; (2) to transmit obscene, indecent, or profane words; (3) to intentionally interfere with other users/operators; (4) to advertise or solicit the sale of any goods or services; (5) to transmit music, whistling, or sound effects; (6) cumbersome in such a manner as to prevent others from contacting the device; (7) for any purpose other than official company business; (8) representative of behavior inappropriate for the workplace; (9) to transmit coded messages with hidden meanings ("10" codes are permissible); or (10) to transmit false or deceptive messages.

Professionalism

All communications are conducted through devices that are the property of the security company or its clients and are the equivalent of face-to-face communication. Any behavior or language with these devices, either verbal or physical, not within any applicable security company policy will not be tolerated. Any act that violates these policies may result in disciplinary action up to and including termination of employment.

Chapter 52

Sexual Harassment

It is unlawful to harass a person (an applicant or employee) because of that person's sex. Harassment can include "sexual harassment" or unwelcome sexual advances, requests for sexual favors, and other verbal or physical harassment of a sexual nature.[1]

Harassment of any kind is bothersome, demeaning, irritating, and annoying behavior. Sexual harassment is specifically harassment of a sexual nature. Most sexual harassment is disrespectful behavior toward others. The involved parties can be men or women, supervisors, subordinates, or peers.

We all suffer when our workplace tolerates abusive and demeaning behavior. To eliminate sexual harassment, we need to understand it.

Quid pro quo is Latin for "that for this" or "something for something" and refers to an exchange. In this case, the exchange is between employees, where one is asked to provide sexual favors in exchange for something else, such as favorable treatment in work assignments, pay, or promotion.

The workplace differs from the broader community because at work, some people have authority over others, and this authority relationship can lead to coercion. People at work are not as free to come and go as they are elsewhere, and since they have to work where they are assigned, they are entitled to an environment free of sexual harassment.

- Sexual harassment is a behavior, and adults are responsible for their own behavior and its consequences.
- We each have the responsibility to treat others with respect.
- A hostile work environment is one in which unwelcome conduct of a sexual nature creates an uncomfortable work environment for some employees.

 DOI: 10.4324/9781003402718-53

Examples of this conduct may include

- Sexually explicit talk or e-mails, sexually provocative images, comments on physical attributes, or inappropriate touching

The following may contribute to creating a hostile environment:

- Posters, cartoons, drawings, calendars, pinups, and pictures of a sexual nature
- Electronic bulletin boards/computer graphics of a sexual nature
- Leaning over, invading a person's space
- Inappropriately touching a person or person's clothing
- Accidentally brushing sexual parts of the body
- Indecent exposure, mooning, or flashing
- Blocking someone's path to make a sexual advance
- Uninvited neck massaging
- Deliberately touching sexually, or brushing up against, or pinching
- Pressing or rubbing up against a person
- Stalking
- Grabbing
- Kissing, hugging, patting, and stroking
- Actual or attempted sexual assault
- Derogatory comments of a sexual nature or based on gender
- Comments about clothing, personal behavior, or a person's body
- Sexual or gender-based jokes or teasing
- Requests for sexual favors
- Request(s) for a date or dates
- Terms of endearment, such as honey, dear, sweetheart, and babe
- References to an adult as girl, boy, doll, or hunk
- Sexual innuendoes or stories
- Leers, grunts, wolf whistles, cat calls, hoots, sucking noises, lip-smacks, or other animal noises
- Tales of one's partner's sexual inadequacies or prowess
- Tales of sexual exploitation
- Graphic descriptions of pornography
- Demands such as "Hey, baby, give me a smile"
- Exaggerated, mocking "courtesy"
- Obscene phone calls or e-mails
- Lies or rumors about a person's personal or sex life

Unwelcomeness: What Does It Mean?

Some questions to ask yourself are

- Would my spouse, parent, child, or sibling like to be treated this way?
- Would I like my behavior published in the organization newsletter?
- Could my behavior offend or hurt other members of the workgroup?
- Could someone misinterpret my behavior as intentionally harmful or harassing?

The most critical factor in determining if the behavior is sexual harassment is whether it is unwelcome. The workplace is not an entirely free and voluntary environment, and people have to work at designated locations near each other. In these circumstances, behavior that is comfortable between direct participants may be unwelcome to others close by (third parties) who cannot avoid observing it.

Note

1 Sexual Harassment. Retrieved on Dec. 17, 2022 from: https://www.eeoc.gov/sexual-harassment

Chapter 53

Creating a Report

Written reports are official documents that detail how evidence was collected and preserved during an investigation. They are an important part of the chain of custody.

The report writing technique can be learned by anyone who possesses the two basic qualities of fundamental communication skills and a trained ability to observe. To be a competent investigator, you must write reports clearly so that everyone who reads them will know what you did and why. Often, the report is needed long after the crime or incident occurred and will be interpreted by many people unfamiliar with the crime or incident. Interviewers must write the report so that the prosecutor and courts can fully understand what happened.

Clear expression is not difficult to achieve, but it does take practice. Always write just the facts when taking notes or writing your report. A statement is the literal reproduction of the actual words spoken by the interviewee. Be a creative listener, use skillful phrases, and ask questions politely. First, listen and then write notes. Be supportive and encouraging.

There are five basic steps in writing a report.

1. Gather the facts (investigate, interview, and interrogate). What are you going to tell us?
2. Take notes and record the facts as soon as possible.
3. Organize the facts; create an outline and bullet points.
4. Write the report – just the facts. Decide how many words you want to write for each part of the report.
5. Edit and revise your report.

Good notes are a prerequisite for a good report, and they share many of the same characteristics of a good report. When taking notes, organize your information, then

DOI: 10.4324/9781003402718-54

report it in chronologically arranged paragraphs. Keep your writing straightforward and simple.

Characteristics of a Well-Written Report

A well-written report indicates that you have done your job and recognize your responsibilities to your client, corporation, or community. A well-written report reflects positively on your education, competence, and professionalism. It communicates better than a poorly prepared report.

Well-written reports share the following characteristics:

- **Factual**
  Facts make up the backbone of all reports. A fact is a statement that can be verified and known as a certainty. *Black's Law Dictionary* defines a fact as a thing done, an action performed or an incident transpiring, an event or circumstance, or an actual occurrence. Present your facts, draw your conclusion, and stipulate which is which. A well-written report does not contain unidentified opinions.
- **Accurate**
  Just as there are rules for spelling, capitalization, and punctuation, there are rules for word choice. Ensure accuracy by being specific in your language and choosing the most appropriate words for each situation. Avoid jargon, which creates confusion.
- **Objective**
  A good report is fair and impartial. Subjective writing might be more colorful than objective writing, but it has no place in a report. You can ensure objectivity in your reports by including all relevant facts and by avoiding words with emotional overtones. Specific crimes or incidents require different information, but you will frequently need certain general information. You will want to include the *who, what, when*, and *where* questions that factual statements should answer. The *how* and *why* statements may require inferences on your part. When this is the case, and especially when addressing the question of motive, clearly label your opinions. Avoid personal opinions.
- **Complete**
  A report should give as full an account as possible. To avoid slanting your report, record all possible motives reported to you, no matter how implausible they may seem.
- **Concise**
  The information you choose to include should be worded as concisely as possible; no one wants to read a wordy report. You can reduce wordiness in two ways: (1) leave out unnecessary information and (2) use as few words as possible to record the necessary facts. Avoid vague phrases such as "a long time

ago" or "sometime in the winter." You need to create a detailed report, and these phrases do not provide such detail.

- **Clear**
  Clarity is one of the most important characteristics of a well-written report.
- **Mechanically correct**
  Use correct spelling, capitalization, and punctuation in your report. A report with errors in these areas gives a poor impression of its writer and the writer's actions.
- **Written in standard English**
  When you translate your ideas into words, follow the rules for correct writing. Use the past tense, complete sentences, and good grammar. Keep your sentences short and the language simple and concise. Do not use jargon or texting phrases that are not complete sentences.
- **Legible**
  An illegible report gives a poor impression of the writer and a distorted explanation of who said what. Reread and edit your report, or even better, have another person proofread your report for accuracy and grammatical errors.
- **On time**
  A report that is submitted late reflects negatively on the report writer.
  Like all other communications, make your reports as clear and direct as possible. The following suggestions will help ensure that your reports can be easily understood:
  - Use the first person. That is, write *I* instead of *the investigator* or *the interviewer*. First-person writing is recommended for law enforcement reports because it is direct.
  - Write in past tense throughout your report.
  - Write in active voice. For example, say, "I asked Jane Smith …" rather than "Jane Smith was asked …." The active voice indicates who performed the action.
  - Be objective.
  - Correctly modify details to be included.
  - When using pronouns, be sure it is clear to whom they refer.
  - Don't use police lingo.
  - Don't use slang.
  - Use parallelism. That is, use the same structure for similar parts of a sentence.
  - Choose your words carefully. Avoid legal, technical, unfamiliar, and slang words.
  - Include specific, concrete facts and details.
  - Keep descriptive words and phrases as close as possible to the words they describe. Use correct grammar.
  - Use diagrams and sketches to clarify a complex description.
  - Quality reports are always typed, using paragraphs, past tense, and first person. Remember that all reports are a permanent written record of your case.

Investigation Report Writing Guideline Sheet

Over the years, we have written hundreds of reports; they must address the who, the where, the when, the why, and the how. We don't want this to be an English class like in school, but these concepts carry over to your everyday life as an investigator. Remember that the nine-page report may not be used in court for two or three years.

An Effective Investigation Report

- It should be easy to read and follow.
- It must be detailed enough so that someone unfamiliar with the case can understand what has happened and cover all the facts.
- It documents the findings and facts of an investigation.
- It demonstrates that all allegations were addressed.
- It includes recommendations and a follow-up of corrective action taken.
- It is written, without grammatical, spelling, and factual errors.

What Goes into a Report?

Every investigation report should include the following sections:

- How and when the incident occurred.
- The date that the complaint was reported.
- The date that the investigation started.
- Names and information for those who conducted the investigation.
- A summary of the investigation process used.
- A summary of the allegations investigated.
- Documentation of interviews, which includes a list of the people interviewed, their titles, and contact information.
- The location of each interview.
- List of anyone who refused to be interviewed or couldn't be interviewed and why.
- List of any follow-up interviews that occurred and the interview details.

Evidence

- Complete list of the evidence collected and reviewed allegations and findings.
- Allegations investigated and responses.
- Facts of the event(s) that occurred.
- Factual discrepancies uncovered.
- Reasons why or why not someone's statements are considered to be truthful.

Chapter 54

Military Time: The 24-Hour Clock*

Law enforcement agencies and security officers typically use military time based on a 24-hour clock. It is a method of keeping hours in which the day runs from midnight to midnight and is divided into 24-hour increments.

When keeping hours in military time, the day starts at midnight and is written as 00:00. The last minute of the day is written as 23:59, or one minute before the next midnight. Sometimes, you may see 00:00 written as 24:00, but both are acceptable.

The following is a side-by-side chart to convert a 12-hour clock to a 24-hour clock:

12-Hour AM–PM Clock	24-Hour Military Time
12:00 midnight	00:00
1:00 am	01:00
2:00 am	02:00
3:00 am	03:00
4:00 am	04:00
5:00 am	05:00
6:00 am	06:00

* Military Time Chart. Retrieved on Dec. 17, 2022 from: https://militarytimechart.com/

DOI: 10.4324/9781003402718-55

12-Hour AM–PM Clock	24-Hour Military Time
7:00 am	07:00
8:00 am	08:00
9:00 am	09:00
10:00 am	10:00
11:00 am	11:00
12:00 pm	12:00
1:00 pm	13:00
2:00 pm	14:00
3:00 pm	15:00
4:00 pm	16:00
5:00 pm	17:00
6:00 pm	18:00
7:00 pm	19:00
8:00 pm	20:00
9:00 pm	21:00
10:00 pm	22:00
11:00 pm	23:00
12:00 midnight	24:00

Chapter 55

The Phonetic Alphabet*

The Police Phonetic Alphabet comes from the April 1940 newsletter released by the Association of Public-Safety Communications Officials-International (APCO).

Phonetic alphabets are meant for law enforcement and security officers who use radios to be able to pronounce and understand strings of letters and numbers regardless of signal quality.

The Police Alphabet is unique to American law enforcement officers. It is more concise than the Military Phonetic Alphabet. It is useful for clearly communicating information like names and license plates over the radio. Similar letters like Ds and Bs may sound the same over fuzzy radio traffic. Using the Police Phonetic Alphabet makes what you're trying to say more obvious and minimizes errors by clarifying the letters.

Below is a table of the Phonetic Law Enforcement Alphabet:

A – ADAM	H – HENRY	O – OCEAN	V – VICTOR
B – BOY	I – IDA	P – PAUL	W – WILLIAM
C – CHARLES	J – JOHN	Q – QUEEN	X – X-RAY
D – DAVID	K – KING	R – ROBERT	Y – YOUNG
E – EDWARD	L – LINCOLN	S – SAM	Z – ZEBRA
F – FRANK	M – MARY	T – TOM	
G – GEORGE	N – NORA	U – UNION	

* The police alphabet: an important 'language' for LEOs. Retrieved on Dec. 17, 2022 from: https://www.police1.com/communications/articles/the-police-alphabet-an-important-language-for-leos-YEwuPNi2NsYGlvVh/

DOI: 10.4324/9781003402718-56

Popular codes like "10-4" ("Affirmative") are recognized everywhere, but police radio codes can vary among different areas. Law enforcement agencies now more commonly use plain English when communicating by radio because they often work with other agencies who may not share their language of 10-codes.

Having a standard radio code system for large-scale events like natural disasters or mass shootings requires teamwork between different agencies. During these incidents, everyone must communicate clearly and eliminate confusion and unnecessary radio transmissions.

Chapter 56

Using a Fire Extinguisher

With proper education and training, fire extinguishers can save lives and property. Security officers should be trained on when to use a fire extinguisher and how to use one. Fire extinguisher use is part of the emergency operations procedures in your post orders. Become familiar with the procedures for your particular facility. Never attempt to fight a fire until you have notified someone of the emergency.

When to Use a Fire Extinguisher

Use a fire extinguisher only when you can answer "yes" to the following questions:

- Have I alerted others in the building that there's a fire?
- Has someone called the fire department?
- Am I physically able to use a fire extinguisher?
- Is the fire small and contained in a single object (like a pan or a wastebasket)?
- Am I safe from the fire's toxic smoke?
- Do I have a clear escape route?

OSHA (Occupational Safety and Health Administration) 1910.157(d)(1) states, "Portable fire extinguishers shall be provided for employee use and selected and distributed based on the classes of anticipated workplace fires and on the size and degree of hazard which would affect their use."[1]

OSHA 1910.157(g)(1) states that

> Where the employer has provided portable fire extinguishers for employee use in the workplace, the employer shall also provide an educational program to familiarize employees with the general principles

DOI: 10.4324/9781003402718-57

of fire extinguisher use and the hazards involved with incipient stage firefighting.[2]

Different Classes of Fires

Fires are categorized by what caused the fire or what the fire is using as fuel, and understanding the different classes of fire will help you assess the fire risks at your facility.

- **Class A**: Solid materials such as wood or paper, fabric, and some plastics.
- **Class B**: Liquids or gases such as alcohol, ether, gasoline, or grease.
- **Class C**: Electrical failure from appliances, electronic equipment, and wiring.
- **Class D**: Metallic substances such as sodium, titanium, zirconium, or magnesium.
- **Class K**: Grease or oil fires, specifically from cooking.

For a fire to occur, three things must happen at the same time:

1. Enough **Oxygen** to sustain combustion.
2. Enough **Heat** to reach ignition temperature.
3. Some **Fuel** or combustible material.

Together, oxygen, heat, and fuel produce the chemical reaction that is fire (Figure 56.1). Take away any of these, and the fire will be extinguished.

Figure 56.1 The fire triangle.

Used with permission and courtesy of Shutterstock.com.

How to Use a Fire Extinguisher – Think PASS

P – PULL THE PIN at the top of the extinguisher. The pin releases a locking mechanism and will allow you to discharge the extinguisher.

A – AIM at the base of the fire and not at the flames. You must extinguish the fuel to the fire.

S – SQUEEZE the lever. This will release the extinguishing agent in the extinguisher. If the handle is released, the discharge will stop.

S – SWEEP from side to side. Using a sweeping motion, move the fire extinguisher back and forth until the fire is completely out.[3]

Checking fire extinguishers is a routine part of security officer safety/security inspections while on patrol. Refer to your post orders for specific information.

Remember that portable fire extinguishers are designed for incipient-stage firefighting only and as a security officer, you should be familiar with how to properly assess a fire situation.

Generally, don't attempt to use a portable fire extinguisher to combat fires larger than you are. Assess the fire's location (Is it fully visible or has it spread behind walls or equipment?), levels of heat (Is the room too hot to remain in comfortably?), presence of thick smoke or fumes, and the availability of sufficient exit routes.

Notes

1 Occupational Safety and Health Administration. Retrieved on 01-23-23 from: https://www.osha.gov/laws-regs/regulations/standardnumber/1910/1910.157

2 Ibid.

3 Fire Extinguisher PASS. Retrieved on 01-23-23 from: https://emilms.fema.gov/is_0026/groups/159.html

Chapter 57

When Emergency Medical Personnel Arrive, Part 1: Introduction*

Michael J. Fagel

Introduction

Law enforcement, fire, and Emergency Medical Services (EMS) rescue may arrive on the scene from converging departments. There may be no time to wait for Special Weapons and Tactics (SWAT) protocols, but rather initial contact teams that form up to neutralize the threat. Also, there will be other emergency medical, fire, and rescue personnel arriving, but based on predetermined protocols that should be practiced well in advance, they will usually stage "outside-the-perimeter" awaiting entry request/guidance.

The individuals involved in the incident may be required to provide immediate life-saving care to assist in the life-threatening injuries. Normal EMS protocols may be superseded, and the normal standard of care we enjoy throughout the United States today may be diminished.

Planning, practice, and preparedness are the keys to survival

A plan is a continuous process; it is never complete. All affected parties, agencies, and members of the various entities must be part of the planning team.

* Reprinted with permission by Michael J. Fagel on 01-30-23.

 DOI: 10.4324/9781003402718-58

An effective Emergency Response Plan (ERP) needs the involvement of all stakeholders across all works of life. All departments in your organization must have an active role as well as all outside stakeholders. This must include police, EMS, fire, public health, public works, legal, human resources, and administration at all levels.

An effective ERP should include

- An effective method for reporting threats and other emergencies.
- An evacuation plan that is practiced with posted policies and procedures.
- Appropriately signed and marked emergency escape procedures and route assignments (i.e., floor plans and safe areas).
- Up-to-date contact information for/and responsibilities of individuals to be contacted under ERP.
- Contact information concerning local area hospitals (i.e., name, telephone number, and distance from your location).
- An emergency notification system to alert various parties of an emergency, including:
  - Individuals at remote locations within premises.
  - Local law enforcement.
  - Local area hospitals.

In addition, the ERP specifies responsibilities and key contact information within your organization. The ERP should also include an emergency notification.

If evacuation is necessary, your facilities should have at least two evacuation routes that are conspicuous and well marked.

With an effective ERP and training, you and your staff will be better.

Chapter 58

When Emergency Medical Personnel Arrive, Part 2: Facility Manager's Responsibilities*

Michael J. Fagel

As part of the Emergency Response Plan, your facility managers should

- Implement and understand site security procedures. Institute security access controls (e.g., keys, security system codes, and passcodes):
  - Key fobs and door codes.
- Distribute critical items to appropriate managers/employees, including
  - Pocket-sized floor plans. In "break glass" cabinets.
  - Keys and other access control measures.
  - Facility personnel lists and cell telephone numbers.
  - Daily schedule.
- Assemble crisis kits containing
  - Radios, tested and rotated batteries, and chemical light sticks.
  - Floor plans.
  - Employee roster and emergency contact numbers.
  - Appropriate first aid kits.
  - Flashlights.

* Reprinted with permission by Michael J. Fagel on 01-30-23.

 DOI: 10.4324/9781003402718-59

- Activate the emergency notification system when an emergency situation occurs as well as a backup plan.
- Ensure that the facility has at least two evacuation routes.
- Coordinate with the facility's security department to ensure the physical security of the location as well as an alternate route.
- Advise according to plans and protocols, and if in higher education, timely clear notification.
- Secure doors.
- Order area supervisors to immediately direct all personnel (employees, customers, visitors, vendors, etc.) to evacuate the facility if it can be done safely and with caution.
- Keep personnel as calm as possible and try to notify 911 (using cell phones or telephones) of your location, number of occupants, and status. Turn all cell phones silent!
- Remain in the room until an appropriate all-clear signal or law enforcement arrives.
- Prepare an incident report documenting personal observations.
- Post evacuation routes in conspicuous locations throughout the facility.
- Place up-to-date and secure removable floor plans near entrances and exits for emergency responders.
- Include local first responders during training exercises.
- The training must be as realistic as possible.
- Encourage all emergency responders, including Special Weapons and Tactics (SWAT) teams, canine teams, and bomb squads, an active violence scenario at their locations.
- Foster a "respect" workplace.
- Beware of early indications of potential workplace violence and follow appropriate protocols as trained for the specific situation.

Chapter 59

When Emergency Medical Personnel Arrive, Part 3: Human Resources Responsibilities*

Michael J. Fagel

Human Resources Responsibilities

As part of your Emergency Response Plan, your human resources (HR) department must also plan for emergency situations involving an active shooter scenario.

Planning for various situations may help to mitigate the likelihood of an incident by establishing processes such as

- Conducting effective employee screening and background checks.
- Creating an effective system for reporting signs of potentially violent employee behavior.
- Making appropriate Employee Assistance Program (EAP) counseling services available to employees.

* Reprinted with permission by Michael J. Fagel on 01-30-23.

DOI: 10.4324/9781003402718-60

Training

Once the emergency response process is ready for testing, you and your staff should be trained to prepare to respond to active violence situations, including the use of exercises that involve local law enforcement.

You and your personnel need to establish an effective education and training program and be effectively and appropriately trained in its protocols and procedures so that you and your team can act effectively if you are ever confronted with an active shooter situation.

One commonly used effective training practice in responding to an active violence situation for you and your team is to conduct well-planned and implemented active violence training exercises.

Security consultants trained in active violence situations, and local response agencies, will be valuable resources as you prepare an effective training scenario appropriate to your situation.

In addition to your immediate security staff, your employees should also be trained in

- Recognizing the sound of gunshots.
- Reacting quickly when gunshots are heard and/or when a shooting is witnessed. Training should cover
  - Knowing how to evacuate the area.
  - Knowing how to hide out.
  - Knowing how to take action against the shooter as a last resort.
  - Knowing when to call 911 immediately.
  - Knowing how to respond when law enforcement arrives. Keep your hands visible at all times. Keep your fingers spread. Drop any objects in your hands. Respond to official commands. Do not reach for or grab responders.
  - Knowing how to adopt a survival mindset during times of crisis.

Meeting the Needs of Those with Disabilities

In addition to developing the Emergency Response Plan and ongoing process and conducting regularly held evacuation instructions and any other retraining exercises, you should ensure that your plans, evacuation instructions, and any other relevant information include provisions for managing the requirements of individuals with special needs and/or disabilities. It is also important to ensure that your building is accessible for individuals with disabilities and is in compliance with Americans with Disabilities Act (ADA) requirements.

Adopting these proactive measures to anticipate security concerns before they materialize can be achieved by creating an effective security strategy based on a robust Emergency Response Plan and practice that may well result in resiliency for your organization. This is essential to deter potential threats.

Adversaries (including active shooters) generally attack the most vulnerable targets (i.e., "targets of opportunity" or "soft" targets). Therefore, mitigating the risk to your facility by minimizing external threats outside your secure perimeter is paramount. Having an effective security program in place will reduce the likelihood of being perceived by your adversary as vulnerable and could help dissuade such potential threats from selecting your facility as a target, such as when an individual engages in purchase of suspicious weapons and ammunition and stockpiling,

Thus, private sector security and law enforcement agencies may use a variety of protective measures to help disrupt or mitigate a potential active shooter attack during the four initial pre-incident phases, such as when an individual engages in suspicious weapons and ammunition purchases, stockpiling, target selection and surveillance, and approaching the intended target.

Chapter 60

Training

Training standards,[1] where they exist at all, are inconsistent at best. There is no standard curriculum within the United States, nor is there a standard number of training hours for individual topics or the training course. Some states mandate security guard (aka: security officer) certification, while others do not. New York, for instance, passed the Security Guard Act in 1992, which requires the training and registration of security guards and state approval of all security training programs. In Alabama, security officers are not registered or licensed at all. In some states where training is mandated, the employer can defer training for a set period. Deferred training, coupled with the high turnover rate in the private security services industry, makes it possible for security officers to drift from one employer to another without ever being trained. Security officers employed by the military in war zones are an exception. To qualify for the work, they must undergo meaningful training, much of which is paramilitary in nature.

Topics suitable for entry-level security officer training include the following:

- The role of a private security officer
- Legal aspects of private security
- Use of force
- Note taking and report writing
- Court testimony
- Conduct and appearance
- Interpersonal communication skills
- Ethics
- Access control procedures
- Emergency response procedures
- Life safety procedures
- Patrol operations

DOI: 10.4324/9781003402718-61

- Intrusion detection and response
- Workplace violence response procedures
- First aid, advanced first aid, cardiopulmonary resuscitation (CPR), and automated external defibrillator (AED)

It is positive that ASIS International has developed a set of training topics recommended to its members. In addition to entry-level training, the client of a contract private security services company may require training appropriate for the client's business, e.g., orientation to

- The physical layout of the protected premises
- The names, faces, and positions of senior management
- The client's policies with respect to harassment, discrimination, diversity, etc.
- Substance abuse
- Telephone protocol
- Demeanor and behavior
- The key rules of a labor-management agreement, if any

Training can be administered in three ways:

- Classroom
- On the job
- Online

Classroom training methods include lectures, demonstrations, the use of audiovisuals, and practical exercises. Professional trainers agree that retention of knowledge and acquisition of skills is greatly increased when practical exercises are used. Examples of practical exercises are how to administer first aid, CPR, AED, directing traffic, self-defense techniques, verbal de-escalation, use of force, applying handcuffs, searching persons and property, inspecting parcels and packages, protecting a crime scene, using communication equipment, and, for armed guards, safety and nomenclature of the weapon issued and extensive practice at a firing range.

On-the-job training (OJT) is an excellent method for teaching all of the above. The downside is that an experienced officer or supervisor has to be removed from their normal duties to conduct the OJT and monitor the officer's job performance.

Online training, a method of instruction relatively new to training security officers, is an excellent method for imparting knowledge. The advantages are as follows:

- Training occurs wherever a PC or laptop is available.
- Learning proceeds at the student's pace.
- Can be done at any time and any place (even at the officer's home, if allowed).

The method does not permit the trainee to move forward in study until all material has been covered, and the training content is uniform for everyone. The method is enhanced when the instruction is augmented with audiovisuals and progress questions are presented throughout the course so that the student can assess his/her learning. Accessibility to an instructor or course administrator by television, phone, e-mail, or in person is also recommended. The contract security company can also free itself from maintaining a record of training because the software of the online learning system does it automatically. The downside of online training is the impossibility of conducting hands-on training. However, the cost of online training is significantly less than other instructional methods, and the trainee can be placed on the job without a long delay. OJT would then pick up the slack for tasks that are hands-on oriented.

A private contract security company will find it difficult to rely exclusively on classroom training because of the issues of scheduling the classes and the students. Sporadic hiring is the nature of the contract security industry, and teaching in a classroom where there are few people to be taught at one time can be costly and not helpful in quickly filling vacant positions. To overcome the problem, some companies (despite rules against it) will brief the individual on the job's tasks, show a film, and test the individual on paper. If the individual fails the test, it is administered until passed. States that regulate the industry usually require the security services company to submit a statement to the regulatory agency affirming that the training has been completed. Little or nothing is done about the quality of the instruction. Finally, the regulatory agency rarely conducts inspections to verify that the security services company is meeting the mandated requirements.

Proper training can go a long way toward preventing or reducing liability. A few points to be considered regarding training are

- All personnel who perform crucial, significant job tasks must be trained to perform those tasks.
- All personnel should also be trained in properly using all equipment and weapons they use on the job.
- Training should approximate the actual task performance conditions as much as possible.
- Training programs must be well researched and planned.
- Training must be delivered seriously so that subordinates do not scoff at it.
- Training in human relations, public relations, customer relations, conflict resolution, and crisis intervention is crucial for the effective, user-friendly human interaction that prevents crisis situations from developing and helps diffuse unavoidable situations.
- There should be some validation or evaluation of the training to determine if the trainees are competent in the tasks they have been trained in.

- Training helps to establish a professional image and a climate of excellence within an organization, which can help reduce the number of complaints and lawsuits.
- The least capable employee is the one most likely to be the primary causal factor in a lawsuit – the capability of this person must be increased to an acceptable level as they are not on trial; the training program is.
- Documentation – class rosters are a good start. Rosters must specify who was trained in what, when they were trained, where they were trained, and who trained them. Additional notes on specific learning experiences are also important to record.
- Instructor qualifications, credentials, or certification should be clearly and unequivocally demonstrable.

Note

1 Fay, John J and Patterson, David. *Contemporary Security Management, Fourth Edition*, Boston: Elsevier Publishers, 2018.

Chapter 61

Pre-patrol Intelligence

Before beginning a shift, a security officer – if not formally briefed by a supervisor or previous officer – should read the patrol log (in either paper or electronic format) for the previous shift. An officer should pay particular note of anything unusual that was reported. This reported activity may be a prelude to additional threats to the protected assets. Security officers should be aware of criminal activity and other unusual news events in the surrounding area of the property he/she is protecting. This activity may indicate increased awareness, and additional patrol oversight may be needed during their shift. Lastly, any reports that were generated by the previous shift should be read by the officer to have an understanding of what occurred before them beginning patrol.

DOI: 10.4324/9781003402718-62

Chapter 62

Effective Patrol Techniques

Effective patrol programs are designed around findings, usually based on a security assessment or survey. These studies look at threats that exist for the assets that are to be protected. These threats can be man-made or natural. Part of the assessment process is to identify vulnerabilities that exist and to make recommendations to mitigate the vulnerabilities. Another part of the assessment is to review the existing security measures in place and make recommendations to enhance security operations, generally through various measures, including that of a physical security patrol presence.

To have an effective security program, both technical and physical needs must be coordinated in such a way as to fit into the environment being protected and, at the same time, display a secure presence. Since different settings require different security applications and modes of patrol, a security assessment is extremely important before deploying security officers.

After the security assessment has been completed and vulnerabilities identified, the security solutions can be implemented. Regardless of what those solutions are, security patrol will be based on the protection of assets – people, property, operations, and information.

Mobile Patrol

A mobile patrol is just as it sounds. A security officer is assigned to be active and mobile during their shift and may perform patrol either on foot or using a motorized

DOI: 10.4324/9781003402718-63

vehicle, a bicycle, horse, Segway, or some other type of mobile means. In other assignments, mobile patrol may be conducted by boat or helicopter. Regardless of the mode of transportation, a security officer on patrol must ensure his/her designated area is thoroughly patrolled and inspected by conducting pre-planned or assigned "tours." It is important to note that mobile patrol tours should be varied and not conducted in the same order.

Virtual Patrol

Given technological advancements and more frequent use, a security officer may be positioned inside a command center where security cameras monitor access control, burglary, fire, and environmental alarms. A security officer assigned to monitor this technology should conduct virtual tours by going through each camera view to support any mobile officers on patrol. When no security officers are deployed, a command center officer should conduct these "virtual tours" as if they were on patrol. Stationary views should be examined, and pan–tilt–zoom (PTZ) cameras may be utilized. Moreover, the alarm systems should be examined to ensure all door, window, motion, and environmental sensors register correctly and are not in "trouble mode" or inadvertently bypassed. Video surveillance may also include analytics, a technology that uses algorithms to assist with security-related functions. There are three common types of video analytics:

- Fixed algorithm analytics
- Artificial intelligence learning algorithms
- Facial recognition systems[1]

Fixed algorithm analytics and artificial intelligence learning algorithms have basically the same function – to determine if an unwanted or suspicious behavior is occurring within the field of view of a camera, and the algorithm notifies the console security officer of the incident. Examples of these algorithms are an individual crossing a line, moving in the wrong direction down a corridor (e.g., airport exit route), leaving or picking up an article/object, or loitering in a specific area. Each of these algorithms is searching for a specific identified behavior.

Artificial intelligence learning algorithms begin essentially as a blank slate. After they are connected to a camera for a specified time, they issue alerts and alarms. The system is learning what is normal for that area during different times of the day and night. The system issues alerts when it detects things inconsistent with previous activity in that area.

Facial recognition systems match specific points on an individual's face with a sample stored in a database and will alert if a match is found. If the face does not match a stored record, it creates a new one.

Regardless of the type of patrol duties or post where a security officer is assigned, it is important that adequate training is conducted to ensure that the officer understands the responsibilities and functions of their job, knows how to operate equipment, and has the tools necessary to perform job tasks.

Note

1 Electronic Elements. Retrieved on 01-31-23 from: https://www.sciencedirect.com/topics/computer-science/video-analytics

Chapter 63

Equipment Check*

Before each shift, a security officer should perform a radio test to ensure their radio is transmitting and receiving radio communications. Flashlights need to be checked to safeguard against drained or dead batteries. Security belts should be examined for leather fatigue, so important items, such as keys, don't come loose during patrol.

If cameras are being monitored by a command center, the security officer monitoring them should check to see which cameras are not functioning so special attention to that area can be delivered during patrol.

Patrol vehicles should have a full tank of gas and be supplied with the proper equipment such as a first aid kit, fire extinguisher, and an automated external defibrillator (AED). These pieces of equipment should also be inspected to ensure they are in the "ready" position and are in working order.

* Reprinted by permission from John O'Rourke.

DOI: 10.4324/9781003402718-64

Chapter 64

Prevention of Crime

As a security officer, you are responsible for preventing crime on the property you are assigned to protect. This should not, however, be confused with the enforcement of law. You are not a law enforcement officer. Your presence, being in proper uniform and presenting an official and professional image, is a crime deterrent. When a crime does occur, you should notify law enforcement and accurately relay information to them and assist them as needed.

DOI: 10.4324/9781003402718-65

Chapter 65

Crime Analysis

Crime analysis is effective in identifying past problems and *future trends*. Consider getting copies of the incident reports from the past 12 months. Then, break them down into categories such as property and personal crime. Identify problem areas such as parking lots, parking garages, the front entrance, and the employee entrance. Include reports of suspicious activity as well. Look for patterns, trends, similarities, and repeat issues.

If thefts are in an area of concern, identify locations, time of day, and day of the week. For example, if a car is stolen every Friday night between 6 pm and 10 pm, now you have a trend and can do something about it. Maybe, you may need to trim bushes so there is more natural surveillance or there is an area without adequate lighting. These are issues that can be corrected with some landscaping maintenance, increased lighting, directed patrol, or additional security coverage at the location. Consider hiring law enforcement to periodically patrol problem areas. BE PROACTIVE.

DOI: 10.4324/9781003402718-66

Chapter 66

Deter, Detect, Delay, Deny*

This methodology provides for the protection of hardened critical assets by considering the four primary protection elements. A properly orchestrated security program will have designed its protective measures around what is known in the industry as the "**Four Ds of Security**."

Whether using technology or a security officer, physical protective measures are built around the principles of Deter, Detect, Delay, and Deny. The primary elements of an effective protection plan design are as follows:

1. **Deter** – Discouraging an adversary from attempting an assault by reducing the likelihood of a successful attack.
2. **Detect** – Determining that an undesirable event has occurred or is occurring. Detection includes sensing the event, communicating the alarm to an attended location, and assessing the alarm.
3. **Delay** – Impeding adversary penetration into a protected area.
4. **Deny** – Prevent an adversary from committing a crime.

As a security officer, there is an additional element. You will

Respond – To counteract adversarial activity and interrupt the undesirable event.

A security officer should deliver their protective services with the same principle in mind.

* Basic Physical Security Concepts. Retrieved on 02-07-23 from: https://www.irs.gov/irm/part10/irm_10-002-011.

 DOI: 10.4324/9781003402718-67

Deter

Measures in place that can deter unwanted behavior or criminal activity are locked doors, restricted areas, security cameras, fencing, and security patrols. Policies and procedures are also part of the deter methodology. Moreover, a properly designed physical security system will layer the protective measures. For example, a fence may be the first layer, a locked exterior door would be another layer, and a burglar alarm system another layer. Security cameras add additional layers to security. Interior layers of security would be additional locked doors, alarm systems, and safes. Someone with malevolent intentions seeing such security measures in place may be dissuaded from their intentions.

A security officer is part of a layered security system. The purpose of a security officer on patrol is to have a physical presence protecting the assets. Most often, a security officer is part of a greater security program. However, there are times when a security officer is the only physical security measure utilized. There is more a security officer can do rather than be part of a layered system. A security officer can become a deterrent in and of themselves.

An alert and attentive security officer can be a powerful deterrent against unwanted behavior, including possible criminal activity. Security officers must strictly enforce policies and not be permissive to clearly defined wrong behavior. An example would be allowing an employee to tailgate another employee rather than using their access card. Another example would be allowing employees to keep a door ajar while they temporarily go outside to get something out of their car or smoke a cigarette. Enforcing compliance with organizational policy by all employees, regardless of their position, is a strong deterrent against more troubling behavior. Those watching, wishing to penetrate the security system or take advantage of their employer, will be less inclined to do so with a security officer who upholds strict compliance with the organizational rules.

Part of an officer's patrol responsibilities, and a deterrent method, is having security officers test and inspect fire and burglary alarm systems. A security officer should periodically check alarms, locks, security cameras, and lighting to ensure measures that have been put in place are functioning correctly. Any item that is nonfunctional should be reported to the appropriate department for repair and/or replacement.

Detect

Detecting unwanted or criminal activity can be challenging, especially for a security officer on patrol. Nonetheless, this is the fundamental reason a security officer is utilized. Officers must have the requisite skills to patrol diligently and be able to identify activity which is contrary to policy or criminal in nature. Often, the signs of criminal or unauthorized behavior are subtle, not overt. A well-trained and versed security officer will be aware of this fact and be alert to all activity taking place during their post or patrol.

Whether out on patrol, on a post, or inside a command center watching security monitors, a security officer should be alert and aware of activity in and around their patrol assignment. Security camera technology has improved to create alerts that notify a security officer of activity taking place on the screen. This technology has improved with the aid of facial recognition and item identification with a memory of past events. It can also acquire a memory of what a certain camera view should look like. When that view changes, and if for instance someone places a backpack down and leaves it there, the system can send an alert to security. A security officer should take full advantage of the technology available to them at the specific site they are protecting. Regardless of the technology available, whether it be smart analytics or a simple security camera system, management should ensure the technology is set up appropriately to aid the security officer in their duties.

To aid a security officer with detecting unwanted or criminal behavior, it is important that officers have the proper equipment needed for the assignments they have been given. Flashlights, binoculars, and night vision technology are tools that enhance a security officer's ability to detect activity taking place in and around their patrol assignment(s).

Delay

The second part of the "Four Ds" is to Deter unwanted behavior, trespassing, and criminal behavior. The security features mentioned in the Deter section also help to delay unwanted intruders from gaining access. Fencing creates a physical barrier that requires either an intruder to climb over or cut through. In doing so, entry by the perpetrator is delayed, which can become a deterrent and displace the intruder to another location where security measures are not as robust. Regardless, if the intruder is not discouraged, the physical barrier delays access. The longer access can be delayed, the more likely the activity will be observed. And, the longer the delay, the more of a deterrent the barrier becomes. Security measures work together to thwart unwanted behavior.

A security officer well versed in creating delay methods during patrol will be a powerful tool in deterring unwanted behavior and delaying the actions of those wishing to gain access to an unauthorized area or commit unauthorized activity. Furthermore, a security officer who can recognize security features and understand burglary ratings and categories can coordinate patrol patterns with the security measures in place.

Often, security officers and their supervisors designing patrol patterns don't understand security features built around the assets they are protecting. For example, a prominent company in New York City has fine art paintings on its corridor wall, each valued upward of $100,000.00. To protect these valuable art pieces, they have placed frame locking devices on each painting. These locking devices are not armed but have a burglary rating of 45 minutes. This rating indicates the degree of protection that the locking device delivers. In this case, the rating indicates that it would take a person 45 minutes to defeat the lock and gain access to the painting. Other security features on the company floor are access control doors and a night security guard. On the surface, there appears to be adequate protection. But, as anyone who ever has been in an office building knows, access-controlled doors are often left ajar, and sometimes doors fall out of alignment and don't close on their own. However, upon further review of their protocols, it was discovered that the security officer was assigned to patrol the floor every two hours. It was abundantly clear management, and the security guard was unfamiliar with burglary ratings and the ratings of those locks they had at their place of business. If they did, a two-hour patrol sweep would not have been set up because it allows plenty of time for a burglar to thwart the layered security and defeat the 45-minute delay feature of the lock on the valuable art.

When delivering security patrol services, a program should be set up to complement the security features for the protected assets. Setting up a security program and deploying officers should be done in an informed way to exist effectively with the overall protective measures.

Deny

Each preceding "D" in the "Four Ds" works to achieve the objective of denying access to the assets being protected. The whole concept of protection is focused on denying unauthorized entry to the asset or assets being protected. It is the ideal outcome for protecting assets and can be the hardest goal to achieve. Each operation of a patrol program is designed to aid in denying access, policy violations, thefts, and other unwanted behavior. Nonetheless, burglary ratings and categories illustrate the difficulty in achieving the objective of denying access. Burglary safes, fire safes, locking mechanisms, and even safe rooms have ratings that indicate how long the protective measure will hold up before penetration or degradation to the protective layer occurs.

It is imperative that a security officer understand this concept. The goal is to protect and deny access to the assets being protected. However, a security officer who understands each security measure in place can be ultimately defeated. Whether it be a fence, a locked door, or a safe, a security officer should conduct their patrol to compliment and become an added layer to the security features.

Chapter 67

Lighting*

Primary Lighting Sources

Incandescent is the least efficient and most expensive lighting to operate and it has a very short lifespan.

Fluorescent lamps are more efficient than incandescent lamps but are not used extensively outdoors. They are inefficient in cold weather but have a long life span.

Halogen and quartz halogen provide 25% better efficiency and life than ordinary incandescent bulbs.

Mercury vapor takes several minutes to produce full light output but has a long life.

Metal halide imitates daylight. It works well with video surveillance but is expensive to install and maintain.

High-pressure sodium is energy efficient and has a long life.

Low-pressure sodium is more efficient than high-pressure sodium but expensive to maintain.

Light emitting diode (LED) is one of the newest light sources where light is emitted from a semiconductor. It has a greater resistance to shock, vibration, and wear, so its lifespan is increased significantly. LED lights can come in various "color" outputs with one being "daylight." Daylight LED lights are used by almost all video applications, including broadcast videography. LED lighting has the potential to furnish a cost-effective alternative that lasts longer without sacrificing illumination.

Induction has a long life and is similar to fluorescent lamps.

Infrared is invisible to the naked eye but may be useful for video surveillance illumination.

---

* National Crime Prevention Institute (NCPI) 2008, Physical Security Seminar.

DOI: 10.4324/9781003402718-68

There are seven basic types of protective lighting:

Continuous – Fixed and most common
Standby – Turns on with alarm activation
Movable – Manually operated searchlights
Emergency – Can duplicate other lighting systems in the event of an emergency
Controlled – Used outside a perimeter
Area – Used in open areas and parking lots
Surface – Frequently used on the surface of structures and buildings

Some key points about lighting to remember while you're on patrol:

- Lighting equipment must be inspected and maintained regularly.
- All lighting fixtures should be numbered so that they are easily identified to report nonoperational lighting.
- Ensure that vegetation is not obstructing the light.
- Ensure that lighting is sufficient for camera operation.
- Ensure that the lamps are operational with no signs of breakage or vandalism.
- Ensure that lamps are clean and positioned at the proper angle.
- Ensure that the lighting intensity meets security requirements and that no shadows or dark areas need illumination.

Chapter 68

Deterrents

By definition, a deterrent is "serving to discourage, prevent, or inhibit."[1]

Category One

- Network security surveillance system to prevent crime in private and public locations
- Crime Prevention through Environmental Design (CPTED) principles and concepts
- Defensible space principles and concepts
- Situational crime prevention principles and concepts
- Lighting that meets standards and design by increased visibility
- Biometrics and access control to specific areas
- Signage
- Padlocks, door locks, and door viewers
- Intrusion alarms and alarm signage

Category Two

- Security officers and law enforcement officers in uniform who may deduce that a crime is about to be committed and deter the incident
- Security officers on patrol – on foot, by vehicle, or virtually to protect assets
- Bollards or barricades to close off areas
- Hardening soft targets

DOI: 10.4324/9781003402718-69

CPTED Strategies

1. Natural access control
2. Natural surveillance
3. Territorial reinforcement (Crowe 1999).

CPTED Landscape Principles

1. For natural surveillance, trim bushes/shrubs to a height of 3 ft or less and tree canopies to 8 ft from the ground.
2. Chain-link fencing to a height of 8 ft plus three strands of barbed wire.
3. Height of a stone wall – 8 ft.
4. A least 10 ft of clear space on both sides of the fence or wall.[2]

Environmental security differs from CPTED in that it uses a broader range of crime control strategies, including social management, social media, target hardening, activity support, and law enforcement.

Notes

1 Deterrent. Retrieved on 02-07-23 from: https://www.merriam-webster.com/dictionary/deterrent

2 James F. Broder., *CPP Risk Analysis and the Security Survey*, 3rd edition, 2006 Elsevier.

Chapter 69

Fraternization

Workplace relationships can be difficult. A fraternization policy aims to minimize the impact of potentially negative results of a romantic relationship in the workplace.

Security officers should never fraternize with their employer/client, client/employees/customers, or security officers with the same duty assignment. The bottom line is be professional – pleasant friendly, but never overly familiar. This will ensure that all interactions with fellow officers, the client/employer, their employees, and customers will be conducted fairly and objectively. Keep in mind that contact on social media may also be considered unauthorized fraternization. Social relationships outside of work with the client/employer or their employees and customers may undermine your ability to perform your duties.

Most organizations have a fraternization policy to send a clear message against sexual harassment, especially when there are workplace relationships among subordinates and supervisors. If and when a workplace relationship ends, the subordinate may claim that the relationship resulted from an unwelcome advance, which may place the client/employer at risk. A workplace relationship may also initiate a claim of a hostile work environment or favoritism. Additionally, the productivity of those involved in the workplace relationship may suffer if their relationship is pursued during work hours. This may lead to reassignment or possibly termination.

A fraternization policy is difficult to "police" and may raise personal and legal concerns. It's important to remember that as a security officer, you are a professional authority figure and you should not engage in potentially inappropriate behavior in the workplace.

 DOI: 10.4324/9781003402718-70

Chapter 70

Bomb Threat Checklist

- Exact time and date of call:

  ____

- Exact words of the caller:

  ____

- Ask them to repeat the message, if necessary, and write as much as possible.
- Keep calm.
- Keep talking.
- Don't hang up.
- Signal a co-worker to get on an extension and notify management and/or the local police.
- Ask when and where the bomb is going to explode:

  ____

- Ask what the bomb looks like and where on the property it is:

  ____

- Ask what type of a bomb it is:

  ____

- Ask what will cause it to detonate:

  ____

- Ask why they are doing this:

  ____

DOI: 10.4324/9781003402718-71

- Ask where they are calling from:

  ____

- Try to get the caller's full name:

  ____

- Try to get caller's exact location and phone number:

  ____

- Listen carefully to the voice; note whether it's a man or a woman, pitch, accent, etc.
- Circle the following: Calm, Slow, Nasal, Angry, Broke, Stutter, Disguised, Lisp, Sincere, Rapid, Giggler, Deep, Crying, Squeaky, Excited, Stressed, Accent, Loud, Slurred, Normal
- If the voice is familiar, who did it sound like?

  ____

- Background noises heard (cars, trains, etc.):

  ____

- Any other pertinent information:

  ____

- Person receiving the call:

  ____

- Telephone number call received at:

  ____

Chapter 71

Incident Report Form

To be completed immediately after the incident is secured and forwarded to the security supervisor before the end of the shift.

- Reports must include who, what, when, where, how, action taken, and the end result.
- Who – employee, visitor, contractor, vendor or customer.
- Type of incident – conduct/missing or stolen property/medical/slip and fall, etc.
- Full name – first and last and contact information - address, phone number, etc.
- Date and time of incident.
- Date and time incident reported/written.
- Where – complete address of facility.
- What room or area – lobby, parking lot, hallway, home, etc.
- All details pertinent to incident.
- Action taken – What did you do? What did others do? What was the end result – paramedic transport; received service; left building without being processed; arrested.
- If EMS or fire department was called and on-site, names of first responders. If police involved – name of officer, district, generated report number, and copy of written report.
- Type of incident – conduct/missing or stolen property/medical/slip and fall, etc.
- Full name – first and last.
- Date and time of incident.
- Date and time of incident reported/written.
- Where – complete address of facility.
- Print legibly.
- Sign and date document.

DOI: 10.4324/9781003402718-72

Chapter 72

Target Hardening

The emphasis on design and use deviates from the traditional target-hardening approach to crime prevention. Traditional target hardening focuses on denying access to a crime target through physical or artificial barrier techniques (such as locks, alarms, fences, and gates). Target hardening often leads to constraints on the hardened environment's use, access, and enjoyment. Moreover, the traditional approach overlooks opportunities for natural access control and surveillance. The term *natural* refers to deriving access control and surveillance results as a by-product of the normal and routine use of the environment. It is possible to adapt normal and natural uses of the environment to accomplish the effects of artificial or mechanical hardening and surveillance. Nevertheless, Crime Prevention through Environmental Design (CPTED) employs pure target-hardening strategies, either to test their effectiveness as compared to natural strategies or when they appear to be justified as not unduly impairing the effective use of the environment.

As an example, a design strategy of improved street lighting must be planned, efficient, and evaluated in terms of the behavior it promotes or deters and the use impact of the lighted (and related) areas in terms of all users of the area (offenders, victims, and other permanent or casual users). Any strategies related to the lighting strategy (e.g., block-watch or neighborhood watch, 911 emergency service, and police patrol) must be evaluated in the same regard. This reflects the comprehensiveness of the CPTED design approach in focusing on both the proper design and effective use of the physical environment. Additionally, the concept of proper design and effective use emphasizes the design relationship among strategies to ensure the desired results are achieved. It has been observed that improved street lighting alone (a design strategy) is ineffective against crime without the conscious and active support of citizens (in reporting what they see) and police (in responding and conducting surveillance). CPTED involves integrating design, citizen and community action, and law enforcement strategies to accomplish surveillance consistent with the design and use of the environment.

 DOI: 10.4324/9781003402718-73

Chapter 73

Grooming and Uniform Standards

Grooming

Female Employees

On-duty uniformed female security officers shall arrange their hair so that it does not interfere with vision or extend below the bottom edge of the collar in normal posture. Hair color should be natural or of a subdued mild color (no bright or unusual coloration) and neat, clean, and orderly. The hairstyle must allow for the proper wear of the uniform hat if it is part of the uniform. The hat should fit snugly and even on the head, with the bill resting 1–2 inches above the eyebrows.

Male Employees

Security officers shall keep their hair properly trimmed. The hair shall be at least moderately tapered, shall not extend below the top of the shirt collar or cover the ear, and shall not interfere with vision in any way.

Sideburns shall not exceed beyond a point even with the bottom of the ear lobe and shall extend in a clean-shaven, horizontal line. The sideburn shall be trimmed and neat in appearance.

A short, neatly trimmed mustache of natural color may be worn. Security officers shall be clean-shaven when reporting for duty. The growth of whiskers shall be permitted for medical reasons with documentation from a medical doctor stating the specific medical reason.

DOI: 10.4324/9781003402718-74

Exceptions to the hair standards for both males and females may be made for medical or religious reasons as a reasonable accommodation. Hairpins/clasps can be worn, but they must be black, neutral, or the same color.

Visible tattoos or body art is prohibited. Tattoos or body art must be covered by your uniform or by makeup of the same or similar color as your natural skin color.

Security officers' fingernails shall be clean and kept to a length that will not interfere in any way with the performance of assigned duties

Security officers may wear lipstick, nail polish, and other appropriate cosmetics, lightly applied, providing the colors are natural and subdued.

Jewelry

On-duty uniformed security officers shall wear only conservative jewelry. A wedding or engagement ring is appropriate, not a ring on every finger or thumb. No "body piercing" through the nose, tongue, eyebrows, nor any visible area not concealed by a regulation uniform may be worn while on duty. Looped/dangle earrings or jewelry will not be worn on duty. Only one pair of post or studded earrings may be worn while on duty and worn in the earlobe only. Chains and chain jewelry should not be visible.

Uniforms

The uniform will fit properly, be clean, and be free of excess wrinkles. Uniform accessories will be properly worn, cleaned, polished, or maintained as appropriate. All security officers are subject to the requirements of the company uniform policy. The purpose of this policy is to ensure that individuals employed as security officers exhibit uniformity in appearance so that the client, their customers, employees, contractors and vendors, and the general public can identify and recognize the status and authority of the Officer. Adherence to this policy by security officers shall provide for the safety, security, and protection of people and property.

- Security officers shall wear black rubber-soled shoes (not tennis shoes or sneakers) while in uniform unless other footwear is approved by the client or employer.
- All security officers shall be required to wear client or company-issued uniforms while on duty unless "street clothes" are required for a specific assignment.
- The uniform policy applies to all security officers regardless of gender.
- Failure to wear the issued uniform by this policy shall result in disciplinary action. Repeated violations of this policy may result in disciplinary up to and including termination.
- Sneakers/tennis shoes, jeans, shorts, sweatpants, and/or T-shirts are not acceptable attire for any security officers in uniform while on duty.

- Security officers are expected to report for work physically clean, neat, and well-groomed and remain presentable while on duty.
- Each security officer may be responsible for maintaining, clean and properly care for maintaining, cleaning and properly caring for his/her uniform at his/her own cost.
- The client or company may not be responsible for replacing a uniform that has been lost or stolen as a result of negligence. A security officer who has been deemed negligent by the client or company in the maintenance and/or storage of his/her uniform shall bear the full replacement cost.

The company, individual post or specific client may require certain uniform and grooming standards for security officers assigned to a designated assignment.

It is important that security officers present a professional image and exhibit the organization's culture.

Chapter 74

Risk Management and Security Master Planning for Events and Festivals

A risk management plan is an essential aspect of organizing any event, so all potential risks that may arise from holding an event and the steps that will be taken to reduce or mitigate identified risks must be identified.

Over the years, we have both been involved in helping organize security for events and festivals, so we decided to put together a set of guidelines or an operational plan. Your objective is to coordinate with various departments and individuals to ensure a safe and enjoyable event for everyone.

A risk can mean many things. For community events, the main risks to consider are anything that could

- Cause harm to another person.
- Cause damage to equipment, infrastructure, or the event site.
- Harm the future of the event organizing committee and/or the event itself.

Some risks are out of the event organizer's control. In this case, the risk management plan details who is responsible for coordinating the safety of every person must something that is out of the control of the event organizer occurs.

To assess a risk, consider

- Existing risks of the site
- Risks the event creates

 DOI: 10.4324/9781003402718-75

- External risks the event organizer has little control over but may need to be managed at the event

At the event site itself:

- Will moving vehicles be near the event site and could this pose a risk to pedestrians?
- Is there anything on the site that could become dangerous if there is inclement weather?
- Is there a body of water on or near the event site?
- Is there infrastructure being brought on to the event site? Who will ensure it is safely secured?
- Are you bringing vehicles on site? If so, how will you manage the safety of people who are setting up near vehicles?
- Will there be children's activities, such as an inflatable bouncy house or carnival rides, and how will the safety of event guests be ensured when on or near rides?
- A risk assessment of all external risks.
- If an evacuation of the event site is required, who is responsible for ensuring all people are calmly and safely moved?
- Are the likely guests at your event at a higher risk of requiring emergency services? If so, have you advised local emergency services?

To begin your security master plan, organize the following:

- Describe the activities at the event in detail.
- Describe in detail the location of the event.
- Identify where the operations center will be located.
- Determine if video surveillance will be deployed and if it will be monitored from the operations center.
- List law enforcement agencies, other government service providers, and local community organizations that you expect to be involved with, along with their contact information. Event staff should be introduced to any outside agency team members.
- Identify area hotels and list the contact person with their phone number.
- Identify all airports, bus depots, and train services and list who in security is in charge of each.
- Design a traffic management plan. Identify drop-off and parking areas for personally owned vehicles (POVs), law enforcement vehicles, Emergency Medical Services (EMS) vehicles and ambulances, buses, and Uber/ride-share/taxi services.
- Plan for adequate lighting as well as emergency lighting.

- Identify public and private access points along with site perimeter security.
- Determine if you will be screening people, vehicles, equipment, and packages that are brought into the event area. If magnetometers (either walk-through or hand wands) are used, and bag checks are being done, ensure all personnel are trained.
- Determine the number of security personnel needed (with event staff uniforms) and identify area responsibilities.
- Establish a communications plan – radios, cell phones, public address system, etc., to ensure all coordinators at the event can communicate. If the event is multi-jurisdictional, effective communications are critical.
- Create emergency action plans (including lost children, active shooter, and bomb threat) and coordinate these plans with law enforcement and emergency medical personnel.
- Prepare signage to direct patrons to different areas of the event.
- Arrange for portable restrooms with adequate lighting and security personnel.
- Identify who will be responsible for waste removal and site clean-up.
- Prepare maps of the site with key areas identified.

A venue emergency operations plan (VEOP) is similar to an emergency action plan (EAP) but focuses on a specific venue. There will be more specific response procedures for that location.

An incident action plan (IAP) is developed in coordination with the VEOP and the EAP and will address different situations.

- The IAP utilizes the Incident Command System; each individual needs to be advised of their specific assignments and immediate supervisor.
- The IAP should give clear and simple instructions for individuals working at the event.
- IAPs are specific about security access control points (ACP), traffic control points (TCP), communications, and staffing.
- Staff assigned to a specific post or location should be advised of specific job tasks and understand what time they should be on post when they can take breaks, and when their shift ends.
- Staff working at the event must be briefed and given a copy of the IAP. They need to know where everyone at the event is assigned.
- The IAP and VEOP work in coordination with each other. Detailed response procedures, such as for active shooters, are in the VEOP.
- Individuals scheduled to work at the event should be briefed on the IAP at the pre-event briefing. The pre-event briefing of the IAP is critical to ensure effectiveness.
- There should be updates on any recent or last-minute changes to staffing, schedule, or new/specific threats.

- If credentials are being issued, staff must see them and know exactly what they mean – all access, media access, etc.

The most important part of creating a risk management plan is that you should reduce potential risks as much as possible and have thought about what you would need to do in an emergency during your event. An after-action report should be completed so planners can determine what worked well (and what didn't) and what lessons were learned. It is important to remember that every event is different and has different resources available.

Chapter 75

Active Violence/Active Shooter Guidelines: Run, Hide, Fight*

Security officers who are on the scene (including off-duty law enforcement officers) may be able to help prevent casualties or possibly stop an attack. But remember, if you try to disrupt a shooting, you will more than likely place yourself in the direct line of fire, so use caution.

Information to provide to law enforcement or 911 operators:

- Location of the active shooter.
- Number of shooters, if more than one.
- Physical description of shooter(s).
- Number and type of weapons held by the shooter(s).
- Number of potential victims at the location.

During an active shooter scenario, the roles of security officers differ greatly depending upon whether or not you are armed or unarmed, as well as your personal level of training and experience.

If you are armed, carefully and quickly confront the shooter or shooters to neutralize at the first opportunity, just like a responding law enforcement officer. The question, however, is whether or not the armed security officer has enough training for an active shooter situation to be able to approach and use

* Active Shooter – How to Respond. Retrieved on 10-11-23 from: https://www.dhs.gov/xlibrary/assets/active_shooter_booklet.pdf

DOI: 10.4324/9781003402718-76

their weapon without harming any bystanders in the process. It should never be assumed that you have trained for this because you are a security officer with a firearm. Whether or not a security officer confronts the shooter should be discussed as part of the emergency action plan's (EAP) active shooter response plan – before an incident occurs.

If a security officer is unarmed, you should not approach the shooter and you need to try to evacuate along with other bystanders. The unarmed security officer can serve a critical role in assisting armed law enforcement officers with locations on the property and even access if security badges are required to enter certain doors.

Be aware also that someone may choose to be an "active bystander"[1] and intervene in an active violence situation and take action to interact with the perpetrator in an attempt to de-escalate the situation or provide care to victims. This may help or hinder the action taken by a security officer at the scene.

A shooter will usually plan their attack carefully, and in many of the cases, they may kill themselves or will be prepared to die during the shooting. A security officer must be very aware of their own surroundings and others since they will be an obstacle for the shooter and might be included in the plan. You cannot act as a line of defense if you become a victim, so it's important to recognize danger before it's too late. It is also important to know the location you are protecting – inside and out. Consider creating a map to keep on you at all times so you can respond quickly when notified of an active shooter in the area or so you can assist law enforcement in where to go. Update your map frequently for any changes to the property.

If you cannot escape from the line of fire, your best option may be to attack the shooter and attempt to incapacitate the shooter as quickly as possible. Use caution when disarming or disabling a shooter. Use the surrounding area to your advantage. In other words, use the environment for concealment. Do not approach a shooter straight on, if at all possible. For the greatest chance of success, groups of individuals working together are the best option to take out the shooter. Tackle the shooter from multiple directions at once and get them on the ground. Stopping a shooter alone is riskier than in a group, but it may still be successful.

When law enforcement officers arrive:

- Remain calm and follow officers' instructions.
- Put down any items in your hands (i.e., bags and jackets).
- Immediately raise hands and spread fingers.
- Keep hands visible at all times.
- Avoid making quick movements toward officers, such as holding on to them for safety.
- Avoid pointing, screaming, and/or yelling.
- Do not stop to ask officers for help or direction when evacuating; proceed in the direction from which officers are entering the premises.

Run, Hide, Fight[2]

Run, Hide, Fight is based on the premise that during an active shooter situation, there are steps that you follow when you hear gunshots fired.

Run

- Find a path and attempt to evacuate.
- Evacuate whether others agree or not.
- Leave your belongings.
- Help others evacuate.
- Prevent others from entering.
- Call 911.

If you are not able to run, then you are encouraged to:

Hide

- Lock or block the door.
- Silence cell phone.
- Hide behind large objects.
- Remain quiet.
- Stay out of the shooter's view.
- Provide protection if shots are fired in your direction.
- Do not trap or restrict your options or movement.

If you do not have the ability to hide, then the last option is to

Fight

- Attempt to incapacitate the shooter.
- Act with physical aggression.
- Improvise weapons.
- Commit to your actions.

To best prepare for an active shooter situation, create an EAP and conduct training exercises. Together, the EAP and training exercises will prepare you to effectively respond to an active shooter situation.

Notes

1 Active Bystanders. Retrieved on December 20, 2023 from: Active Bystanders: Definition & Philosophy (mit.edu) and decide.

2 How to Respond During an Active Shooter Situation. Retrieved on December 20, 2023 from: www.dhses.ny.gov/system/files/documents/2021/12/run-hide-fight

Chapter 76

Traditional Physical Security Countermeasures (Crime Prevention) vs. Crime Prevention through Environmental Design (CPTED)

What Is Crime Prevention Utilizing Traditional Physical Security Countermeasures?

Traditional security countermeasures are typically "target-hardening" approaches. Target hardening focuses on denying potential criminal access to a crime target by using some type of barrier – either physical or artificial. This is typically thought of as "guards, guns, and gates."

Different organizations have different definitions of crime prevention. For example:

> Crime prevention is the anticipation, recognition and appraisal of a crime risk and the initiation of some action to remove or reduce it.
>
> (National Crime Prevention Institute, 1972)

DOI: 10.4324/9781003402718-77

> Crime prevention is a pattern of attitudes and behaviors directed at reducing the threat of crime and enhancing the sense of safety and security, to positively influence the quality of life in our society and to develop environments in which crime cannot flourish.
>
> (National Crime Prevention Council, 1990)

What Is Crime Prevention through Environmental Design (CPTED)?

CPTED (pronounced sep-ted) is a short form for the proactive crime-fighting technique known as Crime Prevention through Environmental Design. CPTED is based on the theory that: **"The proper design and effective use of the built environment can lead to a reduction in the incidence and fear of crime, and an improvement in the quality of life."** CPTED's underlying objective is to help the various disciplines better achieve their primary objectives, with the added by-product of improved security and loss prevention. This objective is based on the belief that crime and loss are a by-product of human functions that are not working.[1]

Target hardening is another element often mentioned in connection with CPTED. This means making a building or property more difficult to enter forcibly.

The use of deadbolt locks is one example of target hardening. The locks should have hardened steel bolts extending at least one inch into the door jamb to be effective. When deadbolts are installed on a wooden frame door, the screws that fasten the strikes should also penetrate at least 1 inch into the door frame.

Protective window films are another example of target hardening. Buildings with plate glass windows are vulnerable to "smash and grab" burglaries. But, plate glass can stop a sledgehammer when a protective film is properly installed.

A CPTED approach focuses on how the environment is designed and used and is a set of design principles used to discourage crime. The concept is that buildings and properties should be designed to prevent crime. CPTED strategies are based on anticipating the thought processes of a potential offender and creating an environment that will discourage them from committing a crime at the same time the same environment will encourage honest citizens to report suspicious behavior and enforce territoriality. CPTED strategies can be used during the design and construction of new buildings or retrofitted into existing buildings and properties.

There are four basic principles of CPTED:

- Natural surveillance
- Natural access control
- Territorial reinforcement
- Maintenance

Natural surveillance is a design strategy directed primarily at keeping intruders under observation. This strategy works because criminals will not commit crimes in areas where they feel exposed to observers. If a crime occurs, there is a greater chance that it will be witnessed and reported to the police.

Criminals do not like being seen or recognized, so they choose situations where they can hide and escape easily. Here are some ways to incorporate natural surveillance into a business environment:

- Keep areas well lit. Building entrances should be bright at all times and provide a clear line of sight from both inside and outside.
- Eliminate hiding spots. Cut down hedges and remove trees, bushes, fences, dumpsters, etc., that create blind spots or hiding places.
- Low, thorny hedges work well around windows because they don't obstruct the view in or out, and they don't provide a comfortable place to hide.
- Use video surveillance to view areas without natural sight lines. Put up public monitors so visitors know they are being watched. The last thing a criminal wants to see when entering a building is their face on a security monitor.

The result: A potential offender should feel like they are being watched and that the surroundings offer no easy escape routes.

Natural access control is a design strategy directed at decreasing crime opportunities. Access control is the physical guidance of people coming and going from a space by placing entrances, exits, fencing, landscaping, locks, and other barriers. This strategy works because it makes the inappropriate behavior obvious to citizens passing by, and they can notify the police.

Criminals like to feel that they are in control. However, this sense of control can be denied by clearly marking the approaches to buildings and properties and channeling visitors into a defined area. Here are a few tips for creating natural access control:

- Use maze entrances in public lobbies. The goal is to cut off straight-line access to a potential target, such as a bank teller or cashier. We're not talking about barbed wire – even tension barriers that must be jumped or navigated around can discourage the bad guys.
- Use curbing and landscaping to direct automobile and foot traffic into a controlled, visible area (Figure 76.1).

The result: a criminal should never feel like they have the upper hand when approaching a facility.

A component of access control is "target hardening," which refers to deadbolt locks, intrusion detection systems, and window locks. This strategy is more closely aligned with traditional physical security countermeasures (Figures 76.2 and 76.3).

Figure 76.1 A change in the surface here designed as a pedestrian crossing.

Photo by Marianna Perry.

Figure 76.2 Planters used as bollards.

Image used with permission and courtesy of Shutterstock.com.

Figure 76.3 Bollards used as vehicle barriers.

Photo by Marianna Perry.

Territorial reinforcement is a design strategy that realizes that physical design can create or extend a sphere of influence so that users develop a sense of proprietorship or territoriality.

The use of buildings, fences, signs, pavement, or other objects to express ownership clearly delineates the transition from public space to private space. This strategy works because it suggests someone present who is responsible for the space and may observe criminal activity.

This principle aims to create a clear distinction between public and private property. This is important for two reasons: Legitimate occupants have a sense of ownership and will notice, and even challenge, people who don't belong; intruders, on the other hand, have a harder time blending in.

Here are some ways to implement territorial reinforcement:

- Make sure receptionists have clear sight lines to all entrances and the ability to quickly and discreetly call for help. A panic button that calls a central station or signals for help via an alarm light in a separate building section works well.
- Make sure security signage is visible at all entrances.
- Implement a visitor badging system and ensure all visitors are properly escorted.

The result: Employees gain a feeling that "this is my space," while intruders are immediately put on the defensive.

The term "natural" refers to deriving surveillance and access control as a by-product of the normal and routine use of the environment. Natural surveillance and access control can be ultimately subdivided into three categories. These are natural, mechanical, and organized means.

Mechanical forms of natural surveillance and access control commonly use traditional target-hardening techniques. These techniques are limited to situations where the effective use of the environment is not unduly impaired.

An area's upkeep and day-to-day maintenance demonstrate that someone cares and is watching. This strategy works because of what is known as the "Broken Windows Theory." This theory suggests that a neglected space will elicit mistreatment by people, while a maintained space will elicit proper treatment.

Maintenance is related to territorial reinforcement. A well-maintained area sends the message that people notice and care about what happens in an area. This, in turn, discourages vandalism and other crimes.

Security practitioners refer to the "Broken Windows Theory" – the idea that one broken window will entice vandals to break another. A vandalized area then becomes more inviting to higher levels of crime. Property should be well maintained as a matter of safety and pride.

Target Hardening

CPTED differs from traditional crime prevention techniques, which are and often do not consider opportunities for natural access control and surveillance (either video or human) and place restrictions on the use, access, and enjoyment of the "target-hardened" environment.

To determine which CPTED strategies are needed for a particular environment, you must first assess the space you are evaluating. To do this, the Three D Approach is normally used. This approach is based on the following functions:

- All human space has some DESIGNATED purpose.
- All human space has social, cultural, legal, or physical DEFINITIONS that prescribe the desired and acceptable behaviors.
- All human space is DESIGNED to support and control the desired behavior.

The primary goal of CPTED is to provide individuals (law enforcement, business developers and owners, homeowners, and security professionals) with information needed to create their own initiatives to prevent crime through environmental design.

CPTED encourages collaboration with law enforcement and community leaders in resolving issues that include reshaping and reimagining the environment of neighborhoods, businesses, houses, and apartments (Roberg, 2009).

Note

1 What is CPTED? Retrieved on 08-23-17 from: https://www.peelpolice.ca/en/crime prevention/resources/whatiscpted.pdf

Chapter 77

Dealing with Difficult People and Situations

Sometimes, it may be difficult to provide good customer service to individuals who are impatient, uncooperative, or just plain rude. Everyone in the public and private sector has had to deal with challenging individuals at one time or another. As a security officer, you want to protect yourself from complaints and violence but meet the customer's needs.

The following tips will help you prevent an interaction from becoming toxic and de-escalate one that does:

- As a security officer, you represent authority. Treat everyone with dignity and respect, and don't ever threaten anyone. ASK someone to do something – don't TELL them. Part of treating someone with respect is listening to what they have to say. You can't figure out what's wrong if you're talking. When you tell someone to "calm down," what you're really saying is that they are out of control and have a behavior problem. Saying this will not "calm down" the situation.
- Provide relevant information to the individual who asks "why" when explaining the rules or procedures that must be followed. When you give someone an explanation and they still will not comply, give them options and allow them to "save face." Give them options to do what is in their best interest. Explain the negative consequences of noncompliance – contacting law enforcement, being banned from the property, etc.
- Body language researcher Albert Mehrabian determined that 55% of communication is nonverbal, 38% vocal, and 7% words only.[1] If you rely only on words for communication, you're likely missing key information. If you're

DOI: 10.4324/9781003402718-78

texting while talking to someone, you're really telling them that they're not important. Pay close attention to the tone of your voice as well. You shouldn't respond to an individual with sarcasm or in a disinterested monotone. Many complaints against security officers come from tone. Most people are unaware of the messages they send through their facial expressions or body language. Research also shows that men and women are more attracted to people who make eye contact and smile.[2] A smile and just the right amount of eye contact can help you effectively de-escalate a situation.
- People want to know that you care about them. If someone is upset, tell them that you understand and will do everything you can to help them with the situation. The ability to empathize may be the most important thing that you can do to de-escalate a situation.

Today, everyone has a camera phone, so expect to be recorded. Ensure you remain professional and do everything you can to de-escalate the situation. This way, you won't have to fear witnesses or be unable to defend yourself in a complaint. At the same time, you will be providing excellent customer service and be seen as a professional security officer who is a problem solver.

Notes

1 How much Communication is Non-Verbal? Retrieved on 04-25-23 from: https://online.utpb.edu/about-us/articles/communication/how-much-of-communication-is-nonverbal/
2 Ibid.

Chapter 78

Motivation

Help your security officers reach their potential. As a manager, it's your responsibility to ensure your team is motivated and performing at a high level. But, recent data reveals abysmal engagement levels among workers around the globe. How do you fix the problem – before your most talented people walk out the door? Understanding what drains your employees can increase their job satisfaction and push them toward achieving their goals. Give employees advice to help them find meaning in their work, build on their strengths, and produce the best results for the organization. Learn how to

- Pinpoint the root causes of lackluster performance.
- Tailor rewards and recognition to individuals.
- Connect routine work activities to a higher purpose.
- Support your employees' growth and development and prevent burnout – especially in your top performers.
- Create a culture of engagement.

How to Engage and Empower Protection Officers

A great way to engage and empower protection officers is through education about security and how they can learn to do their jobs more effectively. We've all heard that knowledge is power, so apply it to security. Through this knowledge, the protection officer will begin to look at things in his/her environment differently and, at the same time, provide more productive customer service. Teaching them about Crime Prevention through Environmental Design (CPTED) is a great starting point. CPTED is a multidisciplinary approach to deterring criminal behavior through environmental design.[1]

 DOI: 10.4324/9781003402718-79

CPTED is about the proper design and effective use of the built environment to reduce the incidence and fear of crime and improve the quality of life. Emphasis is placed on the physical environment, productive use of space, and people's behavior to create environments that are absent of environmental cues that cause opportunities for crime. Educating security officers about CPTED is a good starting point because much of it is common sense.

Note

1 Crime Prevention Through Environmental Design (CPTED). Retrieved on January 15, 2019 from: https://www.niagarapolice.ca/en/community/Crime-Prevention-Through-Environmental-Design--CPTED-.aspx#

Chapter 79

Rest, Relaxation, and Exercise

Security officers should ensure they are well rested before starting their shift. For security officers working rotating or overnight shifts, this can be problematic. Nonetheless, officers should allow themselves to get the proper sleep needed to stay alert and awake during their shift. While off duty, security officers should relax and enjoy their leisure time. A well-lived lifestyle is not only healthy for the security officer but also produces an individual who is eager and ready to get back to work when their shift begins. Lastly, not only is exercise necessary for good health and mobility but it will also help the security officer in performing his/her duties more quickly and efficiently.

DOI: 10.4324/9781003402718-80

Chapter 80

Legal Liability and Inadequate Security

Inadequate security is generally referred to as premises security liability, that is, the civil liability of the owners for the foreseeable criminal acts of third persons.

Inadequate security claims arise when a property owner fails to provide a reasonably safe environment, and as a result, someone is victimized by the criminal conduct of another person.

A property owner may be held liable for a crime if there has been a *crime pattern* on or around the property. The owner may be found by a court to have a legal duty to use reasonable security measures designed to prevent or deter crimes, such as

- Perimeter protection
- Increased lighting or better lighting
- Security officers
- Better locks or additional locks
- A new video surveillance system to replace the old one that was not recording
- A new alarm system to replace the one that didn't work
- Controlled access to parking areas

If the property owner is found by the court to have known about the pattern of crime yet did not provide adequate security, the owner may be found liable for the injuries or death at the site.

DOI: 10.4324/9781003402718-81

Chapter 81

Effective Trainers

Some time ago, we were with a group of trainers, and we asked them for their training "secrets" and their training style because we felt this would be valuable information to include in this book. This is what we were told:

1. Set the dress code in advance. You don't want to be that person in blue jeans when everyone else is in a suit – or vice versa. Publish the dress code to everyone in advance.
2. Facilitate and encourage interaction during breaks. Spot those introverts who usually hang around at the coffee table, draw them into conversation with other class participants, and seek opportunities to put together individuals who could do business.
3. Give external resources to provide the participants with further learning, practical examples, and context to your training. This can include books, e-books, downloads, web links, social media links, etc.
4. Finish 10 minutes early. Finishing 10 minutes early is like giving the gift of time to a class participant. Offer to chat informally after or let them get away and beat the rush.
5. Draw out key burning issues at the start of the training. Collect the key issues the participants want covered – the bits they came along to hear and make sure you cover them earlier in the day. And, if you can't cover one of the points, acknowledge it and agree on a way to cover that point with the participant after the event.
6. Recap at the end of the day. Start with the key points identified in the item above and then draw out your key learning points delivered during the day.
7. In multi-day training, recap at the start of each day. Again, this is blindingly obvious, but if the group has not stayed overnight (or if they've had a long

DOI: 10.4324/9781003402718-82

night!), they will be grateful for a reminder of yesterday's key points and the chance to raise questions on them before diving into today's agenda.

8. If the students are staying over, recommend restaurants or evening activities.
9. Ensure your training is structured well with defined objectives that can be measured and assessed at the end of the training.
10. Use a variety of techniques and practical exercises so that participants have several opportunities to demonstrate their understanding of the content to make the training engaging and learner-centric.
11. Ensure the training is relevant to the audience.
12. To keep participants engaged, start each session with a question so there will be active learning instead of inactive learning.
13. Be a storyteller! Talk about past experiences and how the material covered worked or didn't work. Discuss what could have been done to make it more effective.
14. Make the material presented interesting.

The bottom line is that people don't learn when they are bored.

Chapter 82

Five Steps for Violence Prevention

Experience has shown there are only a few key time periods for violence prevention in the workplace. They are at hiring, at firing, and at any point in between those polar opposites when threats or intimidations are alleged. However, there are at least five simple steps supervisors can take to avert the likelihood of violence. Let's take them one by one:

1. **Conduct your due diligence and prescreening of potential employees before they are hired. Why hire a problem employee when you don't have to?**

   Today, background checks typically entail a simple investigation of one or two references, if that, and a reliance on employee resumes. But, as we know, references, especially former employers, are not saying too much about former employees because of increased defamation litigation. Personnel firms tell us that four out of five resumes and/or applications contain false or embellished information that employers base their hiring decisions on.

   The question employers should ask themselves is: Is this prospective employee who he/she says he/she is? As the Kiplinger Washington Letter recently remarked, "More employers insist on full background checks before hiring. Unfortunately, it's a sign of the times."

   Background checks should include social security verification, driving records, credit histories, educational affiliations, civil litigation, and criminal history of applicants. The next person you hire may majorly contribute to your company's growth or failure. The best predictor of his/her behavior is his/her past history or behavior.

DOI: 10.4324/9781003402718-83

2. **Practice zero percent tolerance for threats: investigate and assess them.**
   Threat assessment investigations are direct inquiries into an employee's past and present behavior outside the workplace. What is the subject's likelihood of following through on threats? Does the subject have a history of violence? Does he/she own a gun or have access to a gun? Has he/she been abusing drugs or alcohol? Does he/she have a history of domestic abuse? Again, past behavior is a predictor of present risk and future behavior.
3. **Conduct investigations immediately.**
   Remember that management leads, but management may not be present when a potentially violent episode erupts. Training the entire workforce to report incidents, rumors, and allegations and then taking immediate action to investigate them are key components of a proactive approach to violence prevention. It's a fact that violence escalates. A threat or intimidation usually precedes the physical assault.
   Give employees and management a written policy outlining how to treat any allegations. Give employees a telephone hotline to report potential incidents involving violence. Then, take those allegations seriously.
   Next, communicate that you are taking action to investigate. Use either internal or external assistance from experienced professionals who can interview participants skillfully, professionally, and objectively. Then, if the allegations prove true, make the results known. Was the perpetrator terminated, transferred, or put on notice? Whatever action was deemed commensurate with the offense, make it an example for the entire company.
4. **Establish employee assistance programs.**
   The following kinds of workplaces are ripe for violence: frequent labor disputes, numerous grievance claims, excessive overtime requests and/or demands, high levels of employee stress, and/or authoritarian management structures.
   Some indicators of violence-prone individuals are those involved in drug and alcohol abuse and domestic conflicts. It is estimated that 20% of all workers use drugs on the job and another 10% use them at home before going to work. Workplace violence may go unreported because of fear of recrimination.[1]
   Employee assistance programs have been around for years. Is yours a truly interactive and proactive environment for workers to air their concerns? Besides having an effective policy, employee assistance programs are the next best deterrent to violence on the job. Do your employees know who they can turn to if they have a problem?
5. **Treat employees respectfully at termination and be prepared for volatile emotions.**
   Many psychologists place the loss of a job at the top of the list for stress, alongside death, divorce, and moving. How you treat your employees at termination will have much to do with how they view your company and you after they leave. Do you treat them with dignity and decorum? Do you take

simple precautions to protect other employees from terminated employees' reactions?

Follow common sense: avoid termination, for instance, when employees undergo severe stress in their personal lives. Do not expect them to act rationally during the termination process. Be business-like and precise about the reasons for termination, not straying into other topics of conversation. Collect all keys and security cards before they leave the building. Notify terminated employees that they are not allowed to return to the worksite. Identify a contact person for future communications with the former employee.

Finally, with violence escalating in the workplace, employers are legally responsible for protecting their personnel, property, and assets.

Note

1 Workplace Violence Prevention and Response. Retrieved on December 20, 2023 from: https://www.shrm.org/resourcesandtools/tools-and-samples/toolkits/pages/workplace-violence-prevention-and-response.aspx

Chapter 83

Disinformation

Disinformation – false information that is intentionally spread – is not a new phenomenon, but the ability to spread disinformation globally is a more recent development thanks to the use of the internet and social media.[1]

By using social media, an attacker no longer has to rely solely on breaching an organization's physical or cyber perimeter – an organization's reputation may be damaged, and the additional stress to the organization causes more damage. When using social media, people often pay no attention to ridiculous rumors, and angry, cynical individuals build on this distrust to continue the damage.

One of the duties of the security department is to help create a holistic response to threats against an organization's reputation. Human resources and other departments can help identify appropriate language to respond to various scenarios and help identify and stop potential insider threats.

Note

1 Redesigning Pandora's Box: Another Reason to Leave Siloed Security Behind. Retrieved on August 10, 2023 from: https://www.asisonline.org/security-management-magazine/articles/2023/02/reputation-security/redesigning-pandoras-box/?ct=YTo1OntzOjY6InNvdXJjZSI7YToyOntpOjA7czo1OiJlbWFpbCI7aToxO2k6MTgyMDt9czo1OiJlbWFpbCI7aToxODIwO3M6NDoic3RhdCI7czoyMjoiNjNlZjg5YzU0YjFhZDU4MjY5ODczMCI7czo0OiJsZWFkIjtzOjU6Ijg1MzIzIjtzOjc6ImNoYW5uZWwiO2E6MTp7czo1OiJlbWFpbCI7aToxODIwO319

DOI: 10.4324/9781003402718-84

Chapter 84

Vehicular Accidents Involving a Company Vehicle

1. Stop immediately.
2. Report the accident to the police and call for medical assistance if needed.
3. Obtain the **names**, **addresses**, and telephone numbers of any injured person, the owners of any damaged property, and **witnesses**.
4. If another vehicle is involved in the accident, obtain the names, addresses, and telephone numbers of the driver and the owner.
5. Obtain the policy number, name of the agent or carrier, and phone number if possible.
6. DO NOT ACCEPT FAULT FOR THE ACCIDENT.
7. Only discuss the facts of the accident with the police or your company.
8. Contact your supervisor or manager immediately.
9. Take photographs of all vehicles involved and the accident scene. It's better to take too many than not enough.

Reporting the Accident

When reporting an accident, the following additional information will be helpful to the insurance company:

1. Provide your name, address, and phone number where you can be reached.

DOI: 10.4324/9781003402718-85

2. The area of damage to your car. Is it drivable? If not, where is the vehicle or where did it get towed?
3. The name of the law enforcement agency investigating the accident and the REPORT NUMBER!

For additional information, refer to the post orders.

Chapter 85

Bullying in the Workplace

To begin with, what is workplace bullying?

The Workplace Bullying Institute (WBI) defines workplace bullying as "repeated, health-harming mistreatment of one or more persons (the targets) by one or more perpetrators. It is abusive conduct that is:

- Threatening, humiliating, or intimidating, or
- Work interference – sabotage – which prevents work from getting done or
- Verbal abuse."[1]

The Society for Human Resource Management (SHRM) defines workplace bullying as: "Persistent, offensive, abusive, intimidating or insulting behavior or unfair actions directed at another individual, causing the recipient to feel threatened, abused, humiliated or vulnerable."[2]

As with all investigations, investigations of workplace bullying should be conducted following a standard format and should

- Be investigated promptly and thoroughly.
- Be fair and impartial.
- Be sensitive to all parties' interests and maintain confidentiality.
- Be focused on finding facts and evidence, including interviews with the complainant, the alleged bully, and any witnesses.

Workplace bullying is very similar to harassment, but in the workplace, harassment often connotes sexual misconduct and a hostile work environment. There are state and federal civil rights laws that are designed to protect workers from discriminatory and disparate mistreatment if they are members of a protected status group. There are seven in the United States and 11 in Canada, e.g., gender, race, religion,

 DOI: 10.4324/9781003402718-86

and ethnicity, etc.and mistreatment of protected groups or individual group members is documented.[3] Contact the company Human Resources Department and/or company legal counsel if you feel the bullying allegations are harassment or discrimination.

Workplace bullying investigations are unique because, many times, witnesses that may corroborate the alleged bullying incidents were not physically present when the bullying occurred. As the investigator, you must develop a framework for identifying and locating witnesses. Workplace bullies are often bosses who practice unfair and inconsistent treatment of subordinates. When the boss targets specific employees, others in the workplace may not hear the actual verbal abuse or profanities directed toward the victim. Still, they may be present for "left-handed compliments" intended to shame the employee in front of others. These colleagues, customers, or clients who are not your typical "witnesses" in an investigation may feel embarrassment with the victim. Sometimes, these "witnesses" may encounter the bullying victim in the restroom or another area when the victim, out of desperation, confides in them.

When you are investigating alleged bullying in the workplace, be sure to ask the victim if he/she confided in anyone at work about the bullying or if anyone saw them physically upset after an incident. If so, these employees, customers, and clients are your witnesses.

Workplace grievances, accident reports, excessive sick leave requests, exit interviews, and even employee assistance program (EAP) statistics may provide data or names of other potential witnesses who are reluctant to come forward during the investigation. Also, don't forget about "digital witnesses," such as e-mails or text messages between the alleged victim and the bully around or after the time of the alleged incident(s) occurred. This paper and electronic information may provide the evidence needed to support or disprove allegations of bullying or harassment.

Lastly, do not forget the alleged bully. He/she may respond to the investigation that allows the investigator to obtain first-hand credible knowledge and become a "witness" to the allegations.

The purpose of your investigation is to determine what happened, so ensure that you follow these steps:[4]

1. Review the workplace policies and procedures on bullying and/or harassment and determine if the alleged behavior meets the definition of workplace bullying and/or harassment.
2. Meet with each party separately to explain the investigation process.
3. Gather evidence by speaking separately with both the complainant and the alleged bully.
4. Interview witnesses or other involved parties.
5. Review the evidence and make a decision based on the evidence, whether bullying occurred.
6. Discuss the findings of your investigation with the employer, manager, or supervisor.

7. Take corrective action by
   - Updating the workplace policy statement, putting new preventive steps in place.
   - Updating and providing training, education, and information for all workers.
   - Reminding supervisors and workers of their duties regarding bullying.
8. Keep a record of the investigation and all supporting documentation.

Notes

1 The WBI Definition of Workplace Bullying. Retrieved on March 4, 2017 from: http://www.workplacebullying.org/individuals/problem/definition/

2 Investigations: Bullying: How do I conduct a workplace investigation of bullying when there are no witnesses? Retrieved on March 4,2017 from: https://www.shrm.org/resourcesandtools/tools-and-samples/hr-qa/pages/investigationintobullying.aspx

3 Workplace Bullying Institute. Retrieved on March 4, 2017 from: http://www.workplacebullying.org/faq/

4 Investigations Guide: Workplace Bullying and Harassment. Retrieved on March 4, 2017 from: http://c.ymcdn.com/sites/www.naecp.net/resource/collection/450702AF-D141-4381-B417-3C97E97AA330/Garde_07_BH_InvestigationsGuide.pdf

Chapter 86

Burglary: Still the Common Crime

Do you ever wonder why one house or business was broken into and the one next door wasn't? Thieves often look for a home or business to break into – based simply on the opportunity and the likelihood that they won't be caught. Security officers are a deterrent to criminals. Criminals make decisions the same way that many of us do. It's a risk versus benefit decision.

- If a residence, are there newspapers in the driveway or on the front porch?
- Are there high bushes and thick trees compared to bushes that are only 3′ tall and tree branches trimmed 8′ from the ground around buildings, parking structures and parking lots?
- If a residence, is there a barking dog?
- Is there a car in the driveway or are parking areas monitored?
- Is there a sliding glass door with no dowel rod in the door track or another secondary device to prevent opening or removal?
- Are doors left unlocked or propped open?
- Is the home or business house well lit at night, and are light sensors or timers used so lights are not on during the day?
- Is the neighborhood considered a "hot spot" by the local police department?
- Is there a culture of security and security awareness?
- Is there an active neighborhood or business watch?

Make your home or business a "hard" target. Don't be a "soft" target. Reduce criminal opportunity by not making it easy for them. Reduce your risk and think about prevention!

DOI: 10.4324/9781003402718-87

Priorities and design opportunities differ vastly from one location to another and Crime Prevention through Environmental Design (CPTED) strategies can be effective only if they are sensitive to special design and use requirements and constraints at each site. It is imperative that crime prevention be consistent with other quality-of-life objectives.

Chapter 87

Preventing Vehicle Crimes

- Lock your car doors and close your windows, even if it's in your driveway or front of your home.
- Never leave your car running or the keys in the ignition when you're away from it, even for "just a minute."
- **NEVER, NEVER, NEVER** leave your child unattended in your car – not even for a moment. Many cars with children in them have been stolen.
- Carry the registration and insurance card with you. Don't leave personal identification documents or credit cards in your vehicle.
- Never leave valuables in plain view, even if your car is locked. Please put them in the trunk or at least out of sight. Remember, briefcases, sunglasses, clothing, keys, gym bags, and small change are all tempting to a thief. If you do, ensure they are kept out of plain sight – under the seat or better yet, in the trunk. Numerous break-ins are crimes of opportunity.
- When transporting valuables, place them in the trunk before you arrive at your parking spot. Don't transfer them in open view of other people.
- Don't leave your garage door opener on the dashboard or front seat. Please put it in your glove box, hide it, or take it with you.
- At night, always try to park in a busy, well-lighted area.
- Remove portable electronic devices such as smartphones and GPS navigation systems – including a suction cup or bean bag-type mounts (Even the visible appearance of a suction cup ring on the glass windshield can entice a thief to break in and look for the GPS system.). When you leave your car, put these items in the trunk or take them with you.
- Leave only the ignition key (or valet key) with the parking attendant in a commercial parking lot or when your vehicle is serviced. Make sure no personal information is attached.
- Lock your car doors, whether driving or parked.

DOI: 10.4324/9781003402718-88

- Do not hide a key in or on your vehicle.
- Observe your surroundings before exiting your vehicle.
- Look for strangers or danger signs as you approach your car. If it looks wrong, walk past your car and call the police.
- If possible, walk to your car with someone else.
- Know how to use the panic alarm on your car keys. Please keep it in your hand while walking to your car.
- BE AWARE of your surroundings at all times. **STAY OFF YOUR CELL PHONE** while you walk. Remember, ***holding a smartphone is the same as holding several hundred dollars in cash***.

Carjacking

Carjacking is stealing a car by force. Statistically, your chances of being a carjacking victim are relatively slim, but you can take some preventative actions to reduce the risk even more.

- First rule – **NEVER go with a carjacker**. Your survival chances decrease dramatically if you are kidnapped. Give them the car, but YOU get out.
- If the carjacker has a weapon, give up the car with no questions asked. Your life is worth more than a car.
- Don't speed away if the carjacker has a gun pointed at you. The sudden movement may cause him/her to shoot. Get out and give up the car.
- If someone attempts to get in your car, drive away. Run the light, make a U-turn, or do whatever is necessary to escape them.
- When driving, keep your car doors locked and windows always rolled up.
- Be especially alert at intersections, gas stations, ATMs, shopping malls, convenience, and grocery stores – all are windows of opportunity for carjackers.
- At night, park in well-lighted areas with good visibility, close to walkways, stores, and people.
- When you stop at a traffic light or stop sign, **leave enough distance to pull out of the line of traffic and drive away**. DO NOT pull within 2–3 ft of the car in front of you because you may be trapped.
- Be familiar with a panic alarm if you have one. Know exactly how to push the button.
- NEVER leave your car running when you get out at a gas station, etc.
- If a stranger flags you down, **DON'T STOP**, regardless of how desperate they look. Call the police and give them the stranger's location.
- Beware of "bump and rob." If you get hit in a minor collision and suspect something is wrong, drive to a safe location and call the police. If you stop, don't get out or roll your window down. Call the police immediately.

- Be aware of individuals impersonating police officers. Look for emergency lights and ask to see their badge and ID card. Unmarked/plainclothes officers should be more than willing to call a marked car to the scene before you exit the car.
- **NEVER** let someone take your car with a child in it. Scream, kick, fight, gouge eyes, and do whatever it takes to stop them.

Call 911 as soon as a crime occurs.

Chapter 88

If Something Doesn't Look Right, Tell Someone!

Solutions – ten things you need to know:

1. Have a professional assessment of your property completed by a security professional who can detect potential risks, risks, and vulnerabilities and provide solutions.
2. The assessment should include your corporate mission statement and your master plan.
3. The assessment should be designed to include training regarding safety and security issues. Training should include scenarios and drills to reinforce training.
4. Review your policies, procedures, and post orders and update them as necessary or at least annually. Emergency procedures should be included if it isn't a separate document.
5. Formulate partnerships with police, fire, Emergency Medical Services (EMS), and community organizations. Discuss potential threats and risks. Learn what resources are available. Discuss your overall security concerns and daily operations. Plan, practice, and prepare.
6. Develop a visitor policy with enforced procedures. Ensure security officers posted at the main entrance of your building/property or on patrol understand suspicious behavior. It's important to meet and greet visitors. For this reason, retail stores, hospitals, universities, and even churches have greeters at their entrances.
7. Some companies have a "no bag" or "clear bag" policy to reduce risk, and it becomes a part of their daily operations.

 DOI: 10.4324/9781003402718-89

8. Plainclothes security coverage is ideal for detecting suspicious activity and behavior.
9. Mass communication through e-mail or other means can quickly notify everyone on site of a potentially dangerous situation or emergency issue.
10. All security devices need to be monitored to ensure they are operational:
    - Is every video camera recording properly?
    - Are keys or access control devices controlled and up to date?
    - Are doors and emergency exit devices operational?
    - Are fire alarm systems – extinguishers, sprinklers, etc., checked and operational?
    - Is there an unobstructed view of the perimeter of the property?
    - Are all lights operational?
    - Is the mass notification system operational?

Target hardening has an initial cost as well as an ongoing maintenance and repair cost to consider. It's best practice to look at a return on investment (ROI) and make decisions about countermeasures that integrate well with other components, address identified vulnerabilities, and are energy efficient. One example of this is the installation of cost-effective lighting. Leadership in Energy and Environmental Design (LEED) is the most widely used green building rating system and will provide a framework for healthy, highly efficient, and cost-saving green buildings.

Chapter 89

Community Policing

Community policing has three key components: community partnerships, organizational transformation, and problem-solving. Collaborative partnerships between law enforcement agencies and the individuals and organizations they serve can help to develop solutions to problems. Security officers should be a part of this community collaboration. Management within the law enforcement agency should be designed to support community partnerships and proactive problem-solving. Law enforcement and community groups can work to identify problems and evaluate effective responses.

Community policing is geographically specific – no two communities or areas are exactly alike. As a result, no two communities will require exactly the same method of community policing service delivery. Investigation and enforcement are still essential elements of community policing, but how services are delivered to the community will depend upon the nature of crime and social problems identified in the community, the resources (both human and financial) available to the community to solve these problems, the needs expressed by community members, and the community's cultural makeup and diversity.[1]

There are a few essential factors of community policing that can serve as a guideline to those responsible for its implementation in any individual community.[2]

Direct Service Delivery

- **Identify the community, or communities, present in an area**. A community consists of people who share certain elements: geographical location, cultural or racial background, socioeconomic status, common interests or goals, or concern with the same crime or social issues. People may belong to more than one community group (e.g., a person may consider themselves a member of an Aboriginal community and a specific residential community area), and

 DOI: 10.4324/9781003402718-90

there may be more than one community of people within a detachment or city boundary. Each group must be identified by the police so that the needs of the community members can be met.

- **Work with the community.** The police must establish a partnership with the community to cooperatively address its problems and needs. Community consultative groups, with representatives from all communities identified, are an effective and successful way to initiate and carry out communication and cooperation between the police and their community.
- **Identify common problems and concerns.** The police are providing a policing service to the community and must be aware of its concerns, needs, and expectations so that their efforts are community oriented and community driven. The community must be aware of the concerns, abilities, and limitations of the police so that their demands are appropriate and able to be met by the police. Once each group understands the other, they can reach compromises and agreements on which problems are most important.
- **Resolve the identified problems.** A problem is defined as a group of incidents that are similar and are of concern to both the police and the community. Problem incidents may be similar in terms of crime, victim, time of day, or year. The responsibility for resolving problems must be shared by both the police and the citizens, and all abilities and resources within the community must be directed toward finding and carrying out effective and innovative solutions. Solutions must be directed toward finding and carrying out effective and innovative solutions. Solutions must attack and remove the root cause of the problem so that the problem itself, not just its symptoms, is removed.
- **Empower police officers to make decisions and take action.** Community policing often involves innovative approaches to problem-solving, which have, in the past, not been considered part of "traditional policing." Empowerment involves delegating a certain level of authority and enabling factors (proper training, guidance, and information). Managers must trust their employees and take the risk to allow general duty officers, in daily personal contact with the community, to be able to make necessary, appropriate, and innovative decisions and take the initiative to act to address the concerns of the public.
- **Support the general duty officer.** The general duty officer has the most direct contact with the community and must be regarded as the most important member of the policing service. The efforts of all other specialized members of the force must be directed toward supporting this community service position.
- **Make patrol, enforcement, and investigation work effective and directed.** There should be no such thing as a random or preventive patrol. When a member leaves the detachment, it should be with a purpose: monitoring traffic in a problem area; liaising with local farmers, business owners, or people

on the street; or attending to a complaint. Law enforcement and investigation (often the focus of contemporary, reactive policing) are still necessary in police work, but they are only one part. The police must get back to crime reduction, not just crime control. Through community consultation, police services can determine the amount of time to spend on these efforts and the problems of concern to both the community and the police, which should be concentrated on.

Administrative Organization:

- **Decentralize**. The police cannot meet the needs of a community effectively if their actions and decisions are dictated to them from above. The members working in a community are the most qualified people to decide how best to serve that community. Authority and decision-making on programs, resource deployment, and budgeting must be delegated to the detachment level.
- **Use modern management concepts**. Problem resolution, innovative resource deployment, risk management, downward delegation of authority, flattening organization hierarchy, participative management, and client consultation can be used to ensure that the service provided to the client community is efficient, effective, and responsive to its needs. Each detachment should provide a custom-designed service directed to the needs, concerns, and problems of its community.
- **Create an enhanced generalist career path**. In community policing, the general duty officer, who is in direct daily contact with the client community, is the most important position within the police service. The existing generalist position may be augmented to allow and encourage experienced and tenured members to remain there and continue to direct their expertise toward serving the community while still being rewarded for their service and initiative.
- **Reduce paper burden**. A large amount of police time is presently spent on administrative "paperwork" tasks. The statistical and paperwork demands, from both internal and external sources, must be reduced to allow more time for direct community service.
- **Evaluate effectiveness through citizen satisfaction surveys**. The community's satisfaction is the best indicator of the success of its policing service; if the client is happy, the job is well done. Some statistical data, such as crime rates, will still be required but should be balanced against the concerns of the community in deciding how to direct police resources.
- **Be proactive and think of solutions**. Community policing is effective when citizens are involved with law enforcement and everyone works together in partnership to address identified problems and provide crime prevention solutions. Security officers can be critical partners in addressing crime and reducing criminal opportunities.

Notes

1 Community Policing Defined. Retrieved on February 3, 2022 from: https://cops.usdoj.gov/RIC/Publications/cops-p157-pub.pdf
2 RCMP Community Policing.

Chapter 90

Mental Health Issues and CPTED

Research has shown that green spaces reduce depression.

Design Council, UK 2017

We all know someone who is affected by some form of a mental health condition. Should it be a close friend or relative, the concern becomes greater for their safety and security. When it comes to living environments and mental health, most security practitioners don't have a clue.

Can Crime Prevention through Environmental Design (CPTED) and urban design create a safer and healthier community?

Yes, it can …

Mental health and living environments need to be a priority and address urban living conditions because those living in our cities are at an increased risk of depression and a double risk of developing schizophrenia compared to those living in the country. Some causes are density, overcrowding, noise, smell, sight, disarray, pollution, feeling overloaded, lack of brain stimulation, and fear of crime.

As early as 1986, the Ottawa Charter of the World Health Organization (WHO) stated that people's living environment is where most health is created. The Ottawa Charter states that

> Health promotion works through concrete and effective community action in setting priorities, making decisions, planning strategies and implementing them to achieve better health. At the heart of this process is the empowerment of communities – their ownership and control of their own endeavors and destinies. Community development draws on

DOI: 10.4324/9781003402718-91

the community's existing human and material resources to enhance self-help and social support, and to develop flexible systems for strengthening public participation in and direction of health matters.[1]

With the growth of mental health issues, especially among adolescents and senior citizens, these concerns must be met with changes in the environments where people live. This can be accomplished by developing local communities that are more inclusive and socially supportive so that people can live a higher quality of life.[2] The primary focus needs to be on favorable living environments and good neighborhoods. Planning and designing communities that are socially supportive are critical to achieve a higher quality of life.

Symptoms of Dementia

Dementia symptoms vary depending on the cause, but common signs and symptoms include the following:

Cognitive Changes

- Memory loss, which is usually noticed by a spouse or someone else
- Difficulty communicating or finding words
- Difficulty reasoning or problem-solving
- Difficulty handling complex tasks
- Difficulty with planning and organizing
- Difficulty with coordination and motor functions
- Confusion and disorientation

Psychological Changes

- Personality changes
- Depression
- Anxiety
- Inappropriate behavior
- Paranoia
- Agitation
- Hallucinations

According to the Mayo Clinic,[3] dementia develops in adults with damaged nerve cells in their brains. Many people with Alzheimer's disease display a buildup of plaque in certain brain areas, which affects memory. This blood vessel damage impacts the brain's blood supply.

Dementia Solutions – Aside from Medical

Regular physical exercise may help lower the risk of some types of dementia. Research has shown that exercise may directly benefit brain cells by increasing blood and oxygen flow to the brain. There are some solutions that may help someone who is suffering from dementia or other mental health issues, including the development of green space to help reduce depression.

The following list is based on research from the Design Council in the United Kingdom (www.designcouncil.org.uk/news-opinion/designing-good-mental-health[4] and www.webmd.com[5]).

1. Areas for regular exercise, walking, or swimming. Exercise can be just as effective as anti-depressant medication for mild and moderate depression. It can also reduce stress and anxiety and help alleviate some of the symptoms associated with Attention-Deficit/Hyperactivity Disorder (ADHD), dementia, and even schizophrenia.
2. Reduce dark corners or hidden spots and create natural surveillance or sight lines.
3. Reduce feeling unsafe or the fear of crime.
4. Maintain this area and create a positive image.
5. Community activity is an important part of mental health. Please read below the section on *The Villages* and the variety of activities they have.
6. Good street lighting increases the perception of safety.
7. In landscape architecture, the built environment is understood to mean a human-made landscape, as distinguished from the natural environment; e.g., a city park is a built environment.[6]
8. One study in Denmark found health benefits for bicycle commuting far beyond calories burned. Bike commuters also ate healthier diets and felt less stress at work, among other positive effects. If we could make biking transportation fully safe and accessible in our cities, the health impacts would be immense.[7]
9. Eat healthy foods such as fruits and whole grains, take vitamin D, and limit caffeine.
10. Listen to soft music, get a pet, have therapeutic massages, and get exercise.
11. Utilize urban design using CPTED concepts.

It is our intention, with the items above, to pass on information needed to aid in the improvement of the quality of life of those affected by these mental health issues.

According to the Crime Prevention Coalition of America, preventing crime involves law enforcement, cooperation/collaboration by all elements of the community, education, tailoring responses to local needs/conditions, and continual evaluation and improvement. The philosophy of the Crime Prevention Coalition of America states that preventing crime (as well as the fear of crime) is

- Everyone's business
- More than just traditional security
- A responsibility of all levels and agencies of government
- Linked with solving social problems
- Cost effective[8]

These prevention techniques and philosophy go hand-in-hand with addressing the mental health needs of the community and improving quality of life by preventing crime and the fear of crime and having environments that are conducive to social interaction and a sense of community.

Current Trends

The goal of effective urban design is to create sustainable urban environments with long-lasting structures, buildings, and overall livability for legitimate users of the environment. Walkable urbanism is another idea defined by the *Charter of New Urbanism.* It aims to reduce environmental impacts by altering the built environment to create smart cities that support sustainable transport.[9] Compact urban neighborhoods encourage residents to drive less. This encourages residents to go outside, walk, and connect with others. Additionally, these neighborhoods have significantly lower environmental impacts when compared to sprawling suburbs.[10]

As a result of the recent New Classical Architecture movement, sustainable construction aims to develop smart growth, walkability, architectural tradition, and classical design.[11] When we look at the great architecture of 100, 500, or 2000 years ago, its power is undiminished. It contrasts with modernist and globally uniform architecture.[12] In the 1980s, urban design began to oppose this increasing solitary housing estates and suburban sprawl we had become accustomed to.[13]

Urban Designers[14]

Urban designers are similar to urban planners when preparing design guidelines, regulatory frameworks, legislation, advertising, etc. Urban planners also overlap with architects, landscape architects, transportation engineers, and industrial designers. They must also deal with "place management" to guide and assist in the use and maintenance of urban areas and public spaces.

There are professionals who identify themselves specifically as urban designers and, through architecture, landscape, and planning programs, incorporate urban design theory into their projects. There is hope for the future because there are an increasing number of university programs offering degrees in urban design.

Urban Design Considers

- Pedestrian zones – To encourage walkability and connectivity.
- Incorporation of nature within a city – To reduce mental issues, such as depression.
- Aesthetics – To increase territorial reinforcement by residents.
- Urban structure – Arrangement and relation of business and people.
- Urban typology, density, and sustainability – Spatial types and changes related to intensity of use, consumption of resources, and production and maintenance of viable communities.
- Accessibility – Safe and easy transportation.
- Legibility and wayfinding – Accessible information about travel and destinations.
- Animation – Designing places to stimulate public activity.
- Function and fit – Places support their varied intended uses.
- Complementary mixed uses – Locating activities to allow constructive interaction between them.
- Character and meaning – Recognizing differences between places.
- Order and incident – Balancing consistency and variety in the urban environment.
- Continuity and change – Locating people in time and place and respecting heritage and contemporary culture.
- Civil society – People are free to interact as civic equals.

The Villages Calls Itself the Healthiest Hometown in America

Alice Grimes, a good friend of ours, told us about the community she lives in and the activities they have. We asked her to take a minute and tell us in detail about all the activities; below is her reply:

"The Villages now has over 300 activities, such as heated swimming pools and recreation centers – all within one or two miles. There are 38 executive golf courses with nine holes, and 12 championship courses with 18 holes. The executive courses are included in our dues of $148 a month along with all the activities, pools, and common maintenance. Classes are taught by volunteers who are retired people, experienced in that field. What's great is that there should be something for everyone.

If they don't like to exercise, there are social activities, like card games, groups making things for charities, clubs for train enthusiasts, etc. Most streets have frequent get-togethers with their neighbors, whether it's monthly Flamingo parties in the street (a Flamingo is placed in the front yard when that person is hosting), groups meals out, or parties for events such as Super Bowl, etc. If anyone has surgery, loses a partner, etc., the neighbors all rally around and take food and give support. This is a great place for widows and widowers because there's so much going on and it's easy to make friends and keep busy. The other thing is that if there isn't an activity or club someone is interested in, they can start one! We even have support groups for those with diseases like Parkinson's, so they can learn from each other. Oh, and I forgot the three town squares with restaurants and shops, and free, live entertainment every night except Thanksgiving and Christmas Day, where people can go to watch or dance."

See the following links for more information on *The Villages*: https://www.thevillages.com/lifestyle/marketSquare.asp

https://www.thevillages.com/Calendar/index.html

First-Generation CPTED

The basic idea when developing a CPTED program is that the physical environment can be manipulated to produce behavioral effects that will reduce the incidence as well as the fear of crime, so that the quality of life will be improved. These behavioral effects can be accomplished by reducing the inclination of the physical environment to support criminal behavior. In a CPTED program, there is a strong relationship between humans and their environment. The term *environment* includes the people and their physical and social surroundings. The term *design* includes physical, social, management, and law enforcement directives that seek to affect positively human behavior as people interact with their environment. The desired result of a CPTED program is to prevent crime and fear of crime within a specific environment by manipulating variables.

CPTED relies not only on physical and urban design but also on contemporary thinking about behavioral and social science, law enforcement, and community organization. The concepts of CPTED continue to evolve, but traditional (First-Generation) CPTED involves the following concepts: natural surveillance, territoriality, access control, activity support, and image/maintenance.[15] Jane Jacobs' idea of "eyes on the street" influenced the concept of natural surveillance and believed that the safest urban place is one that is continuously watched by human beings.[16] Research was later done by Oscar Newman on "defensible space" and he found that crimes more likely occurred in spaces where there was no natural surveillance by residents. Both Jacobs and Newman used urban planning and design to help develop places with close-knit social networks to develop voluntary community guardianship.[17]

There are some problems if high levels of fear of crime keep residents from going outside and spending time in public spaces. This in turn decreases physical activity levels which can lead to physical and mental health issues. When CPTED concepts are used to reduce fear of crime and in turn increase outdoor activities and active living, this will help improve the quality of life. There is a relationship between neighborhood conditions and health and there are direct and indirect effects on individual and public health. Direct effects include violence, homicide, dangerous driving, and substance abuse. Indirect effects include stress, fear of crime, repeat victimization, and social isolation. Research shows that residents' fear of crime negatively influences their active lifestyles, particularly by minimizing their time spent walking outdoors and eventually affecting their physical and psychological health.[18]

Target Hardening

The emphasis on design and use deviates from the traditional target-hardening approach to crime prevention. Traditional target hardening focuses predominantly on denying access to a crime target through physical or artificial barrier techniques (such as locks, alarms, fences, and gates). Target hardening often leads to constraints on the use, access, and enjoyment of the "hardened" environment. Moreover, the traditional approach tends to overlook opportunities for natural access control and surveillance. The term *natural* refers to deriving access control and surveillance as a secondary result of the normal and routine use of the environment.

These three original concepts of First-Generation CPTED – natural surveillance, natural access control, and territorial reinforcement – are reinforced by the activity support of legitimate users of the space to increase eyes on the street[19] and target hardenings, such as locks and alarms. CPTED emphasizes "natural" strategies as the preferred approach; these can be supplemented (as needed) by organized and mechanical strategies.[20]

Second-Generation CPTED

Second-Generation CPTED *"seeks to cultivate while building or rebuilding our Urban Areas"* (Saville & Cleveland 2008).

There are few opportunities for positive and social interactions between people and groups within the community (Green et al., 1998; Saville and Clear 2000).

What are the concepts of Second-Generation CPTED?

1. Social cohesion
2. Connectivity
3. Community culture
4. Threshold capacity

Second-Generation CPTED reduces crime motives by dealing with the cultural, social, and emotional needs of people at the specific locales where crime is or may be most acute.

Social Cohesion

A few of the characteristics that define social cohesion include

- Participation in local events and organizations
- Presence of self-directed community problem-solving
- Extent to which conflicts are positively resolved within the community, e.g., restorative justice programs
- Prevalence of friendship networks within the community
- Extensive positive relations between friendship networks

Connectivity

Connectivity means the neighborhood has positive relations and influence with external agencies such as government funding sources.

Some characteristics of connectivity include

- Existence of networks with outside agencies, e.g., shared websites
- Grant writer or access to a grant writing service
- Formal activities with outside groups, organizations, and neighborhood
- Adequate transport facilities (ride-sharing, bicycle paths, public transit) to link with outside areas

CPTED practitioners sometimes forget what is significant about Jane Jacobs' "eyes on the street,"[21] not the sight lines of the streets – but the eyes. We don't need neighborhoods of watchers; we need a sense of community where people care about who they are watching. Community culture brings people together for a common purpose. This is how local residents begin to share a sense of place and why they bother to exert territorial control in the first place (Adams and Goldbard, 2001).

A few characteristics that define culture within a community include

- Presence and effectiveness of gender and minority equality strategies
- Gender-based programs, e.g., violence against women
- Extent of social and cultural diversities within a neighborhood
- Prevalence of special places, festivals, and events
- Extent of community traditions and cultural activities, e.g., art fairs and sports role models

- A unique sense of pride or distinctiveness based on the attributes or characteristics of the residents, occupants, or users of the space involved

Research indicates that there is a relationship between mental health and the physical living environment. These issues can be partially addressed through proper urban design and planning utilizing CPTED concepts. Certain environments increase the fear of crime and are associated with negative health and well-being issues. Changes in the physical environment may discourage criminal behavior and, at the same time, encourage human interaction and social connectivity. When individuals are isolated and fear prevents interaction and outside activity with others, mental health may deteriorate.

Notes

1 Living Environments. Retrieved on April 09, 2018 from: https://www.ntnu.edu/chpr/living-environments
2 The Coordination Reform. Retrieved on March 06,2018 from: https://www.regjeringen.no/contentassets/d4f0e16ad32e4bbd8d8ab5c21445a5dc/en-gb/pdfs/stm200820090047000en_pdfs.pdf
3 Dementia. Retrieved on January 6, 2018 from: https://www.mayoclinic.org/diseases-conditions/dementia/symptoms-causes/syc-20352013
4 **D**esigning good mental health into cities: the next frontier for urban design, Design Council, 2017, **Rachel Toms, Insight & Standards Manager, Cities Programme (Secondment)**.
5 What are the Treatments for Dementia? Retrieved on March 13, 2018 from: https://www.webmd.com/alzheimers/dementia-treatments-overview#1
6 Urban Design. Retrieved on February 15, 2018 from: https://en.wikipedia.org/wiki/Urban_design
7 Cycling is Healthier than You Think. Retrieved on February 18, 2018: http://www.cycling-embassy.dk/2015/04/30/cycling-is-healthier-than-you-think/
8 Crime Prevention Coalition of America. Retrieved on April 21, 2018 from: http://archive.ncpc.org/programs/crime-prevention-coalition-of-america.html
9 Boeing; et al. (2014). "LEED-ND and Livability Revisited". *Berkeley Planning Journal*. **27**: 31–55. Retrieved April 15, 2018 from: https://escholarship.org/uc/item/49f234rd
10 Ewing, R "Growing Cooler - the Evidence on Urban Development and Climate Change". Retrieved on: March 16, 2018 from: http://smartgrowthamerica.org
11 The Charter of the New Urbanism. Retrieved on March 8, 2018 from: https://www.cnu.org/who-we-are/charter-new-urbanism
12 "Beauty, Humanism, Continuity between Past and Future". Traditional Architecture Group. Retrieved on March 23, 2018 from: http://www.traditionalarchitecture.co.uk/aims.html
13 Issue Brief: Smart-Growth: Building Livable Communities. American Institute of Architects. Retrieved on March 14, 2018 from: https://www.aia.org/SiteObjects/files/smartgrowth05.pdf
14 Urban Design. Retrieved on February 24, 2018 from: https://en.wikipedia.org/wiki/Urban_design

15 Moffatt, R.E. Crime Prevention through Environmental Design-a Management Perspective. Can. J. Criminal. 1983, 25, 19–31.
16 Jacobs, J. The Death and Life of Great American Cities; Vintage Books: New York, NY, USA, 1961.
17 Marzbali, M.H.; Abdullah, A.; Tilaki, M.J.M. The effectiveness of interventions in the built environment for improving health by addressing fear of crime. Int. J. Law Crim. Justice 2016.
18 Hallal, P.C.; Reis, R.S.; Parra, D.C.; Hoehner, C.; Brownson, R.C.; Simões, E.J. Association between perceived environmental attributes and physical activity among adults in Recife, Brazil. J. Phys. Act. Health 2010.].
19 Eyes on the Street. Retrieved on 02-18-18 from: https://www.npr.org/2016/09/28/495615064/eyes-on-the-street-details-jane-jacobs-efforts-to-put-cities-first
20 Zahm, D. Using Crime Prevention Through Environmental Design in problem solving. Retrieved on February 23, 2018 from: http://www.popcenter.org
21 Eyes on the Street. Retrieved on 02-18-18 from: https://www.npr.org/2016/09/28/495615064/eyes-on-the-street-details-jane-jacobs-efforts-to-put-cities-first

Chapter 91

Do You Fear That Your Job Will Become Obsolete?

Advances in technology are moving at an incredible pace! Smart devices and artificial intelligence (AI) are in the workplace and are also controlling more aspects of our daily lives than ever before, but there are some limitations.

To understand AI, you need to know that there are two distinct "parts" of AI. One is *programmed AI* that is fed data and it can make decisions and determine all possible outcomes before a decision is made. The *machine learning algorithm of AI* knows nothing and collects data as it "learns" from experiences and it gets more knowledgeable.[1] AI has gained more attention since the release of ChatGPT and Dall-E because they increase the potential for AI-driven business applications.[2]

Throughout the years, technological advances have automated many physical tasks like those in a manufacturing or a production facility, but since AI has the capability to "think" more like a human brain, this will undoubtedly affect the jobs of security professionals. According to Per Research Data:[3]

- In 2022, 19% of American workers were in jobs that are the most exposed to AI, in which the most important activities may be either replaced or assisted by AI.
- 23% of workers have jobs that are the least exposed to AI, in which the most important activities are farther from the reach of AI. Other workers, nearly six in ten in all, are likely to have varying levels of exposure to AI.
- Jobs with a high level of exposure to AI tend to be in higher-paying fields where a college education and analytical skills can be a plus.

DOI: 10.4324/9781003402718-92

The Fear of Becoming Obsolete (FOBO) is very real and it's understandable.[4]

- 22% of US workers worry technology will make their jobs obsolete.
- Fear of tech is up seven points since 2021, while other job concerns are stable.
- College-educated workers nearly match non-college workers in their worry about technology.[5]

Security officer functions may be more in danger of being replaced by AI – if AI can assist or independently perform their job duties. An example of this would be obtaining or analyzing information when video analytics or smart alarm sensors are triggered. The customer service aspect of security cannot be replaced by AI and this is a critical component of providing peace of mind and developing a culture of security. AI does not have *feelings*. It cannot feel sympathy or empathy for someone. These are some human capabilities that AI cannot duplicate. AI also doesn't know whether or not the decisions that it makes are right or wrong. Elon Musk stated at an event in the United Kingdom that AI will eventually create a situation where no job is needed.[6] This is unlikely to happen anytime in the near future.

It is very important for security officers to consistently concentrate on professional development. Maintain the right skillsets to be more valuable in the workplace and learn to work in harmony with AI and the changes the new technology brings. Educate yourself by taking classes on the potential of AI and how technology can make you more productive.

It's also critical to understand what AI CAN do as of 2023:[7]

- Write your academic essays – and almost anything else.
- Create visual art.
- Get trained and "learn."
- Make investments
- Analyze phone conversations at scale to find trends

What AI CAN'T do – as of 2023:[8]

- Multitasking.
- Explain its decisions.
- Make moral judgments.
- Feel empathy, sympathy, or anything else for that matter.
- Be creative (on its own, anyway).

It's true that AI can do many things a lot faster than people. It can perform complex, data-related tasks, but all indications are that AI will only completely eliminate those jobs in the workplace that are automated, such as data entry. Other jobs, such as those of a security officer, will continue to progressively work more in conjunction with AI by using advancements in technology to provide a more secure workplace.

Notes

1 11 Things AI Can — and Can't Do (So Far). Retrieved on January 28, 2024 from: https://www.invoca.com/blog/6-things-ai-cant-do-yet
2 Do You Suffer From FOBO? Here's How To Handle It. Retrieved on January 28, 2024 from: https://www.forbes.com/sites/williamarruda/2023/11/28/do-you-suffer-from-fobo-heres-how-to-handle-it/?utm_source=newsletter&utm_medium=email&utm_campaign=dailydozen&cdlcid=6540326a554da33a6bb44fbe§ion=intro&sh=2e9e41424885
3 Which U.S. Workers Are More Exposed to AI on Their Jobs? Retrieved on January 28, 2024 from: https://www.pewresearch.org/social-trends/2023/07/26/which-u-s-workers-are-more-exposed-to-ai-on-their-jobs/
4 More U.S. Workers Fear Technology Making Their Jobs Obsolete. Retrieved on January 28, 2024 from: https://news.gallup.com/poll/510551/workers-fear-technology-making-jobs-obsolete.aspx?utm_source=alert&utm_medium=email&utm_content=morelink&utm_campaign=syndication
5 xx
6 Elon Musk says AI will eventually create a situation where 'no job is needed." Retrieved on January 28, 2024 from: https://www.cnbc.com/2023/11/02/tesla-boss-elon-musk-says-ai-will-create-situation-where-no-job-is-needed.html
7 11 Things AI Can — and Can't Do (So Far). Retrieved on January 28, 2024 from: https://www.invoca.com/blog/6-things-ai-cant-do-yet
8 11 Things AI Can — and Can't Do (So Far). Retrieved on January 28, 2024 from: https://www.invoca.com/blog/6-things-ai-cant-do-yet

Chapter 92

Knowledge and Awareness

Benjamin Franklin once said, "An investment in knowledge pays the best interest."[1] He understood the value of becoming more knowledgeable. Successful people have one thing in common – they invest in their own future by doing something to educate themselves daily. Lifelong learning becomes a part of their daily lives. Everyone needs to be the best version of themselves that they can be and constantly seek to improve on their existing talents.

Security officers should learn their job and learn it well. They should be well versed in patrol methodologies, crisis communication, basic first aid, reporting instructions, areas of responsibility, problematic employees, and vulnerable access points. Officers need to know the environment they are protecting, the people they meet, and the underlying atmosphere of the environment to identify dangerous situations, thievery, trespass, and any other form of unauthorized activity they are charged with preventing. Lastly, security officers should understand the concept of situational awareness.

On the surface, situational awareness seems to be easy to understand. Simply put, it is knowing what is going on around you. However, it is more than just that. Not only does a security officer need to know what is going on around them, but they also need to know the "why" of the activity that is going on around them. For example, a security officer working in parking lot patrol sees a flatbed tow truck pull into the parking lot. The occupant gets out of the truck and, in plain view of the security officer, begins to hook up a luxury car and pull it onto the flatbed of the truck. The driver takes the vehicle away, driving directly in front of the security officer, who simply watches the driver as they exit the property. Several hours later, a call comes in to security reporting a stolen car in the parking lot. The driver returned

DOI: 10.4324/9781003402718-93

to the parking lot to realize his car had been taken. This could be a vehicle theft or possibly a repossession by the creditor.

This illustrates the importance of a security officer understanding not only the "what is happening" but the "why it is happening." The security officer knew the car was being pulled onto a flatbed truck, but did not know why. The security officer figured since it was taking place in the open in the middle of the day, it must be fine. But, a confident car thief may pull into the parking lot with a flatbed or tow truck and commit a crime in plain view of the security officer. Officers must know that situational awareness is understanding the ordinary so that they can spot the unordinary. If something occurs during an officer's shift that doesn't happen daily, he/she needs to investigate it for further evaluation. Tow trucks seldom pull into the parking lot and take away a vehicle. Understanding what is going on in and around the assets being protected is the best tool a security officer takes on patrol.

Note

1 An Investment in Knowledge Pays the Best Interest. Retrieved on June 12, 2023 from: https://selfmadesuccess.com/investment-knowledge-pays-best-interest/

Chapter 93

Proprietary vs. Contract Security Officers

When a company has determined that it wants or needs on-site security, it has to make the decision of whether to hire a security contractor or hire its own security personnel. This is an important decision because security officers are often the first contact that visitors, vendors, contractors, customers, and employees have with the company. Security officers are often excellent PR resources for the company and give everyone a greater sense of safety and security.

Proprietary security officers or in-house security officers work for one company or organization and provide security services for their employer.

Contract security officers are employed by a security company to provide security services to different organizations on a contractual basis. There are pros and cons to each.

Advantages of Proprietary Security

When a company decides to hire proprietary security, the company can determine the post orders and the policies and procedures for the security staff. The company can have requirements for experience, training, and other capabilities to manage the day-to-day operation of the security staff. Proprietary security officers are considered internal employees rather than external contractors, which may affect how internal disputes between security officers and other employees are handled. In most cases, the company can provide better benefits and a more positive image than contract security. Proprietary security positions generally attract higher-quality individuals, and there is less turnover than with contract security. Since they are an employee of

DOI: 10.4324/9781003402718-94

the company, proprietary security officers are generally more dedicated to their jobs and more loyal to the interests and concerns of the company since they are a part of the organization's culture.

Disadvantages of Proprietary Security

Control over daily security operations is positive for many companies, but the most obvious disadvantage of proprietary security officers is the cost of hiring, management, scheduling, training, and equipment. Many times, companies may not know what they need in terms of security processes and do not know the best security policies and procedures to put in place to protect their assets.

Advantages of Contract Security

Security vendors can recommend the best security practices to the company and provide the best contract employees to meet the company's qualifications. Contract security companies may be able to provide protection for company executives traveling in the United States and abroad. When a contract security vendor is responsible for security on a day-to-day basis, there is some liability transfer from the company to the security vendor. Contract security services generally have more resources for additional staffing or special assignments in the event of an emergency situation. Most companies see some cost savings by hiring security contractors over hiring their own security staff because the security vendor handles all of the payroll paperwork and works with the company to develop security post orders.

Disadvantages of Contract Security

One of the disadvantages of using contract security officers is that the company has little or no control over what security officers are assigned to their site. The security company can decide who is assigned to which of their contracted security customers. Contract security vendors generally have a higher turnover rate than proprietary security so individual sites may frequently see different security officers on their property. The customer must work through the security vendor if they want to add or replace security officers.

There are advantages and disadvantages to contract and proprietary security, and a company has to determine what will work best for their company culture, but, regardless, both can help protect company assets – people, property, and information. Whether security officers are proprietary or contract, they must be professional and must demonstrate a high level of skill, training, and professionalism.

Chapter 94

Walking and Working Surfaces Are Critical for a Safe Work Environment

Slips

Falls due to slips occur when there is not enough friction between the walking surface and the person's foot, causing a loss of balance. All flooring or other walking surfaces do not have the same degree of traction in all areas.[1]

Everyone, especially on-duty security officers, should constantly be aware of their environment, particularly walking and working surfaces. Unfortunately, other factors – personal matters, an upcoming meeting, and a conversation with a co-worker, can often affect an individual's concentration and attention to surroundings.

Many walking surfaces, especially smooth or polished surfaces such as marble, tile, or terrazzo, become slippery when wet. Some common sources include freshly mopped or waxed floors (before buffing), plumbing or roof leaks, and spills. Interior floors usually get wet during inclement weather as water is brought in on the soles of people's shoes or even blown in as doors are opened. These problems are compounded when the walking surface is sloped. For these hazards, good housekeeping is the primary tool to prevent slips. **Mark and, if possible, block off the wet portion with proper signage or barriers**. Also, mark any wet areas resulting from a spill and clean them as soon as possible. When the signage or barrier is no longer needed, it becomes a tripping hazard. If signs are repeatedly left out when the floors are dry, they may eventually be ignored.

Rain and snow may cause floors to be wet at building entrances. As with spills, there should be a procedure for placing warning signs and keeping the area as dry

DOI: 10.4324/9781003402718-95

as possible. A porous, non-absorbent mat is placed outside, and an absorbent mat is placed inside the vestibule, with an additional absorbent walk-off mat placed inside. The first mat removes debris from the shoes, allowing water to run through, and the absorbent mats help dry the shoes.

Exterior hazards also require good housekeeping and maintenance. In winter weather, initial ice and snow removal from parking lots and sidewalks is critical, as is follow-up to prevent refreezing. Granular ice-melt pellets or liquid ice-melt can also be used. In warmer weather, wet grass and residual rainwater may cause walking surfaces to be slippery.

Footwear is an important factor in preventing falls from slipping. If working where floors are wet or oily, non-slip footwear is desirable. The specific hazard should be considered when selecting footwear because the non-slip properties of footwear vary, and one type will probably not cover every situation. For example, neoprene soles work well on wet or dry surfaces but not in oily conditions. Crepe soles are acceptable on concrete but not on smooth surfaces such as tile.

During inclement weather, particularly ice and snow, appropriate footwear is essential. Shoes or boots with good traction are preferred to leather or smooth soles. Many outdoor sporting goods stores carry studded ice grippers (such as YakTrax®) that strap on the bottom of shoes to provide traction on ice, but they must be taken off inside where they become a slip hazard on hard floors.

Trips

Like slips, falls from trips occur when an unexpected obstacle causes a loss of balance. Uneven walking surfaces, unfastened carpeting or flooring, clutter or debris, open drawers, and other objects on the floor, such as electrical cords and pipes, are just some of the items that cause individuals to trip. An obstructed view, poor lighting, inattention, and haste, in combination with these objects, are often associated with tripping incidents.

Once again, good housekeeping and proper maintenance are the primary means for preventing trips. Here are some tips to prevent tripping:

- Keep work areas and walking surfaces clean and free of clutter and debris.
- Keep work areas and hallways well lighted. Turn on lights or use a flashlight in unlit areas.
- Close drawers (file or desk) and remove file boxes around furniture and other areas where individuals may walk.
- Do not run electrical cords across walkways or aisles without taping them to the floor or covering them with a proper cord cover. Never cover it with a rug or carpet.

- Make sure that you can see the way ahead. Do not carry or push things that obstruct your view of the travel path.
- Keep sidewalks, parking lots, and other walking surfaces in good condition and free of uneven surfaces, such as cracks, bumps, or holes. Mark and barricade such hazards until they can be repaired.
- Keep stairs in good condition and clear of objects. Check treads for wear and whether secure. Be sure handrails are in good condition and securely fastened.
- Secure loose flooring and carpets. Make sure rugs and mats are not turned up or folded over.[2]

Falls

Falls due to slips and trips are generally called falls from the same level. Other types of falls often involve falling from or to a different level, either from an elevated area or through an opening in the walking surface. As with the other types, these falls result from an excessive shift off the center of balance. For these types of incidents, good housekeeping and proper lighting are essential. Guarding and handrails are generally required.

Personal Fall Prevention

Not all workplaces can be changed, so there are several personal factors that everyone needs to remember to keep from falling. These include, but are not limited to the following:

- Use proper equipment if you must work or reach a higher level, such as a ladder. Do not use chairs or tables.
- Walking at a safe pace, alert to any obstacles that may be ahead. Adjust pace and stride for the condition of the walking surface.
- Wearing proper footwear for the job and work surface conditions.
- Not carrying items that block the view ahead.
- Not jumping from heights. Climb or ease down.
- Promptly reporting any slip, trip, and fall hazards.
- Taking the time to pick up small debris items or clean up minor spills. Never assume somebody else will take care of it.
- Using personal protective equipment where necessary.
- Closing all files and desk drawers immediately.
- Using a flashlight to enter dark areas.
- Storing heavy items down low. Heavy items may be hard to handle on ladders or step stools.[3]

Preventing slips, trips, and falls can be a major challenge for anyone. Using these measures will help reduce the probability. Still, the ultimate responsibility rests with security officers to remain alert, recognize hazards, and take the necessary steps to avoid someone being injured.

Notes

1 Canadian Centre for Occupational Health and Safety Occupational "Prevention of Slip, Trip, and Falls." Retrieved April 13, 2006, from http://www.ccohs.ca/oshanswers/safety_haz/falls.html?oe

2 Walking/Working Surfaces." U.S. Department of Labor, Occupational Safety and Health Administration. (2005, July): Retrieved April 13, 2006, from http://www.osha.gov/SLTC/walkingworkingsurfaces/index.html

3 Ibid.

Chapter 95

Understanding Crime Issues

Crime prevention is the same regardless of the type of business where a security officer is assigned. The philosophy is always consistent – reduce criminal opportunity. A well-rounded crime prevention program will help ensure that all of the client's assets – people, property, information, and reputation – are protected.

How to start:

1. Conduct a security vulnerability assessment to identify vulnerabilities and areas of concern. Develop a security plan that addresses the vulnerabilities.
2. Start a business watch[1]/neighborhood watch program[2] and encourage neighbors and community members to participate. Security officers can network with neighborhood businesses and develop a relationship with local law enforcement.
3. Encourage the community to report crime regardless of the dollar value of the loss. This may cause a slight increase in crime statistics. Conduct a follow-up on every reported crime and see what can be done to reduce criminal opportunity so it doesn't occur again.
4. When you meet with employees, don't just talk to them about security at work, but talk to them about home and personal security and emphasize situational awareness. Please encourage them to report suspicious behavior or people to security officers.
5. Be PROACTIVE with your actions and in your thinking.

DOI: 10.4324/9781003402718-96

Notes

1 Business Watch. Retrieved on May 07, 2023 from: https://www.nnw.org/business-watch
2 Welcome to Neighborhood Watch. Retrieved on May 07, 2023 from: https://www.nnw.org/business-watch

Chapter 96

Crime and Opportunity

Environmental criminology addresses

1. Criminal behavior
2. Process of behavior
3. Using environmental clues
4. Decision to plan a crime
5. Seizing the opportunity
6. Stages of opportunity
7. Stages of decision-making
8. Awareness of space

Case #1: There is a large office area where petty cash was stolen from a four-drawer file cabinet. The Human Resources (HR) Department had about 15 four-drawer file cabinets lined up against the wall. During the investigation, we noticed that the file cabinet at the very end had several keys on a ring that was kept in the lock, and this ring had keys to the file cabinet where the petty cash was taken – even though the cabinet was locked. Locks were changed on the file cabinets since they contained confidential employee information. This situation could have been much worse if the confidential HR information had been accessed instead of the petty cash. This was a simple fix because the opportunity to access the petty cash was removed.

Case #2: At the National Crime Prevention Institute (NCPI), we studied padlocks and learned they should be replaced every 3 to 5 years. Why? Because through the years, it's not uncommon to lose control over the security of the padlock if you're not sure who has the keys.

Case #3: Three people have keys to a closet where cash was stolen. The closet had a high-security lock and key, and all three employees with access were long-term employees of the company. A close look at the door showed marks on the hinge

DOI: 10.4324/9781003402718-97

pins made by a tool – possibly a screwdriver. It appeared as though the pins had been removed, and the door could be opened with the lock still secured. In all high-security applications, nonremovable hinge pins should be used.

Case #4: Petty cash was kept in a locked supervisor's desk, and the desk was secured. The office had only three desks, but one had the same keyway as the supervisor's desk. A temporary employee was using that particular desk, and the cash was missing on her last day with the company. Interestingly enough, this temporary employee had offered to work late on her last day to finish a project. Cylinder numbers on desk locks must be either removed or tracked to ensure that desks do not use the same key.

Case #5: A woman with dementia lived in an assisted living facility. She had an insured, $10,000 diamond ring taken from the top of her dresser. The family was very upset and contacted the local police and the facility administrator to have an investigation done. Two days later, the ring was found on the dresser – exactly where the woman said she had put it.

All of these scenarios describe easy targets. The environment can and will influence a crime when there is an opportunity.

As a security officer, think about prevention at all times! Be proactive by recommending a locked desk or locked file cabinet policy. Don't wait until after a crime has occurred to secure valuables.

Chapter 97

Security/Situational Awareness

After the terrorist attacks of 9/11, awareness was raised throughout the world about the need for competent security professionals. There are more job opportunities in the diverse world of security for those individuals, both male and female, who strive to stay on top of this ever-changing industry by being knowledgeable about current trends and issues and are consistently striving to develop themselves professionally to remain on the cutting edge of the latest innovations and solutions in the industry.[1]

> *Security Awareness* is the method through which an individual is made conscious of, and accepts, his or her own role and responsibilities in the protection of the assets of an organization; i.e., Security Awareness must overcome both ignorance and apathy.
>
> (Draper, 2017)

"*Situational Awareness* is the perception of environmental elements and events with respect to time or space, the comprehension of their meaning, and the projection of their status after some variable has changed, such as time, or some other variable, such as a predetermined event." (US Army Field Manual: FM 3-19.30, 2001)

To put it another way, *Security/Situational Awareness* is

- Paying close attention to what is going on around you.
- The ability to scan the environment and sense danger, challenges, and opportunities while maintaining the ability to conduct normal activities.

DOI: 10.4324/9781003402718-98

The success of any *Security/Situational Awareness* program (SAP) is the measure of intended protective attitudes and behaviors displayed by all those who interact with the organization, including staff, contractors, and even vendors and customers (Draper, 2017).

Purposes of Security Awareness

Security/Situational Awareness supports several important goals. Those who receive security awareness instruction are better able to do the following:

- **Protect company assets.**
  First and foremost, the purpose of the security awareness program is to educate employees on how to help protect company assets and reduce losses. Everything else flows from this prime responsibility.
- **Understand the relationship between security and successful operations.**
  This purpose is the prime one for awareness efforts directed toward executive management. Protection professionals should devote time and talent to demonstrate the program's value and cost-effectiveness.
- **Identify their obligations under the security program.**
  It is important to identify security obligations for all employees and non-employees and present them as reasonable and necessary. Employee orientation and periodic refreshers can teach people precisely which security requirements apply to them.
- **Recognize the connection between security program objectives and selected security measures.**
  This purpose is important to middle management. Unit and department heads must recognize (and, preferably, agree) that security measures are appropriate and necessary.

The illustration shown in Figure 97.1 depicts a triangle that has six sides, three inside and three outside, all critical elements of a Security Master Plan.

Over the Years

Over the years, we have all done security/situational awareness or personal safety and security presentations or training programs in our communities and for various organizations. One of the main reasons we do these types of presentations is to educate the community about better protecting themselves, their property, and corporate assets. This is part of formulating a *Culture of Security* within your corporation.

When you plan to do a presentation or a training program on *Security/Situational Awareness or Personal Safety and Security*, gather the crime statistics for that particular

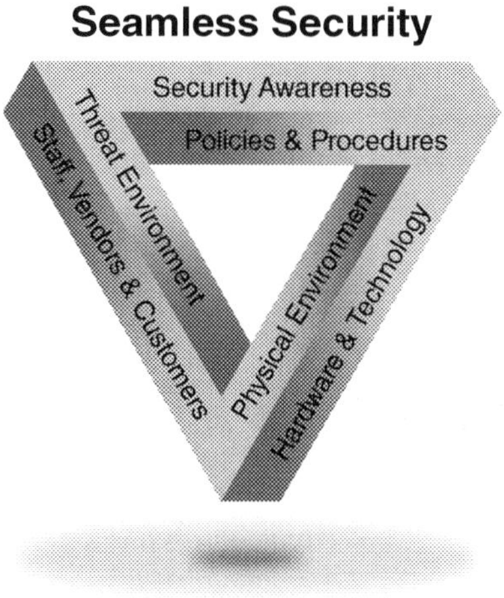

Figure 97.1 Seamless security diagram (Graphic designed and used with permission courtesy of Rick Draper. Adapted from an image in the Protection of Assets Manual (POA), 2017).

state and/or locale. Then, compile statistics on UCR (Uniform Crime Reporting) Part I and Part II crimes within a one-half-mile radius of the location where you will be presenting your program. Next, calculate what the likelihood is that a person will be the victim of different types of crime – both violent crime and property crime (e.g., the chances of becoming a victim of murder in this location is 1 in 150 people, the likelihood of becoming a victim of rape is 1 in 75 people, or the chances of having your car stolen in this location is 1 in 50 people).

During your presentation or training on *Security/Situational Awareness*, emphasize the following:

"In most cases, when a criminal selects a victim, he/she looks for 3 things:

- A person who appears to be weak or vulnerable.
- A person who is unaware of their surroundings and is not paying attention.
- OPPORTUNITY."

(Fennelly, 2014)

This information, together with pertinent crime statistics for their particular area, will make your presentation "personal" to those in attendance, they will understand the need for their Security/Situational Awareness, and they will then see how they "fit" into the overall security program.

Look at crime trends within a specific environment and ask yourself, "How do I put a stop to these problems?" For example, if employees are paid twice a month, on the second and fourth Friday, they cash their checks, have lunch, and go back to work; and women place their purses under their desks. At 5:00 pm on that payday, they go home, and then on Saturday, they realize, "Oh my goodness, I lost my wallet." Maybe, after this happens five or six times, someone may suggest that there is a need for a meeting on staff safety and security.

Monthly Safety or Newsletter

Another good idea is a *Monthly Safety/Security Newsletter* that is relevant to what is happening at that particular time. For example, in September (the typical beginning of the school year), we wrote information on bullying; in October, we developed safety and security tips for Halloween; and in December, we outlined some *Holiday Shopping Safety and Security Issues*. Each month has a different theme and makes it "personal" to the reader. At the end of our information, we always put the words, "Be Proactive. Think Prevention."

Tricks of the Trade or Security Awareness in Depth

A successful *Security Awareness* campaign recognizes that it is easier to engender protective behaviors on behalf of family members first and then expand it to include the business or corporate well-being. Larry Fennelly and Marianna Perry, along with Rick Draper, all believe that one of the techniques of the trade we use is to

1. Discuss *Family and Personal Safety/Security* issues first.
2. Talk about *Protecting Personal Property, Home Security, and Implementing Neighborhood Watch* next.
3. Develop a *Business Watch and Safety/Security Awareness Campaign* in the workplace, emphasizing that work colleagues should look out for one another to keep the work environment safe.
4. Finally, *Corporate Safety/Security* issues to protect corporate assets.

Situational Crime Prevention incorporates other crime prevention and law enforcement strategies in an effort to focus on place-specific crime problems.

Results and Objectives

- Reduce violent crime.
- Reduce property crime.
- Displacement of crime.
- Eliminate the threats and risks.
- Reduce the likelihood of more incidents.
- Eliminate vulnerabilities and protect assets.

Question: "Why get involved in Security Awareness?"

Answer: ***"To educate the community and reduce opportunities for crime to occur."***

Four Essential Components

Security awareness is one of the four essential components of an effective security program that includes physical, electronic, and design security; security staff; security policies, procedures, and protocols; and security education and training. All these elements combine to protect the organization's assets and reduce liability.

Security awareness is the first step that precedes the education and training elements of the security program. For business invitees, licensees' other visitors/guests, and even trespassers, the security awareness effort may be as simple as a warning sign or as complex as a signed document regarding premises security guidelines. For security and other staff, the security awareness may be a series of security or crime alerts relating to an ongoing security and/or crime trend and pattern and specific instructions for both the security staff and other staff to follow.

Security awareness documents usually specify the crime and/or security issue and concern, what you can do to mitigate or prevent the security issue, and what steps the organization is taking to mitigate or prevent the security issue. Depending on the nature of the crime and/or security threat, the organization may need to furnish education and training for specific responses to the threat. For example, workplace violence awareness will usually involve detailed information, instructions, and specific training, including exercises, drills, and tests.

Security awareness efforts interface and integrate with the entire security program of an organization to present a seamless and streamlined system to reduce or eliminate the security and crime threats faced by the organization. To succeed, support from the top management of the organization for security awareness is critical (Dowling, 2017).

What Are Security Awareness Programs?

There is no one simple answer to this question because security is always a situational discipline, in part defined by the ambient threat environment.

On its face, **SAPs** seem simple: *All employees and/or tenants should be trained to be aware of suspicious behavior and what to do when they see it. One cannot assume that everyone knows what constitutes suspicious behavior or what to do when encountered. This requires training.*

SAPs are similar to the basic concepts of the **Neighborhood Watch** program in the workplace.

One of the fundamental objectives of any **SAP** is to be on the lookout for **suspicious behavior**. Where the breakdown often occurs is with the assumption that all participants understand what suspicious behavior looks like. More often than not, this is an inherent weakness of well-intended **SAPs**. Therefore, it is important that rudimentary training equips all employees with the basic skills required to recognize *suspicious behavior*, including the ability to read body language, conversational spontaneity, eye contact patterns, and latency of verbal response. Basic training also includes teaching the ability to know when to retreat and/or how to be a credible witness. Training also includes the ability to recognize the precursors of potential criminal behavior, such as casing the premises for future criminality.

CPTED (Crime Prevention through Environmental Design), in combination with a robust **SAP**, is a cost-efficient duo applicable to almost any security program. Cost efficiency is accomplished by ensuring that the *whole is greater than the sum of the parts*.

Well-designed **Security Awareness Programs**, when supported by the **CPTED**, reinforce the goals of *natural surveillance* and *territoriality*. These **CPTED** strategies are significantly more effective for properties with little or no access control, such as shopping malls, hospitals, and other public institutions. Both SAPs and CPTED are methodologies aimed at enhancing the perception of effective security prescience.

Training and the ability to recognize potential suspicious behavior should be applied at two levels. Fundamental training is applicable to all employees and retail tenants and should focus on the recognition of suspicious behavior. The skill to actually confront suspicious behavior may require a slightly higher level of training, especially when there may be the possibility of basic interaction with a suspect. Typically, this level of training would generally apply to security personnel, including in-store security personnel (William (Bill) Nesbitt, CPP, 2017).

Issues to Keep in Mind

- Management at all levels must set an example.
- Threats will get you nowhere.
- Choose issues likely to respond quickly.
- Don't try too much at once.
- Warn about the increase in reports.
- Speak in brief, "bottom-line" terms to management.

Sell the Benefits

- Reduced number and frequency of losses.
- Improved cost-effectiveness of security.
- Conveys constant security message.

- Sets standards.
- Defines required behaviors and practices (Rick Draper 2017)

Security Awareness is the method through which an individual is made conscious of, and accepts, his or her own role and responsibilities in the protection of the assets of an organization; i.e., Security Awareness must overcome both ignorance and apathy.

The success of any Security Awareness program is the measure of intended protective attitudes and behaviors displayed by all those who interact with the organization, including staff, contractors, and even vendors and customers. (Rick Draper 2017)

Note

1 Women in the Security Profession, Elsevier, Sandi Davies, 2017, p. 253 and. 150 Things You Need To Know About Security, Elsevier, Lawrence J. Fennelly, CPO & CSS, Marianna Perry, CPP, CPO, 2018, p. 219.

Chapter 98

Emotional Intelligence

You may have heard the term "EI," but what does it mean? Author and psychologist Daniel Goleman – who popularized the concept of emotional intelligence (EI) in his 1995 best-seller *Emotional Intelligence: Why It Can Matter More Than IQ* – defines EI as "the ability to recognize, understand and manage our own emotions as well as to recognize, understand and influence the emotions of others."[1]

Goleman outlines EI in four quadrants as in Figure 98.1.[2]

Self-awareness means recognizing your emotions and knowing your strengths and weaknesses. What is important to you, and what are your core values?

Self-management is having a positive reaction when faced with strong emotions. Recognize the emotion that you are feeling, and take time to process it. Allow yourself some time so you can feel calmer and more clear-headed.

Social awareness is trying to connect with your team and understand their needs and feelings. How do you communicate with your team? Practice good listening skills and be supportive.

Relationship management refers to your skill at working to receive desirable responses from others when dealing with change or conflict. Ensure you are clear-headed and have a calm demeanor.

In conclusion, EI is recognizing emotions in yourself and others and using those feelings to guide better decision-making. Security managers and supervisors who exhibit strong EI understand how their actions can affect members of their security team. Set an example for your security officers and work with them so they can develop EI.

Security managers and supervisors who display high EI typically have greater self-awareness, better communication skills, and superior problem-solving abilities, and they incorporate more effective conflict resolution strategies in their day-to-day work lives. EI gives leaders the necessary skills to create a more positive work environment where security officers feel appreciated and valued.[3]

DOI: 10.4324/9781003402718-99

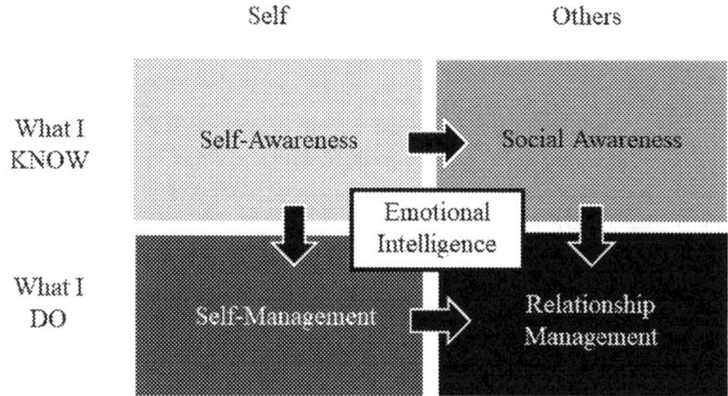

Figure 98.1 This represents the four quadrants of emotional intelligence: "Self-awareness," "Social awareness," "Self-management," and "Relationship management."

There are six key actions you should concentrate on to ensure you're exhibiting high EI:[4]

- Communicate effectively with your security team to build trust and rapport.
- Provide regular feedback using positive reinforcement and constructive criticism.
- Motivate your security officers by understanding what motivates them.
- Handle conflict effectively by staying calm.
- Make decisions quickly and confidently after weighing all options.
- Continue learning and growing and lead by example.

Your goal is to create a healthier workplace where everyone, including other security officers, feels valued to what they contribute to the overall security program.

Notes

1 Emotional Intelligence in the Workplace: What Is It, and How Can It Help During These Times? Retrieved on October 18, 2023 from: https://www.indeed.com/lead/emotional-intelligence-in-the-workplace?gclid=EAIaIQobChMImse9i6mAggMVQpKGCh0UlwZtEAAYAiAAEgL8bfD_BwE&aceid=&gclsrc=aw.ds
2 Ibid.
3 Emotional Intelligence Makes Good Leaders Better. Retrieved on October 18, 2023 from: https://www.paycor.com/resource-center/articles/importance-of-emotional-intelligence-in-leadership/
4 Ibid.

Chapter 99

Stationary or Post Duty

Stationary or post duty is an assignment where a security officer is responsible for maintaining the integrity of a certain area. Security officers on post duty are typically stationed at entry points either onto the property or at building entry points. Officers with these assignments are primarily responsible for access control. They will verify identification and check if the person is authorized to access the area or building. Procedures will vary depending on whether the individual is an employee, visitor, vendor, or contractor. Security officers on post duty may also utilize magnetometers and perform bag searches. Other post assignments can be for traffic detail, pedestrian control, or safeguarding a specific area requiring additional protection. Officers assigned to a post position must strictly adhere to their post unless otherwise instructed.

DOI: 10.4324/9781003402718-100

Chapter 100

Civil Disturbances, Riots, or Protests

Civil disobedience, resulting in riots and protests, has increased throughout the world. Law enforcement officers and security officers must be prepared to protect people and property and ensure the safety of everyone involved. Still, these types of incidents often do pose a challenge for security teams.

It is imperative that security officers maintain control to manage the crowd. This means setting up barricades to control where the crowd may move and the ability to communicate with protest leaders so they understand expectations from a security standpoint. Security officers need to be prepared to provide medical assistance if needed, intervene to prevent altercations from escalating, and know when they need to contact law enforcement for assistance.

Every security operation should have someone who monitors social media and the local news for information about planned protests. Public–private sector partnerships are critical during times of civil unrest and security operations should partner with local law enforcement and keep the lines of communication open.

The emergency plan for this type of incident should include how many security officers and how many law enforcement officers are needed to protect the property safely. Security priorities must be established, knowledge of who and what the security officers are there to protect and defend, and what level of force can be used. The plan should include what should be done if security officers find themselves overwhelmed and need to retreat and where the safe exit routes are located.

Security officers are meant to present a deterrent to protesters that they will protect the property but ensure that this presence does not create a challenge for protesters. Security officers must be trained not to verbally engage in an altercation either for or against the protester's cause.

DOI: 10.4324/9781003402718-101

Security officers should be positioned around the property's perimeter to deter trespassing and possible vandalism or looting.

It is important to note that if armed officers are used, they understand that they cannot use deadly force to defend against property or property damage and that weapons should remain holstered or out of view.

Protecting businesses during civil unrest requires planning, training, and involvement with local law enforcement. Proper training will allow security officers to manage aggressive behavior and, at the same time, ensure the protection of people and property. We suggest you develop a security plan to deal with this issue.

Chapter 101

How to Handle Trespassers

A trespasser on the protected property can often be doing so accidentally, while at other times, trespassing might be just one of many repeated and frequent offenses. There are general guidelines for what to do in each situation to prevent theft and other harmful trespassing behaviors.

Don't overreact. Before taking action against someone you believe is trespassing, ensure they haven't been invited onto the property. This will help alleviate an embarrassing situation for the security officer. Even if they are not supposed to be on the property, it's possible that they aren't aware they are trespassing, and they could have wandered in to ask for directions. Usually, you can determine whether the individual's intentions are harmful by simply asking what they are doing on the premises. This can help the security officer determine how to proceed. You must stay calm and ask them to leave as politely as possible. If they are agreeable, escort them out to the nearest exit. Let them know they were trespassing on private property and what may happen if they return to the property.

The security officer should maintain a respectable distance between the trespasser so that the individual does not feel threatened or cornered. Staying too far away can make the trespasser feel more unsupervised and less likely to listen to the request to leave.

When a trespasser is asked to leave the property, they will be escorted the entire way off the premises. If possible, it's best for two security officers to respond to a trespassing situation so that there is a witness.

If the trespasser is uncooperative, refuses to leave the property, threatens violence, or has a weapon, then the police should be called. Inform the police of the situation that they are responding to. If the trespasser has been violent or unstable,

DOI: 10.4324/9781003402718-102

these pertinent details and others like them should be reported to the police as well. This process is of utmost importance because assisting the police is essential in the relationship between private security and the police.

The security officer should document everything that transpires in a daily log. The trespasser should be given specific time limits and parameters for leaving the property and document this as well. Security must work closely with management in responding to and reporting all trespass situations.

Trespassing is a crime, and it is covered under various local laws. Even though it may not be considered a serious crime, it should be enforced for the safety and security of the protected property.

Chapter 102

Dealing with Homeless Individuals

Homelessness is a growing problem today and will continue to be an issue going forward. As a security officer, it's important that you understand the many facets of homelessness such as poverty, unemployment, mental health issues, addiction, and domestic violence.

Policies and procedures should address how to deal with this issue, followed by training of all security officers on how to handle homeless individuals on the protected property and when to call first responders – law enforcement, the fire department, or emergency medical services – for help.

Some Solutions to Consider to Address Homelessness

1. Seek out solutions from city, county, and town government officials.
2. Appoint someone to develop a liaison with this community in order to communicate with local officials effectively.
3. Develop relationships with local shelters and homeless advocates to connect homeless individuals with resources.
4. Be prepared for different situations such as individuals asking for money to more aggressive panhandling by having strategies in place for these scenarios.
5. Use de-escalation techniques to avoid conflicts. Train about nonconfrontational language, how to stay calm, and knowing when to call for help.
6. Post the property with "No Trespassing" and "No Loitering" signs and that police are instructed to enforce this law. You may want to make a flyer out of the sign and hand them out to homeless individuals. Why do we recommend this? Many jurisdictions have no trespassing laws that require the area to be posted or written notice to be given.

DOI: 10.4324/9781003402718-103

7. Do not start any kind of physical confrontation with homeless individuals.
8. Be aware of television news cameras or reporters in the area.
9. Seek help from local churches and houses of worship.
10. Meet with local law enforcement.
11. Homeless individuals may be under the influence of drugs or alcohol and may not be able to fully process what is going on and may react with violence when told to leave. Don't overreact. Instead, call the police if the homeless person gets violent.
12. Don't allow employees on the site to get involved.
13. Make sure the facility is properly locked down by ensuring that perimeter security components are operational.
14. Utilize cameras for remote surveillance of problematic areas and utilize motion-detection sensors to monitor throughout the facility.
15. During inclement weather, be prepared to move homeless individuals out of garages and outdoor shelters on the protected property.
16. Giving panhandlers food and money will attract more homeless individuals. Consider donating to food banks, charities, and nonprofit organizations.
17. Do not allow encampments or shopping carts, bedding, and other personal items to stay on the protected property.
18. Secure dumpsters, storage areas, and exterior power outlets.
19. Keep your property illuminated at night with motion-activated lighting.
20. Make sure any parking areas are properly secured.

One of the most effective ways a security officer can deal with homelessness is to build a positive relationship with homeless individuals. Attempt to establish trust and respect which will make it easier to resolve conflicts and help prevent incidents from escalating. Practice just being kind – things such as smiling or listening will help. In the summer, offering a bottle of water and in the winter offering a warm pair of socks can help build a positive relationship. Be polite, but professional. Perform your assigned duties as required.

Chapter 103

Suspicious Mail or Packages

What Is Suspicious Mail or Packages?[1]

Items addressed to someone no longer with your organization or otherwise outdated may be considered suspicious (Figure 103.1). This includes:

- Items that are handwritten and have no return address or have one that can't be verified as legitimate
- Items containing restrictive endorsements, such as "personal" or "confidential"
- Items of unusual weight relative to their size or that are lopsided or oddly shaped
- Items that are sealed with excessive amounts of tape
- An item containing a postmark that does not match the return address or bears an excessive amount of postage
- A piece of mail that is leaking an unknown powdery substance

Note: When you order postal products through Stamp Fulfillment Services, cornstarch as a white powder is used in the processing function. The packing process includes adding food starch, a non-toxic white powder that inhibits moisture, cracking, and spotting. It protects the archival properties of our products.

What Do I Do with a Suspicious Piece of Mail?

If you receive a suspicious mail piece, **do not handle it, shake it, bump it, or sniff it**.

DOI: 10.4324/9781003402718-104

Follow these steps:

1. Isolate the mail piece.
2. Evacuate the immediate area.
3. Wash your hands thoroughly with soap and water. This also applies to everyone who has handled the mail piece.
4. Notify local law enforcement immediately.

It would be best if you exercised caution and common sense when dealing with the mail or package. When in doubt, call local law enforcement.

If you are notified by someone on the property that they have a suspicious package, obtain the following:

- Type (description) of the suspicious package.
- Location of the suspicious package.
- Call the security supervisor and advise that there is a suspicious package and where it is located.
- Contact property management.

The shift supervisor or security officer will respond to the building and suite of the suspicious package and receive the following information from the person who reported the suspicious package:

- Name
- Work address
- Home address
- Work phone number
- Home number
- Occupation

Position a security officer where the package or letter is located, and another security officer, supervisor, or management will assist the fire department or bomb squad in getting to the suspicious package promptly (Figures 103.1 and 103.2).

After emergency personnel have arrived at the location, security personnel will assist as needed and receive the following information from the emergency responders:

- Name of the emergency personnel.
- Unit number.
- Security officer and supervisor will proceed to the area where the emergency occurred and remain there.

If radio and TV personnel arrive on the premises, make no statements and refer them to property management.

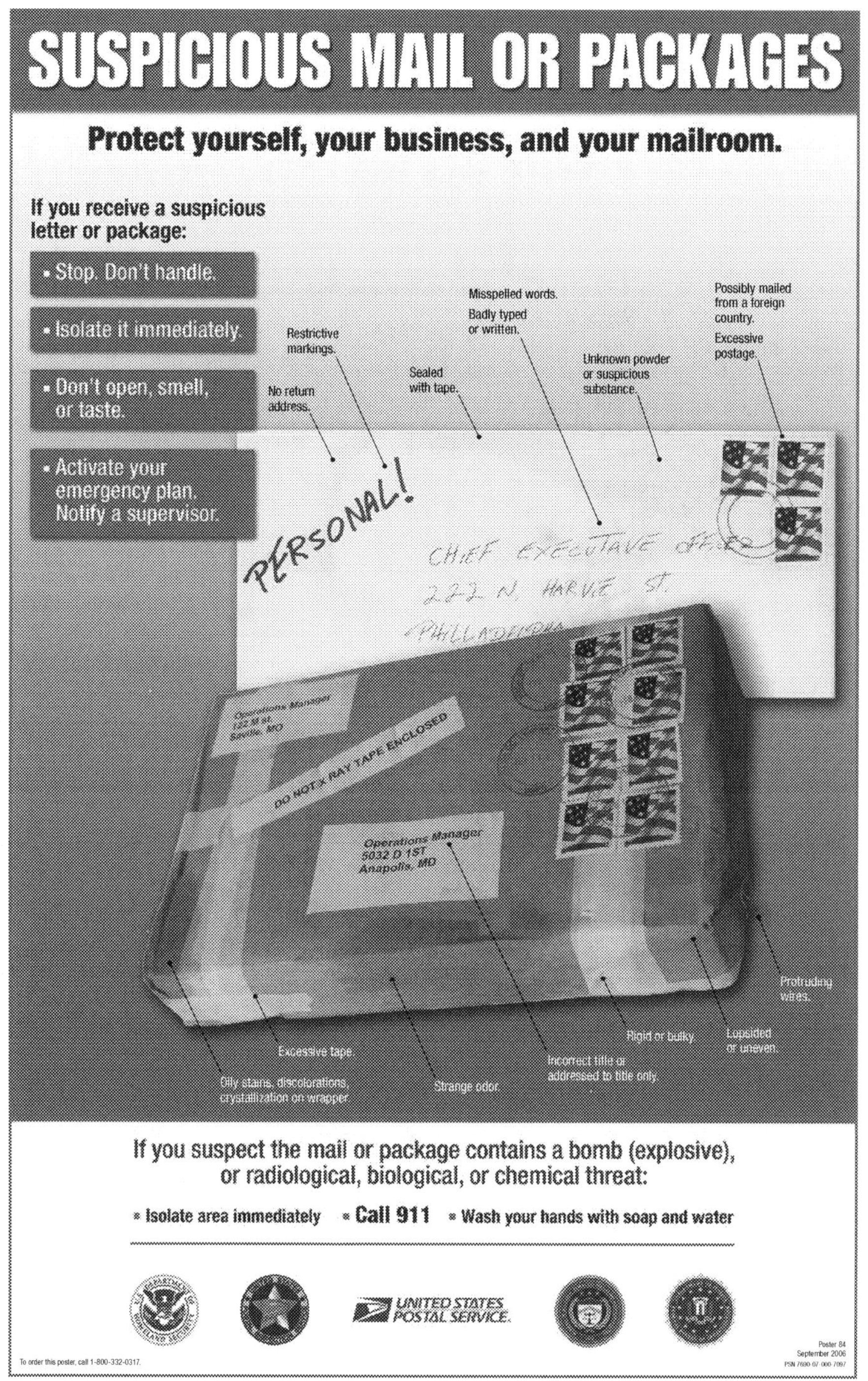

Figure 103.1 How to handle suspicious mail and packages.

Source: U.S. Postal Service.

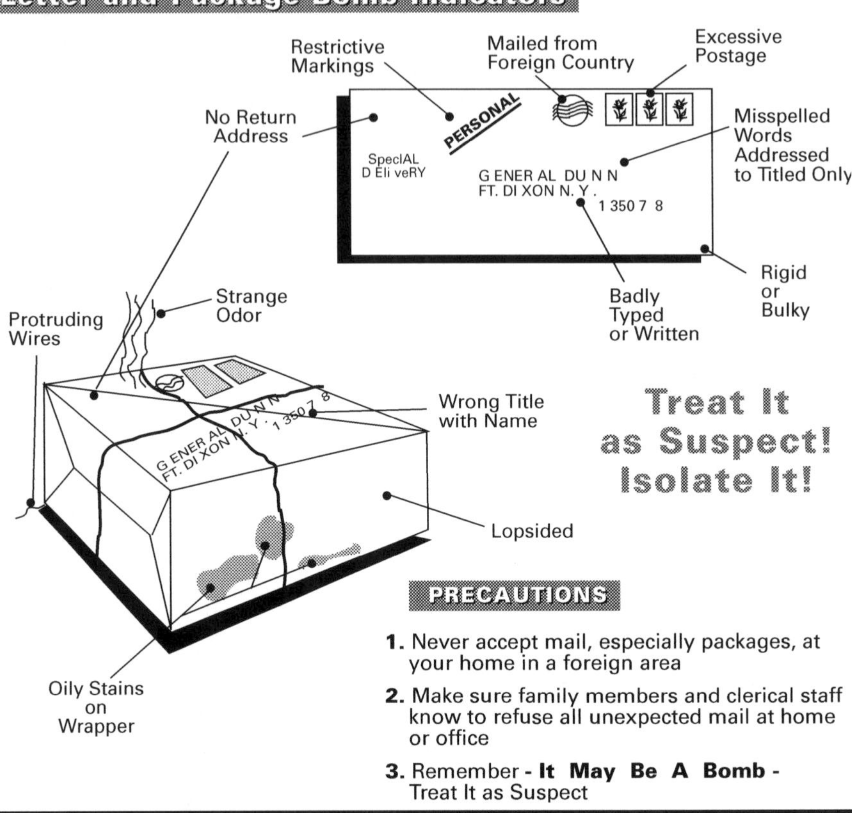

Figure 103.2 FBI letter and package bomb indicators.

Source: FBI.

Note

1 Suspicious Mail. Retrieved on October 26, 2023 from: https://faq.usps.com/s/article/Suspicious-Mail

Chapter 104

Artificial Intelligence (AI) and Security

Artificial intelligence (AI) is the simulation of human intelligence processes by machines, especially computer systems. Specific applications of AI include expert systems, natural language processing, speech recognition, and machine vision.[1] AI requires a foundation of specialized hardware and software for writing and training machine learning algorithms to work effectively, but no single programming language is required.

AI systems ingest large amounts of labeled training data, analyze the data for correlations and patterns, and then use these patterns to predict future states. A chatbot is then fed examples of text to learn to generate lifelike exchanges with people, or an image recognition tool can learn to identify and describe objects in images by reviewing millions of examples. AI can create realistic text, images, music, and other media.[2]

AI programming focuses on cognitive skills that include[3]

Learning
AI programming focuses on acquiring data and creating rules to turn it into actionable information. The rules or algorithms provide computing devices with step-by-step instructions for how to complete a specific task.

Reasoning
AI programming focuses on choosing the right algorithm to reach a desired outcome.

Self-correction
AI programming is designed to continually fine-tune algorithms and ensure they provide the most accurate results possible.

DOI: 10.4324/9781003402718-105

Creativity

AI programming uses neural networks, rules-based systems, statistical methods, and other AI techniques to generate new images, new text, new music, and new ideas.

The convergence of physical security, cybersecurity, and AI is addressing solutions to some of the most challenging security issues. AI can help reduce the labor required to secure people and properties, but physical security is still required to protect not only facilities but also confidential information, software equipment, and company assets. The Internet of Things (IoT) continues to be a cause for security concerns simply because of the large variety and number of connected devices. Still, AI can analyze all of this data efficiently.

Examples of AI for the Security Industry

AI and machine learning are adding a layer of proactive trouble detection to video surveillance.

With the addition of AI, cameras can now spot potential shoplifters and alert security personnel to suspicious behavior. NTT East, a Japanese telecom company, together with Earth Eyes created AI Guardsman, a machine learning system that attempts to catch thieves in the act.[4] AI Guardsman scans live video streams from cameras in retail stores and tracks customers. When it detects suspicious activity, such as a potential thief looking for blind spots or beginning to nervously check their surroundings, the system sends an alert to store security with the person's image and their location in the store. Through AI and machine learning, the system tracks the posture and movement of shoppers and analyses it to match the posture and movement of confirmed shoplifters derived from previous data.

This same technology is also being used on cameras outside of a residence. Home security cameras utilize algorithms to spot suspicious activity, such as an intruder planning to break in or a neighbor trying to steal a package at the front door. According to new market research, the home security market is expected to reach $121.4 billion by 2030.[5] This is attributed to the introduction of AI, deep learning, and the increasing use of IoT-connected devices. Two of the biggest issues faced by home security are false alarms and human error, AI can be used to alert you of intruders or individuals, what pets are doing while you're away, and deliveries and other issues that you may want to know while you're away from home. With deep learning, AI can recognize people living in the home and what activities are considered "normal" for the property.

Evolve Technology[6] is an AI-based system that enables threat screening at large events. Automated surveillance technology with an AI camera with facial recognition can identify a wanted criminal out of a crowd of thousands or aerial drones that use image recognition to predict fights before they take place. The technology utilizes AI and facial recognition software to analyze live footage of approaching visitors to determine if they are approved persons, such as regular visitors, VIPs, employees, and others who should be granted entry. If a visitor is highlighted as not allowed to enter, their profile will be sent to security, and a human security officer can review and verify the data. The technology will allow at least one person entry per second. This technology is not designed to eliminate the human element of threat completely and can be best utilized at locations such as airports, sporting events, and schools, along with security officers. This technology may help end long lines and bottlenecks to entry at large-scale events.

AI can perform some tasks much better than humans and can be used to automate tasks typically done by humans, such as fraud detection. This is especially true when performing repetitive, detail-oriented tasks. AI can often complete jobs quickly and with relatively few errors while processing massive amounts of data.

In the future, AI will continue to be a critical part of effective security operations, make security procedures more efficient, and reduce the labor that is needed to effectively protect people and property, by working in conjunction with security officers.

Notes

1 Artificial Intelligence (AI). Retrieved on October 26, 2023 from: https://www.techtarget.com/searchenterpriseai/definition/AI-Artificial-Intelligence

2 Ibid.

3 Ibid.

4 AI Guardsman Uses Computer Vision to Spot Shoplifters. Retrieved on October 26, 2023 from: https://venturebeat.com/ai/ai-guardsman-uses-computer-vision-to-spot-shoplifters/

5 Home Security Market Research. Retrieved on October 26, 2023 from: Home Security Solutions Market Size, Share and Analysis | Forecast - 2030 (alliedmarketresearch.com).

6 Our Mission: Safer Zones. Retrieved on October 26, 2023 from: https://www.evolvtechnology.com/

Chapter 105

Smart Devices and Network Safety and Security

By 2030, as many as 125 billion devices across the globe will be internet-connected, according to consultants IHG Markit.[1] These smart devices are called the Internet of Things (IoT).

Everything and everyone is vulnerable to a cybersecurity attack. The problem has worsened with the increase in remote work since the pandemic, putting business networks at an even greater risk. Anything that connects to the internet is at risk.

There are five security best practices for Business Network Safety and Security:[2]

1. **Fortify the softest targets.**
   Smart devices often use components made by third parties, which usually rely on embedded software called firmware that may have security flaws. IT teams should update all factory default usernames and passwords, require strong passwords, and consider using two-factor authentication for the most critical network devices.
2. **Know what's on your network.**
   Companies can increase visibility by mapping out all network-connected devices, especially those connected by employees rather than the IT department.
3. **Keep firmware and software up to date.**
   According to Palo Alto Networks 2020 IoT Threat Report, 57% of IoT devices are vulnerable to medium- or high-severity attacks, making connected devices an easy entry point for attackers.

DOI: 10.4324/9781003402718-106

Vulnerabilities in printer software, security cameras, and other connected network devices can give cybercriminals easy access to company data and assets. If IT departments fail to keep this device software and firmware up to date, attackers can exploit long-known vulnerabilities.

4. **Regularly update vendor and supplier lists.**
   No matter how strong your security is, a vendor can still make your network vulnerable. Businesses must keep third-party partner and supplier lists current, deleting old vendors and revoking any permissions that aren't justifiable.
5. **Plan for the worst.**
   Organizations should be ready to take immediate action to identify, investigate, and end any network breach, limiting the damage as much as possible. Similarly, it's important to have a plan to recover from a breach, restore lost data, and begin efforts to repair any damage to the business. This should be a part of the company incident response plan.

Notes

1 Why Your Company's Smart Devices Need Smarter Passwords. Retrieved on October 29, 2023 from: https://www.grainger.com/know-how/trends/kh-smart-devices-need-smarter-passwords

2 Ibid.

Chapter 106

Robots and Drones in the Security Industry

Robotic security has the capability of automating some security duties to increase efficiency and strengthen protection. Security robots can independently perform surveillance tasks, detect threats, and patrol or collaborate with human security officers or other security systems such as cameras and intrusion detection.

Security robots use advanced technologies such as image recognition software or specific sensors to carry out their functions. They can be equipped with high-resolution cameras, motion sensors, heat detection systems, and other surveillance devices that allow them to constantly and accurately monitor the environment.

Robots can quickly respond to dangerous or hazardous situations without endangering human security officers or other first responders. In addition to detecting hazards, security robots can perform patrols and respond to incidents. They use algorithms and artificial intelligence (AI) systems to analyze and process collected information, make decisions, and issue alerts if a threat suspicious activity, or behavior is detected.[1]

There are some benefits to utilizing security robots over human security officers, the most obvious being cost. Robots can work 24/7 with no time off, vacation, or sick days and do not require an expensive employee benefits package. They never grow tired or fatigued and there is no margin of error as with human security officers. Since AI-powered robots continually learn and adapt, they can collect volumes of data and analyze patterns of activity, increasing their effectiveness the longer they are used.[2]

The downside to utilizing security robots without human notification can occur when there is a detected anomaly; the robots lack the ability to interpret and understand the context of a situation. They have difficulty determining if something is a threat because they only detect changes or exceptions to their algorithms and

DOI: 10.4324/9781003402718-107

learned patterns. Human security officers can provide support and guidance to individuals on the property and provide personal interaction.[3]

The best security program is one in which there is the appropriate mix of people, technology, and human security officers. Robots and human security officers can work together to have an effective security program if they capitalize on the strengths of each other.

Unmanned Arial Vehicles (UAVs/Drones)

Drones can be remotely controlled or guided through software-controlled flight plans working with a global positioning system (GPS). DJI, a Chinese technology company, is one of the businesses making consumer drones that executive Randy Braun describes as "flying robots with high-quality cameras attached."[4]

According to the Federal Aviation Administration (FAA)[5]:

- There are no "traditional" pilot requirements for UAVs, but if used for commercial purposes, the operator must have a Remote Pilot Airman Certificate (often referred to as FAA Part 107 certificate), be 16 years old, and must pass Transportation Security Administration (TSA)vetting.
- Cannot fly within five miles of an airport without prior approval from the FAA or Air Traffic Control (often via the LAANV system).
- Must ALWAYS yield the right of way to manned aircraft.
- The operator must keep the aircraft in sight (visual line-of-sight).
- Must undergo a pre-flight check to ensure the UAS is in condition for safe operation.
- Must fly under 400 feet.
- Must fly during the day unless the pilot holds the FAA Part 107 Certificate.
- Must fly at or below 100 mph.
- Must be under 55 lbs and registered if over 0.55 lbs.
- Must yield the right of way to manned aircraft.
- Must NOT fly over people.
- Must NOT fly from a moving vehicle unless the FAA part 107 Certificate.
- Never fly over groups of people.
- Never fly over stadiums or sports events.
- Never fly near emergency response efforts such as fires unless there is a waiver from the FAA for specifically approved emergency responder remote pilots as part of the scene management operations.
- Never fly under the influence of drugs or alcohol.
- Understand airspace restrictions and requirements.
- Must follow any community-based safety guidelines (this is not necessarily applicable to FAA Part 17 Certificate holders but is true for recreational flyers).

Security Applications for Drones (SUAS/UAVs)

Security professionals are constantly discussing how the drone industry will change the security industry. New ways to maximize the use of drones will continue to revolutionize the security industry. Some possible uses for drones in the law enforcement and security industry are:

- Civil security – operations against looters.
- Anti-piracy when deployed by the Coast Guard or water patrols.
- Surveillance by law enforcement of high-crime areas or "hot spots."
- Assist police officers in a foot or vehicle pursuit. Helicopters have been used to support to teams on the ground but are expensive and require time to deploy. A drone could be immediate air support, more cost-effective, and just as successful alternative.
- For surveillance or apprehension, drones can enter narrow and confined spaces, produce minimal noise, and be equipped with night vision cameras and thermal sensors.
- Crime scene photography to aid in investigating crimes and the location of evidence.
- Surveillance of evidence in criminal cases.
- Monitor serious vehicle, train, or airplane crash scenes and ship collisions.
- Monitor traffic for flow to determine alternate routes, vehicle accidents, stranded motorists, inoperable traffic signals, etc.
- Private property and city-owned streets could be monitored for inoperable lighting that needs repair or replacement.
- Drone security teams protecting large areas of property can patrol the perimeter of a property with an infrared camera on a drone instead of having a human security team walk the perimeter. This may be a security/protection officer on private property or used by local, state, or federal law enforcement.
- Ground security cameras in a fixed position can lead to blind spots, but since a drone has the ability to move, security teams can search around corners and get a closer look to avoid blind spots.
- If a security team does find an intruder on the property and the intruder runs, the drone can easily continue monitoring the location of the intruder and the drone operator and relay information to the security team.
- In the corrections industry, prison guards can monitor the prison yard more efficiently and safely with the assistance of a drone. A monitor could send a drone to an area if a fight occurs to assess the situation before correctional officers respond.
- Help identify trespassers who hope to vandalize property. The presence of a drone security camera may also serve as a deterrent for trespassers.

- If security or protection officers patrol an area with vehicles at night, the headlights easily let intruders know the security team is arriving and give them a chance to hide. Utilizing a drone will help apprehend the criminal or intruder.
- The water industry (which includes water engineering, operations, water, and wastewater plant construction), wind farms, and oil pipelines could use drones to protect large infrastructure against acts of terrorism or vandalism.
- Help security or protection officers monitor and protect people and exhibits at open-air museums and help guard historic artifacts and cultural heritage.
- Currently, the FAA does not allow drones to be flown over stadiums when they are in use. At some point, there may be potential to apply for a waiver to operate the drone during the event, but they could still be used for security when the stadium is not being used.
- Drone security teams can patrol the parking lots of large commercial industries and large venues (such as concerts) during and after events.
- On large college or university campuses, drones can be deployed to areas that have become trouble spots, giving staff more eyes, without the expense of hiring more security or protection officers. Drones can more than likely be able to reach destinations quicker than a security or protection officer can.
- Patrol a dockyard for loss prevention and movement and also monitor incoming and outgoing shipments.
- Stop poachers by helping guide animals out of danger or recording and monitoring poachers' actions and location for apprehension and prosecution.
- Monitor activity at borders and be used by US Customs and Border Protection to deter drug smuggling.
- Monitor borders along waterways to detect people coming in on small watercraft.
- Patrol large land areas that aren't bordered by walls and fences, which can lower a company's need for manpower for patrols.
- Help secure foreign embassies and consulates by monitoring the surroundings better than fixed video surveillance.
- For maximum security applications, a team of drones could be deployed instead of just one drone.
- When equipped with cameras, a powerful strobe light, and audio speakers, drones can be used to engage an intruder.
- The presence of a drone flying overhead may be a deterrent for potential offenders.
- Routine patrols could be more efficiently done by a drone with video and an infrared camera rather than a security or protection officer. Drones can cover a much wider area in a short amount of time than a human, although for a limited amount of time. Consider a drone doing a perimeter check around a secure facility.

- With the appropriate learning software, drones could recognize threats and identify who an intruder is and follow the thermal image until human backup personnel can arrive.

Notes

1 What are the Benefits of Using Security Robots in My Organization? Retrieved on October 27, 2023 from: https://robotnik.eu/what-are-the-benefits-of-using-security-robots-in-my-organization/
2 A New Era in Property Protection: Security Officers & Security Robots. Retrieved on October 28, 2023 from: https://www.securitymagazine.com/articles/99157-a-new-era-in-property-protection-security-officers-and-security-robots
3 Ibid.
4 www.theguardian.com/technology/2015/nov/08/dublin-web-summit-things-learned-tinder-drones-apps
5 www.faa.gov/uas/

Chapter 107

What You Should Know About NFPA 730®*

The premise of the **National Fire Protection Association (NFPA) 730, Guide to Premises Security**, is that security issues and potential security risks of a property must be identified to provide a safe environment for employees, residents, vendors, contractors, and visitors.

A security assessment is a loss control procedure that will help identify the risks and add to the security countermeasures and components in place to mitigate risks. The purpose of a security and vulnerability assessment is to provide a safe environment and the protection of property from security threats.

After a risk has been identified, a plan should be implemented to mitigate the identified risks. The plan should become a part of daily operational procedures and post orders with which security officers must comply.

The security plan should include internal and external controls and address the risks associated with each asset. Input from local law enforcement about crime issues and trends in the area should be considered when addressing security threats. There may also be industry-specific risks that should be addressed. The security plan should be customized for the specific site, and the following should be included:

- How the perimeter of the property and the building will be secured.
- How assets on site will be secured and restricted areas will be monitored to prevent theft.

* NFPA Guide for Premises Security: 2023 Edition. Retrieved on October 23, 2023 from: https://www.nfpa.org

DOI: 10.4324/9781003402718-108

- How access to pedestrian and vehicular traffic at the property's perimeter and the building(s) will be controlled.
- How to deny, deter, detect, or delay an attack on the property and the response from management and security officers.
- How shipping to and from the facility will be controlled and how documentation will be provided.
- How procedures and a plan will address insider threats.
- How an Emergency Response Plan will be developed to respond to security incidents. The plan should include a response from site management, security officers, and local law enforcement and/or other government agencies as needed. Effective training is a critical part of the Emergency Response Plan. The security manager or other designated individual responsible for the Emergency Action Plan should be identified.

Chapter 108

Video Analytics

Intelligent video analytics can recognize temporal and spatial events in a video, such as when a person moves suspiciously, when traffic signals are not obeyed, the presence of flames, or the presence of smoke.

Typically, video analytics require real-time monitoring to quickly respond to object changes, movement patterns, or behavior. Video analytics can also analyze historical data and detect trends and patterns.

Examples of utilizing video analytics for security operations would be facial recognition at building and property entrances and license plate recognition at parking facilities. Facial and license plate recognition can identify people and vehicles in real time and make appropriate decisions. For instance, it's possible to search for a suspect in real time and store video footage or recognize authorized personnel and grant access to a secured facility.

Video analytics can be used in airports, shopping malls, hospitals, and stadiums. The crowd observed and monitored in real time. These tools can provide an estimated crowd count and trigger alerts when a certain number of individuals in a particular area is reached. They can also analyze crowd flow to detect movement in unwanted or prohibited directions by comparing it to people's "normal" flow.

Video analytic systems can be trained to detect specific events, such as detecting fires or alerting security officers when someone enters a restricted access area or walks in the opposite direction of traffic. They can also detect unattended bags or items left in public spaces. When video analytics are used for intrusion detection, algorithms can filter out motion caused by animals, wind, rain, or snow.

Video analytics significantly improves the levels of security by tracking objects, securing perimeters, detecting loitering, and observing objects left behind. It also enables scenes to be analyzed for reasons beyond security. For example, to help enhance mobility and safety on roadways, count people in busy scenes, and measure occupancy in parking lots.

DOI: 10.4324/9781003402718-109

Video analytics software can help security officers accurately deal with volumes of information and can monitor and alert security personnel to the following exceptions:

- No-parking zones
- Blocked emergency exit
- Loitering detection
- Left object detection
- Removed object
- Deviate from path
- No-stop area
- Safety in warehouse
- Wrong-way detection
- Parking monitoring
- Railway crossing
- People counting
- Person detection with privacy masking
- Queuing notifications
- Intelligent tracking
- Object detection while moving
- Flood detection
- Fire and smoke detection

Chapter 109

Checklist of Parking Lot or Garage Security Solutions

Not every parking lot or garage is the same, nor do any have the same technological and personnel needs to mitigate risks. Generally, however, what follows are some elements to cover:

- Adequate lighting, vegetation that does not block lighting and surfaces that reflect light.
- Signage, giving direction and information.
- Monitored video surveillance systems with open line-of-sight throughout the facility.
- Electronic access controls.
- Intrusion detection (if the application warrants its use).
- Under-stress automated sound detection alarms and location sensors.
- Emergency phones, duress buttons, and intercoms are connected to the security office or attendant booth.
- Hardened entry/revenue module with revenue collector or security officer inside.
- Patrols throughout the facility with varied routes.
- Parking gates.
- Parking controls and monitors.
- License plate reader cameras.

DOI: 10.4324/9781003402718-110

Chapter 110

Naloxone for an Opioid Overdose

Naloxone (Narcan®) is the opioid-reversing drug that is now commonly carried by most first responders throughout the country and should be available to all security officers to respond to a workplace overdose. Security officers who administer Narcan® should be trained to understand that when the Narcan® takes effect and the victim wakes up they may be upset or even become combative.

Illicit drugs can be in powder, pill, or liquid forms, and to ensure your safety, always use appropriate personal protective equipment (PPE) such as disposable gloves and eye/face protection.

Signs of an opioid overdose include:

- Will not wake up or respond to your voice or touch
- Breathing is slow prolonged, irregular, or has stopped
- Blue skin tinge
- Body very limp
- Face very pale
- Pulse (heartbeat) is slow or not there at all
- Throwing up
- Passing out
- Choking sounds or a gurgling/snoring noise

To respond to a potential opioid overdose[1]:

1. Stimulate them awake by yelling their name and administering a hard sternum rub to the chest plate.

DOI: 10.4324/9781003402718-111

2. If you have naloxone/Narcan®, use it. Administer one dose every two minutes.
3. Nasal: stick the device up one nostril and click the plunger. Make sure the device is inserted fully (medication will be absorbed through the sinuses).
4. Call 911, explain someone is not responsive and not breathing, and that you suspect an opioid overdose.
5. Provide rescue breathing.
6. Get the person on their back, tip their head back to straighten the airway, check to make sure nothing is blocking their airway (food, gum, pills, etc.), pinch their nose, and put your mouth over theirs and form a seal, one breath every five seconds.
7. When the person starts to breathe regularly, roll them into a recovery position on their side.[2]

Naloxone knocks the opiate off of the opiate receptors in the brain and temporarily takes away the "high," giving the person the chance to breathe. Naloxone works in 1–3 minutes and lasts 30–90 minutes. Naloxone can neither be abused nor cause overdose.

Have a Bag Valve Mask (BVM), be trained I how to properly use it, or some other type of face shield device available. Often, people who are suffering from an opioid overdose will stop breathing, and cardiopulmonary resuscitation (CPR) may need to be performed.

Have a sharps box present. Unfortunately, one of the most common ways that opioids are abused is through a needle. The presence of an uncapped needle presents a safety hazard for both anyone responding to aid the victim of an overdose and the victim.[3]

Instead of each security officer carrying Narcan®, overdose response boxes may be set up throughout the facility. Narcan® can often be placed in the cabinet with the automated external defibrillator (AED) or in first aid kits/cabinets.

Security officers in all organizations should be prepared to respond to the worldwide opioid epidemic and take life-saving action. Training should be conducted so security officers can recognize an opioid overdose and respond appropriately.

Notes

1 Narcan® Nasal Spray – Anyone Can Save a Life. Retrieved on October 20, 2023 from: https://Narcan.com/

2 How to Use Narcan® (Naloxone) Step-by-Step Guide. Retrieved on October 20, 2023 from: https://zinniahealth.com/substance-use/blog/how-to-use-Narcan®).

3 The Role of Security in Responding to the Opioid Epidemic in the Work Place. Retrieved on October 20, 2023 from: https://www.linkedin.com/pulse/role-security-responding-opioid-epidemic-work-place-dinapoli-cpp

Chapter 111

License Plate Reader Technology

License plate reader (LPR) cameras are part of a complete surveillance system when you want to track more than just the people entering and exiting your property. New high-resolution cameras with processing units and software can capture images of license plates on vehicles and instantly compare them with millions of records to identify vehicles of interest and alert security officers with an audible or visual alarm when there is a "match." Mobile and fixed license plate reader technology is available, and some IP cameras can be converted to LPR cameras.

LPR technology works well wherever vehicle security measures can add an extra layer of protection. For example, in the parking facilities or entrances/exits in the following locations:

- College campuses
- Casinos and hotels
- Airports
- Military bases
- Apartment complexes
- Warehouses
- Office complexes
- Government facilities

DOI: 10.4324/9781003402718-112

Chapter 112

Physical Security

There are different opinions and interpretations about physical security, but the two definitions below incorporate all the aspects and are all-inclusive.

ASIS (ASIS) International (2005) defines *physical security* as:

> Physical security focuses on the protection of people, property, and facilities through the use of security forces, security systems, and security procedures. Physical security personnel oversee proprietary or contract uniformed security operations, identify security system requirements, assess internal and external threats to assets, and develop policies, plans, procedures, and physical safeguards to counter those threats. Physical security can include the use of barriers, alarms, locks, access control systems, protective lighting, CCTV, and other state-of-the-art security technology.[1]

The Army Field Manual, No. 3–19.30 defines *physical security* as:

> That part of security concerned with physical measures designed to safeguard personnel; to prevent unauthorized access to equipment, installations, material, and documents; and to safeguard against espionage, sabotage, damage, and theft.[2]

When planning perimeter barriers,[3] take into consideration the following:

1. Walls are usually more expensive than fences. Design for observation enclosures and video surveillance systems.
2. Fences and walls provide limited delay against intruders, and the least secure types can only delay a skilled intruder for a few seconds.

DOI: 10.4324/9781003402718-113

3. Perimeter barriers intended to protect against intruders should therefore be considered delay devices only.
4. The combination of a fence or wall with security lighting, an intrusion detection system, a video security surveillance system, and security officers provide layered security.
5. The perimeter should be as short as possible and illuminated.
6. The perimeter should run in straight lines between corner posts, if possible, to facilitate surveillance.
7. Drains or culverts giving access to the perimeter barrier should be protected.
8. The ground on both sides of the perimeter barrier should be cleared to deny cover to an intruder.
9. Emergency gates may be required to provide safe evacuation routes.
10. A sterile zone protected by a double fence may be required for certain intruder detection sensors.

Fence Enhancements

The most commonly used barrier (other than the walls of a building) is a fence. Fences can vary in type, size, use, and effectiveness, and fences can be erected fairly quickly at reasonable costs – depending on the specific type. It is important to balance the costs of the fence with the risk, so be sure that the specific fence type you select meets the organization's specific needs. Fences can be more effective when barbed wire or concertina wire, alarm sensors, and video surveillance are added. Double fences may also be utilized with a clear zone between the fences and a clear zone outside each fence.

Card Access Control Systems

Card access control systems need to be multifunctional.

1. Utilize "smart" cards or devices and integrate them with other systems (e.g., parking garages or lots, time and attendance, and computer systems), if possible.
2. Badges to access restricted or sensitive areas can be controlled to allow access only on specific days and during designated times.
3. Using access card database storage, determine the legal and/or organizational needs based on your specific industry.
4. Have procedures to change access levels when an employee is transferred from one position to another within the organization.
5. Have procedures to remove access for employees who are no longer with the organization and audit for 100% compliance.

6. Expand card access control systems to control multiple sites for one organization.
7. Incorporate sufficient expansion capabilities into card access control systems to allow for the organization's future growth.
8. If a badge is borrowed or used by an unauthorized person(s), have sufficient backup data such as height, weight, and color of eyes and hair included to verify.
9. Assign a department and individual to maintain the database for badges.
10. Identify access levels and authorization.

Consider credentials for retired employees and special badges for contractors and vendors. Decide how you will track visitors on the site.

Using Layers of Protection Analysis (LOPA)

When using risk analysis, the LOPA can also be incorporated to improve the implementation of consequence estimation tools.[4] In addition to the consequence estimation tool, the risk analysis also depends on the estimated frequency of the hazardous event. Any error associated with the consequence severity estimate directly impacts the risk reduction measures. Most security professionals will find that using the LOPA is easy and flexible. attempting to determine priorities based on the estimate of the hazardous event frequency, look carefully at the root causes of events that lead to the hazardous event and the possibility that the safety and security measures may fail. Security professionals will use the experience to determine the right types of protection layers to utilize and use best practices to demonstrate the risk reduction or mitigation techniques that have worked when conducting previous risk analyses. Security professionals will need to determine the root causes (or initiating causes) and analyze those enabling conditions that result in process deviations (or initiating events). This is a critical part of risk analysis since by understanding the likelihood of the types of hazards that may occur and the conditions that enable them; security professionals can then estimate the event frequency.

Security Officers: Day-To-Day Operations and Dealing with False Alarms

Security officers responding to routine and emergencies are important in day-to-day operations. Security Officers monitor communications, video surveillance, radio activity, access control, telephone services, and alarm/fire panels. They are the eyes and ears of the property.

False Alarms

There are three basic reasons for false alarms, and the key to reducing them is to identify the cause and make proactive corrections clearly:

1. Lack of proper education on how to enter and exit the facility, such as improper arming and disarming of the intrusion detection system using a keypad.
2. Weather-related issues.
3. Equipment failure (dead batteries) or poor installation.

Notes

1 www.asisonline.org
2 *Army Field Manual, No. 3–19.30*. Headquarters Department of the Army, Washington, DC and Physical Security 150 Things You Should Know.
3 John J Fay, CPP, B-H. *Model security, policies, plans and procedures*. Elsevier; 1999.
4 Summers AE, Hearn WH. Risk criteria, Protection layers and conditional modifiers paper; 2010.

Chapter 113

What's the Difference Between a Security Officer and a Security Guard?

Being a security officer is a profession – a career choice. It is no longer "just a job until something better comes along." There is more training, more responsibilities, and more expectations for the security officer of today. Security officers are no longer poorly paid night watchmen or "security guards" with no training, education, or experience in protecting people and property.

Professional security officers must have excellent observational skills, be tech-savvy to operate sophisticated security systems, be good report writers and communicators, be trained to perform life-saving skills such as CPR, and have some legal knowledge about their limits of authority. There are a variety of duties for a security officer, including:

- Conducting security assessments to identify vulnerabilities.
- Coordinating emergency procedures.
- Ensuring policies and procedures are followed.
- Patrolling premises regularly to maintain order and establish presence.
- Authorizing the entry of vehicles or people into the building or on the property.
- Securing all exits, doors, and windows.

DOI: 10.4324/9781003402718-114

- Monitoring alarms, cameras, access control systems, and screening systems such as magnetometers.
- Investigating people for suspicious activity or possessions.
- Responding to alarms by investigating and assessing the situation.
- Providing assistance to people in need.
- Submitting reports of daily surveillance activity and important occurrences.
- Providing customer service.

Many licensing agencies don't distinguish between security officers and security guards and use the terms interchangeably. This adds to confusion within the industry and with the general public.

A security officer is, many times, the "face" of an organization and is the first person an employee, visitor, vendor, or contractor sees when they enter a building or are on protected property. It's important that security officers are competent and friendly, yet professional.

Chapter 114

Police Officers vs. Security Officers

Security officers are *not* law enforcement or police officers. Security officers are assigned patrol or stationary posts and are responsible for the property they are assigned to and answer to the client or the security company. Basically, security officers observe and report and also enforce the policies of the employer or client.

Police officers have the authority to serve arrest warrants and make arrests and can legally search buildings and homes with a search warrant. Even though most security officers cannot make arrests or serve search warrants, a critical aspect of the job of security is to report criminal activity on the property they are protecting and alert law enforcement to detain or make an arrest. Generally speaking, security officers have no more power to make an arrest than any other private citizen and only in very specific situations, but ensure that local laws are followed in the performance of day-to-day operations or when dealing with criminal activity.

DOI: 10.4324/9781003402718-115

Chapter 115

Investigations: Luck or Skill?

Over the years, we both have been involved in numerous investigations. Being lucky during an investigation is something we feel needs to be acknowledged. Fred Mullins, CPP, was telling us about a stakeout he was on. He spent five hours at the designated location and nothing. It was 5:00 am, and he decided to head home and go to bed. While traveling toward home on a major highway, the truck and the individuals he had been waiting for passed him on the left. Fred said, "I was lucky." But was it luck or being in the right place at the right time? Was it dedication to the assignment? Was it knowing when to leave a stakeout? Was it a skilled investigator's hunch? Was it a degree of skill and a mixture of all of the above? We do know he completed his assignment, and the individuals were arrested.

The "Sloppy" Investigation

Simply put, this is the complete opposite of an acceptable professional investigation: one in which leads are not thoroughly documented and/or checked; personal bias and prejudice of the investigator slip into the process of data collection; no successful completion whereby a discharge, arrest, or complaint is made; the evidence is overlooked and poorly or improperly handled; and finally, there is an inept selection of the resources to investigate the particular investigation.

Given our mutual experiences and past involvement with the process of investigations, we have never observed anything written on the subject but have acknowledged that many investigations were "sloppy" and poorly managed.

DOI: 10.4324/9781003402718-116

Principal responsibility for a professional or "good" investigation rests with the investigator or case manager. The case manager may frequently be the only resource assigned to the investigation. The manager is accountable for the quality of his or her efforts or the efforts of all involved.

The manager or supervisor must read and review every report, see every piece of evidence and documentation, interview the people, and evaluate the resources assigned or involved with the investigative effort.

Example: A supervisor was reviewing a well-written and complete investigation of a safe that had been locked on a Friday evening with $400.00 inside.

On Monday morning, the money was missing. The assigned investigator had identified two suspects. The case reviewer inquired about the safe manufacturer and reputation. It was determined that the safe in question could be "cracked" by even the most inexperienced thief.

Example: A clerk responsible for petty cash disbursement goes on vacation. Upon returning, she determines that the cash is missing. The investigator found no suspects and no forced entry. It was later determined that the secretary next to the clerk never locked her desk, and a duplicate key was kept in the desk tray.

Example: The efforts of a prolonged undercover investigation were wasted when through the poor judgment by the undercover investigator, he ventured too close to the suspect and was recognized and identified.

Many hold the theory that good investigators are born, not made. Others hold that training and experience can produce a competent investigator. We believe all of these are true with one additional attribute – *common sense*!

A successful investigation is one in which:

- A logical sequence is followed.
- All available physical evidence is legally obtained.
- All witnesses are effectively interviewed.
- All suspects are legally and effectively interrogated.
- All leads are thoroughly developed.
- All details of the case are accurately and completely recorded and reported.

Chapter 116

Testifying in Court

At times, you may be required to testify in court due to some incident at work. When you are called into court for any reason, be serious, avoid laughing, and avoid saying anything about the case until you are on the witness stand.

When you are sworn in as a witness, stand up straight, pay attention to the clerk, and say, "I do" clearly. Then say, "Good Morning, your honor," to the judge.

Below are some helpful hints to assist you if you are required to testify in court:

- Being nervous is nothing new. Even lawyers are nervous. Arrive early before you are to testify.
- Observe where everyone is sitting and where you testify. At this point, do not talk, laugh whisper, or cause any disturbance.
- When called upon, smile and make eye contact with the jurors when you answer the lawyer's questions.
- Remember, it's the jury, not the judge, that is going to decide on the outcome of the case.
- If you can, leave after you testify.
- Be aware that the jury may observe your behavior in the hallway and elevator.
- Finally, remember these six points:
  1. Tell the truth and do not exaggerate.
  2. Look the jurors in the eye; eye contact is important.
  3. Lawyers ask questions, and you answer to the jury.
  4. Give full and complete answers.
  5. During cross-examination, give short, truthful answers.
  6. Sit comfortably in the witness chair and avoid hand motion. Try locking your fingers together as if in prayer.

 DOI: 10.4324/9781003402718-117

Chapter 117

Suspect and Vehicle Descriptions

As a security officer, your job is to protect assets (people and things) on the protected property. Preventing any crime from happening outside that private property is not your job; instead, it is the job of local law enforcement. They can pursue individuals for crimes committed around the private property you are protecting. If an intruder trespasses on the property you are protecting, commits a crime, and then flees the scene, the security officer should contact the police. The police can then intervene to protect the security officer and public officials' safety.

When a situation on the property that you are protecting turns violent, it's time to get law enforcement involved. For example, suppose an intruder is armed or physically abusive. In that case, law enforcement can assist in preventing harm to you, the property you are protecting, or others in the area. Security officers should stay in constant communication with their security team during a dangerous, violent situation.

A good description of a suspect/suspicious person or a suspicious vehicle is critical for police officers who are responding to a report of a crime in progress or that had just occurred. Hence, it's important that the security officer give them as much information as possible so the police can apprehend the suspect. Use the following as a guideline.

Location information

- Observe where you are and the exact location of the crime. Remember if you have seen the suspect in the area before.
- Note the time as precisely as possible.

DOI: 10.4324/9781003402718-118

- Observe if the suspect is carrying a weapon and, if so, what type – handgun, shotgun, knife, etc.
- If the suspect leaves the scene, note the direction of travel.

Vehicle Information

- If the suspect is in a vehicle, note as much of the following information as possible: vehicle type (auto, truck, van, etc.), color, make and model, condition (dirty, damaged, tinted windows, etc.), and license plate numbers.
- Note also if the vehicle has no license plates or if there are any bumper stickers or decals on the vehicle.
- Watch for other vehicles that may be involved or accomplices.

General Description Information About the Suspect

- Gender
- Race or national origin
- Age (estimated)
- Height – use comparisons with your height, a door, or some other standard measure
- Weight (estimated)
- Build – fat, husky, slim, muscular, etc.

Facial information

- Hair – color, texture, hairline, style; note possible dyes or wigs.
- Forehead – forehead height and whether the skin is smooth, creased, or wrinkled.
- Eyes – color, shape (round and slanted), whether clear or bloodshot, and the heaviness of eyelashes and eyebrows.
- Nose – overall shape (long, wide, flat, etc.) and nostrils (wide, narrow, flared) are important.
- Cheeks – is the flesh sunken, filled out, dried, or oily? Are there wrinkles around the nose or mouth? Are cheekbones high or low, wide or narrow?
- Ears – size and prominence (protruding or flat against the head).
- Mouth – are lips thin, medium, and full? Do corners turn up, turn down, or level?
- Chin – what is the shape (round, oval, pointed, and square)? Double chin, dimpled, and cleft?
- Neck – protruding Adam's apple or hanging jowls?
- Complexion – pores, pockmarks, acne, razor rash, and bumps.
- Facial hair – clean-shaven? Unshaven? Beard, mustache, goatee, and sideburns?
- Tattoos – shape and style; on what part of the body.

- Piercings – location and description.
- Scars – if visible and location.
- Glasses – type and description.

Clothing information

- Hat – note color, style, ornaments, and how it is worn (bill forward, backward, and to one side).
- Coat – note color and style (suit coat, jacket, topcoat, and overcoat).
- Shirt/blouse/dress – color, design, sleeves, and collar.
- Pants/slacks/shorts/skirt – color, style, and cuffs.
- Socks – color, pattern, and length.
- Shoes – color, style, brand name for sneakers (if possible), and condition.
- Accessories – sweater, scarf, gloves, necktie, and belt.
- Jewelry – rings, watches, bracelets, and necklaces.
- General appearance – neat or sloppy? Clean or dirty?
- Oddities – look for clothing too large or too small, odd colors, and patchwork.

Other physical features

- Voice – pitch, tone, rasp, and lisp.
- Expression – angry, excited, remorseful, and frightened?
- Speech – articulate, uneducated, accent, and use of slang.
- Gait – slow, fast, and limp.

Chapter 118

The Broken Window Theory: Controlling Physical Deterioration and Disorder

Physical deterioration, wear and tear, and large-scale accumulations of graffiti and trash routinely occur in many older, urban neighborhoods. If people or agencies do not do anything for a significant period of time about such deterioration or accumulations, residents and businesses in the neighborhood feel increasingly vulnerable.

Feeling more concerned for their personal safety, residents and businesses will begin to participate less in the maintenance and order of public places. They are less likely to stop teens or adults who are "messing around," "being rowdy," or "hassling people." Sensing fewer **"eyes on the street"** (Jacobs 1961 & 1968), delinquent preteens and teens in the neighborhood become emboldened and harass or vandalize more frequently. Increasingly convinced they can get away with it, delinquents commit more minor crimes, and youths become increasingly disorderly.

Residents, sensing that some local youths are becoming increasingly troublesome, withdraw further from the public spaces in the neighborhood and become more concerned about protecting their own person and property.[1]

At this point, potential offenders from outside the neighborhood sense the area is vulnerable. They are drawn to the neighborhood because crimes committed there are less likely to be detected and responded to. The neighborhood crime rate increases dramatically.

 DOI: 10.4324/9781003402718-119

Six Points to the Broken Window Theory[2]

1. Increase in unrepaired physical deterioration.
2. Increased concern for personal safety among residents and property owners.
3. Decreased participation in maintaining order on the street.
4. Increased delinquency, rowdiness, vandalism, and disorderly behavior among locals.
5. Further increase in deterioration; further withdrawal from the streets by residents and other locals.
6. Potential offenders from outside the neighborhood, attracted by vulnerability, move into the area.

Crime Prevention Through Environmental Design (CPTED) and the "Broken Window Theory" suggest that one "broken window" or nuisance, if allowed to exist, will lead to others and ultimately to the decline of an entire neighborhood. Neglected and poorly maintained properties are breeding grounds for criminal activity. Formal CPTED-based maintenance plans will help preserve property values and make the neighborhood a safer place.

Notes

1 Physical Environment and Crime. Retrieved on December 21, 2023 from: https://www.ojp.gov/pdffiles/physenv.pdf

2 CPTED Security. Retrieved on December 21, 2023 from: http://cptedsecurity.com/cpted_design_guidelines.htm

Chapter 119

Proactive vs. Reactive Security for an Effective Security Process

How well do businesses manage security risks? Many businesses will consider security processes to protect assets, people, property (tangible and intangible), and information. Will you be proactive and prepared before something happens, or will you react to the situation after something occurs?

Prevention vs. Reaction

There's a difference between crime prevention and crime reaction. However, many take the reactive approach and don't consider purchasing an alarm system, for example, until after they've been burglarized, or have stolen property.

We need to change the way we think. To be effective, crime prevention and security (both policy and procedure) must be a part of the business operation and accepted by everyone in the company. Security policies are objectives, and they list the responsibilities and expectations for personnel. Security procedures are detailed instructions outlining how personnel will carry out the objectives. Security procedures change more often than security policies to meet the changing needs of an organization. For instance, the security policy may state that a particular area is restricted; only authorized personnel are allowed. A security officer is placed at the entrance, visually identifies those who can enter, and allows them access. At some point, this system may become automated; each employee wanting access

DOI: 10.4324/9781003402718-120

must place his/her hand or finger on a biometric reader, and physiological characteristics determine admittance. Video surveillance may also monitor the area for an attempted unauthorized entry. The policy remains the same in this situation, but the procedure has changed.

Changing procedures to meet new needs is an excellent way to be proactive, but the security process shouldn't be so cumbersome that it impedes business operations – instead, it should operate in conjunction with workflow.

Three-Part Security

There are three parts to achieving the desired level of security (the goal of this three-step approach is to reduce the likelihood that a loss will occur and, if a loss does occur, to minimize it):

1. A vulnerability assessment, which a security professional completes to identify the deficiencies and excesses in the security process. In essence, the security professional will consider the probability of an incident and make recommendations to address vulnerabilities and "harden the target." Performing a vulnerability assessment ensures a proactive approach to crime and loss prevention.
2. A cost/benefit analysis will determine if the recommendations are affordable, feasible, and practical. At this point, countermeasures are implemented to reduce or eliminate the deficiencies identified in the vulnerability assessment. These countermeasures may consist of hardware (fencing and locks), software (electronic access control), and people (security officers or employees) who will take on the role of guardian of the company's assets.
3. A test of the system, which ensures that everything is working properly, to determine if changes need to be made to achieve the desired level of security.

The key to an effective security process is having the appropriate mix of physical security, electronic security, and personnel to meet security goals. The strength of one component outweighs the weaknesses in another component. There must be "layers" in your security process so the weaknesses are outweighed by the strengths of another component strength of component outweigh the weaknesses. You may have security policies and procedures in place, a fence around your property, security officers on patrol, exterior lighting, steel doors, high-quality mechanical locks, an intrusion detection system, and video surveillance – but at what point in the process will an intruder be detected?

A professional security risk assessment determines the best way to "harden your targets" and integrate all components of the security process so you have the appropriate level of security.

Chapter 120

Patrolling in Hazardous Areas

As a security officer, you may be required to patrol in areas identified as hazardous. Hazardous areas have the presence of potentially dangerous substances or conditions that can lead to fire, explosion, or other safety hazards. The classification of hazardous areas typically depends on the types of materials or processes involved. The following are common types of situations that may cause an area to be classified as hazardous[1]:

- **Flammable gases or vapors** – Areas where flammable gases, vapors, or mists are present sufficiently to ignite or explode. Examples include areas around fuel storage tanks, gas pipelines, or where volatile chemicals are used or stored.
- **Flammable liquids** – Locations where flammable liquids with low flashpoints are used, stored, or handled. These areas include areas near fueling stations, paint booths, or chemical storage.
- **Reactive chemicals** – Areas where reactive chemicals, such as strong acids, oxidizers, or unstable compounds, are present. These chemicals can react violently with other substances or release toxic gases, leading to hazardous conditions.
- **High-pressure systems** – Areas where high-pressure systems exist, such as pipelines, vessels, or hydraulic systems. The release of pressurized gases or liquids can cause mechanical failure or create dangerous conditions.
- **Confined spaces** – Enclosed or partially enclosed spaces, such as tanks, vessels, or storage bins, where the accumulation of flammable or toxic gases can occur. Lack of ventilation can lead to hazardous atmospheres.

 DOI: 10.4324/9781003402718-121

- **Extreme temperatures** – Areas with extreme temperatures, either very high or very low, can pose risks to personnel or equipment. Examples include furnaces, ovens, or cryogenic storage areas.

When security patrols are required in hazardous areas, remote guarding through video surveillance may be the best option, or a robot may be used to not endanger human security officers. If security officers are patrolling in a hazardous area, it is imperative that they have been trained about the hazards located in the area, supplied with appropriate personal protective equipment (PPE) to be worn while in the area, and know what steps are to be taken if there is an exposure incident or issue. The safety of security officers, other workers in the area, and the property is the primary concern.

Note

1 Understanding Hazardous Areas. Retrieved on October 23, 2023 from: https://blog.msasafety.com/flame-detectors-understanding-hazardous-areas/

Chapter 121

Marijuana and the Security Industry

Crime Prevention Through Environmental Design (CPTED) strategies work well as a security component for marijuana farms and dispensaries. Since the cultivation and use of marijuana for either medicinal or recreational use remains a controversial subject, both farms and dispensaries should be "good neighbors" to those who live and work in the area as well as local government offices. Working together to help ensure the community doesn't want to pose a safety or security threat will be an important aspect of being a part of the community and a proactive problem-solver.

For marijuana farms, the area on each side of the perimeter fence (fences that you should be able to see through – no walls or cement barriers) should be visible so there is a clear line of sight from inside or outside the property. Where there are gates for worker access, the gates should lock, and this area should be well-lit. There should be casual observance and more formal observance by farm workers and/or security officers. Any office buildings with windows on the farm should have windows that face access to the property and the fields. Workers should be able to see down the rows of plants in the field. To discourage trespassers, it may be necessary to place signs (approximately 100 ft apart) stating the area inside the fence is private property. There should be a well-defined point of entry to the farm, and signage should be posted stating that it is private property. It may be necessary to have driveway sensors, video surveillance, and fence sensors to detect activity at that location to help protect the property. Security officers and other guardians should regularly patrol the property, especially around the perimeter to ensure the fence is intact. The farm itself should be well-maintained.

Utilizing CPTED strategies for the security of marijuana dispensaries would be similar to that of other high-risk retail establishments, such as liquor stores. Lighting,

DOI: 10.4324/9781003402718-122

and there should be, again is going to be a critical component, and there should be a clear delineation between public and private space. The parking lot should be well-maintained and well lit, with visibility from all sides to ensure no shadows where someone could hide. The windows of the dispensary should not be cluttered with signs, and they should face the street. There should be a clear line of sight from inside and outside the facility for security officers, law enforcement, dispensary employees, customers, and casual observers. It's important that customers and those in the dispensary neighborhood "feel" safe when they are in the area. Suppose crime in the area becomes a problem. In that case, dispensary owners or managers should work with local law enforcement and community groups to assist with problem-solving or if proactive crime prevention strategies need to be implemented.

Marijuana – Basic Facts

Marijuana is the dried leaves, flowers, stems, and seeds from the hemp plant *Cannabis sativa*. The plant contains the mind-altering chemical delta-9-tetrahydrocannabinol (THC). Extracts with high amounts of THC can also be made from the cannabis plant. The THC in marijuana is the chemical responsible for most of marijuana's psychological effects because it acts much like the cannabinoid chemicals made naturally by the human body. The cannabinoid receptors are concentrated in the areas of the brain associated with thinking, pleasure, coordination, and time perception. The THC in marijuana attaches to these receptors and activates them and affects a person's memory, pleasure, movements, thinking, concentration, coordination, and sensory and time perception.

The legalization of marijuana – whether it is for medical use or recreational use – is a controversial subject. There are pros and cons on both sides of the argument, and each side cites research data supporting their stance on the subject that the other calls "low quality." Proponents say that marijuana helps the economy and the job market, and others say that it causes more crime and puts people at risk.

Chapter 122

Identity Theft

Identity theft is a crime where a thief steals your personal information, such as your name, your social security number (SSN), or your credit card information, to commit fraud. The identity thief can use your information for fraudulent purchases or to fraudulently apply for credit, file taxes, or get medical services. These crimes can damage your credit status and cost you time and money to restore your good name. You may not know that you are the victim of identity theft until you experience a financial consequence (mystery bills, credit collections, and denied loans) from actions that the thief has taken with your stolen identity.[1]

Steps You Can Take to Protect Yourself

- **Be aware of someone taking a picture or a video with their smartphone** – If you are paying at a register or a restaurant, watch for people fidgeting with their phones. They could be trying to take a picture of your card.
- **Keep an eye on your credit card** – Whenever you hand your card to a waitress, clerk, or cashier, pay attention to where it goes and for how long. Card skimming or copying your credit card information may be occurring.
- **Shop with a slim wallet** – Remove everything except one credit card and your driver's license from your wallet. Carrying multiple credit cards increases your risk of identity theft.
- **Be alert for pickpockets** – Tuck your purse under your arm, keep your wallet in your front pocket, and don't put it down where someone else may grab it.
- **If you're shopping online** – If you pay by credit or charge card online, your transaction will be protected by the Fair Credit Billing Act.[2] Under this law, you can dispute charges under certain circumstances and temporarily withhold payment while the creditor investigates them. If someone uses your

 DOI: 10.4324/9781003402718-123

credit card without your permission, your liability is generally limited to the first $50 in charges. Never shop online using a public Wi-Fi network, and shop on secure sites with a URL that begins with "https" instead of "http."

- **If you're making large purchases or electronics purchases** – Most credit cards offer their warranty protection for your purchases just for using a credit card for the transaction. Some of those warranties go beyond what's offered by the manufacturer and offer you extra coverage, which is useful for electronics, appliances, or other large purchases.
- **If you're traveling** – If you're away from home, use your credit card for purchases because debit cards don't offer the same protections. Also, don't carry more cards than necessary.

Steps You Can Take to Protect Yourself from Identity Theft

- Don't carry your social security card in your wallet or write your number on your checks. Only give out your SSN when absolutely necessary.
- Don't respond to unsolicited requests for personal information (your name, birth date, SSN, or bank account number) by phone, mail, or online.
- Watch out for "shoulder surfers." Shield the keypad when typing your passwords on computers and at ATMs.
- Collect mail promptly. Ask the post office to put your mail on hold when you are away from home. Consider paperless billing statements.
- Pay attention to your billing cycles. If bills or financial statements are late, contact the sender.
- Review your receipts. Ask for carbon copies and incorrect charge slips as well. Promptly compare receipts with account statements. Watch for unauthorized transactions.
- Shred receipts, credit offers, account statements, and expired cards to prevent "dumpster divers" from getting your personal information.
- Store personal information in a safe place at home and work.
- Install firewalls and virus-detection software on your home computer.
- Create complex passwords that identity thieves cannot guess easily. Change your passwords if a company that you do business with has a breach of its databases.
- Use multi-factor authentication. This requires two or more credentials to log in to your account. Multi-factor authentication makes it harder for scammers to log in to your accounts if they get your username and password.
- Order your credit report once a year and review it to ensure it doesn't include accounts you have not opened. Check it more frequently if you suspect someone has accessed your account information.

How to Report Identity Theft

If you are a victim of identity theft, report it immediately. The Federal Trade Commission (FTC)[3] and your local police department are critical in the complaint process. The FTC affidavit should be taken to local law enforcement and used to file a police report. These two documents together are your identity theft report. Your identity theft report will be significant as you resolve the problem with creditors, banks, and any other companies where fraudulent accounts were set up in your name.

In addition to government agencies, you should also report the theft to other organizations, such as:

Credit reporting agencies – Contact the three major credit reporting agencies to place fraud alerts or freezes on your accounts so that no one can apply for credit with your name or SSN. Also, get copies of your credit reports to be sure that no one has already tried to get unauthorized credit accounts with your personal information.

Credit bureau contacts – Contact the national credit bureaus to request fraud alerts, credit freezes (security freezes), and opt-outs from pre-screened credit offers.

Equifax
Equifax.com/personal/credit-report-services
800-685-1111

Experian
Experian.com/help
888-EXPERIAN (888-397-3742)

TransUnion
TransUnion.com/credit-help
888-909-8872

Financial institutions – Contact the fraud department at your bank, credit card issuers, and any other places where you have accounts. You may need your ID theft reports from the police and Federal Trade Commission in order to report the fraud.

Retailers and other companies – You will also need to report the fraud to companies where the identity thief created accounts, opened credit accounts, or even applied for jobs in order to clear your name.

State consumer protection offices or attorney general – Your state may offer resources to help you contact creditors, dispute errors, and other helpful resources.

Notes

1 Identity Theft. Retrieved on October 29, 2023 from: https://www.usa.gov/identity-theft
2 What is the Fair Credit Billing Act? Retrieved on October 29, 2023 from: https://www.experian.com/blogs/ask-experian/what-is-the-fair-credit-billing-act/
3 Identity Theft. Retrieved on October 29, 2023 from: https://www.usa.gov/identity-theft

Chapter 123

Insider Threats

As we hear more frequently about domestic and international terrorism attacks on businesses and government agencies, we also hear about the risk of the "Insider Threat." We feel as though it's important to define these terms.

What is an Insider? An insider is a current or former employee, contractor, or business partner who has or had authorized access to the organization's network, systems, or data.[1]

What is an Insider Threat? An insider threat is an insider intentionally or unintentionally misuses access to data that may negatively affect the confidentiality, integrity, or availability of the organization's critical information or systems.[2]

An insider threat is a threat that comes from within an organization. Since "insiders" already have access "inside" the organization, they don't need to breach physical or cybersecurity control measures that are in place to put the organization at risk. Because of this, insider threats are the most difficult to detect and can be expensive. It's the "insider" knowledge of the structure of the company's security measures and the location of critical assets, like data, that make them more dangerous. A security breach may be combined with legitimate business activity, making it harder to detect. It's important to note that not all insider threats are intentional acts. The intent and motivation of the attacker are what determine the type. Awake security identifies the following types of insider threats[3]:

- **Negligent insiders** behave in ways that make it more likely that a threat will occur and act without practicing security awareness. They may not intend to put the organization at risk, but it happens because of their behavior and bad judgment.
- **Collusive insiders** will collaborate with external threats to compromise the organization. Professional cybercriminals may use the dark web to recruit

DOI: 10.4324/9781003402718-124

employees to work as their allies. This type of threat is more difficult to detect since professional cybercriminals are knowledgeable about security technology.

- **Malicious insiders** work toward financial rewards or other personal gains from their attack. Network data may be moved to personal accounts slowly to avoid detection by an angry or discontented employee wanting to intentionally sabotage the company or steal sensitive information.
- **Third-party insiders** may be contractors or vendors that a business has given some type of access to the physical site or the company network. Flaws may also exist in security measures that leave the company property, devices, and systems open to attack.

Detecting insider threats can be challenging. Negligent insiders may be detected by having checks and balances that identify vulnerabilities in systems before they are compromised, identify when a credential is compromised, or detect unusual credential activity. Collusive insiders are usually detected as they communicate with or attempt to move data. Malicious insiders may be detected when they are accessing areas or information they don't need or shouldn't have access to. Third-party insiders are sometimes identified in any of these ways.[4]

Malicious insider threat incidents are increasing – rising by 47% between 2018 and 2020, according to the Ponemon Institute's **2020 Cost of Insider Threats: Global Report.**[5]

To avoid insider threats, it's important to have security policies and procedures in place and to conduct audits to ensure that vulnerabilities in systems and components are detected. One of the most important steps is to limit access to sensitive areas or information within the organization. Restrictions should be in place, and access controls should be in effect to limit physical and network access to critical areas. The bottom line is that if someone doesn't need access to a particular location or information, they shouldn't have it. Additionally, employees should receive training in security awareness and be made aware of how physical or network security breaches occur. Employees must also be educated about secure passwords and what to do if they are solicited for sensitive data.

Notes

1 What is an Insider? Retrieved on July -5, 2021 from: https://www.observeit.com/insider-threat/

2 Ibid.

3 Insider Threat. Retrieved on July 05, 2021 from: https://awakesecurity.com/glossary/insider-threat/

4 Ibid.

5 2020 Cost of Insider Threats: Global Report. Retrieved on July 08, 2021 from: Ponemon Report 2020 Cost of Insider Threats: Global | ObserveIT.

Chapter 124

The Culture of Security

Culture is what gives a society, a nation, or a community its identity. Societies are indeed identifiable through their cultural expressions. Therefore, every society tries to preserve its particular cultural heritage by ensuring that it is passed from one generation to the next.

What is a "culture of security?" Whether they want to admit it, every company, organization, and community has a security culture. When someone says that they don't have a security culture, it's because they don't want to admit that they have a "bad" security culture. A company, organization, or community must make a conscious effort to invest in a security culture. If a security culture is to become sustainable, it has to be more than a one-time event and have its life cycle. This way, there will be a return on investment (ROI). A security culture must become a part of everything done, and the security culture must stay abreast of the current threats.

To determine what type of culture a company, organization, or community has, we suggest you start with a thorough *risk assessment* to identify issues with crime, personal safety concerns, and non-criminal issues. There has to be a social mechanism in place to support the development of a culture of security (Figure 124.1).

As stated in Figure 1, a culture of security is part of an overall *Security Master Plan.*[1] Timothy Giles defines a security master plan as

> a document delineating the organization's security philosophies, strategies, goals, programs, and processes. It is used to guide the organization's development and direction in these areas in a manner that is consistent with the company's overall business plan. It also provides a detailed outline of the risks and the mitigation plans for them in a way that creates a five-year business plan.[2]

DOI: 10.4324/9781003402718-125

Figure 124.1 The factors that go into a culture of security.

A *Step-by-Step Process* will define how the plan will be implemented and how the organization will reach its security goals. A vulnerability or risk assessment will identify issues that will be addressed. A trained security professional must conduct a vulnerability or risk assessment so the organization will know what assets they need to protect and what risks to retain, transfer, or mitigate. When the appropriate countermeasures are implemented, the emphasis will be on the layers of security, security policies and procedures, and security education and training. It may also be helpful to have a safety and security committee.

The formulation of partnerships is a problem-solving approach to the issues identified during the risk or vulnerability assessment. Identify key agencies or businesses that should be in the partnership. Besides law enforcement, community members, and local businesses, partnerships can also include other stakeholders – those who have an identifiable interest or stake in the outcome and can bring something useful to the partnership and its efforts. Possible stakeholders include social service agencies, schools, religious and faith-based organizations, government agencies, and community groups. The membership in the partnership will depend on the nature of the problem but remember that the greater the number of partners, the harder it will be to organize activities or get everyone in the same room simultaneously. It may also be more difficult to decide on goals and strategies and to maintain communication and cooperation. It's usually better to form a partnership with a core group of stakeholders and invite others to join the partnership as other needs arise.[3]

You must design *a blueprint for what security measures* will be implemented to address specific vulnerabilities identified during the risk or vulnerability assessment. Then, you must ensure that each partner understands their role and responsibilities to *educate the community*. To achieve buy-in, support, and participation in your plan, community (or organization) members have to know what they will "get" by being involved or what the ROI for their time and efforts will be. In the situation of criminal activity, *reduced fear of crime* may be the goal so that lifestyle will not be negatively affected. It is interesting to note that there is little evidence to support a link between fear of crime and the likelihood of victimization since there are so many variables involved.

As a part of your overall culture of security, your security program *must be promoted to become ingrained within the company, organization*, or community.

This brings us back to the question, "What is a culture of security?" A culture of security means that security procedures become unconscious, instinctive, and essentially effortless because safe behavior will become a habit.[4] It will become "just the way things are done around here" so that identified vulnerabilities are effectively mitigated. Remember that security policies and procedures have to effectively address the identified threats, so changes will need to be made from time to time so that you have a living, breathing culture of security.

Notes

1 Giles, Timothy D. How to Develop and Implement a Security Master Plan. Florida: Auerbach Publications, 2009.
2 Ibid.
3 Police-Business Partnerships. Retrieved on October 29, 2023 from: https://popcenter.asu.edu/content/tool-guides-partnering-businesses-address-public-safety-problems-page-4
4 What is Security Culture? Retrieved on Feb. 9, 2017 from: https://crimethinc.com/2004/11/01/what-is-security-culture

Chapter 125

The Security Officer of the Future

The security officer role is evolving and the industry has undergone a significant transformation since the events on September 11, 2001 (9/11) when the perception of security changed. It continues to change drastically as advanced technology becomes more of a part of daily operations. There is more emphasis on public–private sector partnerships and how information is shared through different groups. Developments in career paths in security and higher levels of training are helping the industry to be viewed in a more professional light. Today and moving forward, technology will continue to play an even greater role in securing people and property. Technology will help security officer operations be more efficient and allow different components of security processes to work together in conjunction with each other. It will help create a holistic security operation without silos and individual components that work independent of other processes. Security officers will be assigned to facilities based on their individual skill sets, experience, and training. There is not a "typical" security officer. Security officers will be selected and assigned depending on the needs of the facility and the program.

Security officers no longer just react to threats, but now must be proactive and able to assess potential risks. This means enhanced situational awareness and understanding behavior patterns and emerging threats and being able to make informed decisions. Security officers are better trained with more emphasis on the most recent safety and security procedures. Using technology, security officers can collect data and make better, more informed decisions to protect people and property. Robotic security officers are now frequently used for patrol and report back findings in real time to human security officers about conditions so that security is increased. Robots can patrol large areas and can be equipped with 360 field of vision, intruder

 DOI: 10.4324/9781003402718-126

detection, and sensors to detect heat, smoke, chemicals, and other potentially dangerous situations. In some situations, especially hazardous areas, robots are being used as an alternative to human security officers.

Remote guarding – through AI cameras that can detect suspicious activity, recognize faces, and have biometric scanners that can report information to security officers to increase the efficiency of the security operation. The use of enhanced camera systems has improved surveillance functions and by utilizing video analytics, security officers can more effectively secure property.

Security officers many times are the first line during an emergency situation and must be prepared. It could be a medical situation where CPR needs to be done, a natural disaster where people need to be evacuated to a safe location, or an active threat, such as an active shooter where the security officer has to take action to protect lives.

Technology is allowing security operations to provide a higher level of protection and a more efficient and cost-effective way of protecting people and property, but it is critical that the security officer of the future be proficient in operating and troubleshooting this technology.

In addition to the responsibilities of protecting people and securing property, security officers must also be aware of increased diversity with the individuals that they come in contact with. It is now a requirement that security officers understand cultural differences, be able to communicate with individuals from diverse backgrounds, and be well-versed in social norms so that each individual that they come in contact with feels respected and safe.

The demand for qualified security professionals has continued to grow since 9/11 when awareness was raised throughout the world about the need for competent security professionals. There are more job opportunities in the diverse world of security for those individuals who strive to stay on top of this ever-changing industry by being knowledgeable about current trends and issues and consistently striving to develop themselves professionally to remain on the cutting edge of the latest innovations and solutions in the industry. Technology has and will continue to have a great influence on the security industry. The future challenge for security professionals will be to understand the capabilities and the integration of technology into day-to-day security operations. It is important to understand that technology is not the answer to effective security. Technology is just a component within the overall security process. Moving forward, all security professionals will need to be adaptable and have the ability to anticipate change and needs of the future by gathering information, analyzing data, and studying crime trends.

2

SECURITY SUPERVISORS AND MANAGERS

Chapter 126

The Leader as an Agent of Change

As the last link between senior management and security officers, it is the leader's job to assist in implementing change. To do this, certain obstacles must be overcome. There are several strategies for reducing resistance to change. Much resistance to change comes from a lack of trust or people having to operate outside their comfort zone.

Resistance can sometimes be overcome or the impact lessened if the leader takes the following actions:

- Fully explain the upcoming changes.
- Make certain employees or customers fully understand the change.
- When possible, discuss why the change is required.
- Identify and discuss the possible effects with employees or customers.
- Answer questions, or take the information and follow up if you don't know the answer.
- Build trust with your employees; they will better accept the change.
- Be honest and be consistent.

Change can potentially create fear and uncertainty in the organization, so information must be disseminated correctly through the organization by leaders.

Leadership differs from management, but not for the reasons most people think. It has nothing to do with having charisma or other exotic personality traits. It is not only for a chosen few. Leadership is not necessarily better than management or a replacement for it, but instead, are two distinctive and complementary systems of

DOI: 10.4324/9781003402718-128

action. Each has its function and characteristic activities. Both are necessary for success in today's business environment.

Management is about coping with complexity, but leadership, by contrast, is about coping with change. Part of the reason this has become so important in recent years is that the business world has become more competitive and more volatile. More change always demands more leadership.

Most US corporations today are over-managed and under-led. They need to develop their capacity to exercise leadership. Successful corporations don't wait for leaders to come along. They actively seek out people with leadership potential and expose them to career experiences designed to develop that potential. Indeed, with careful selection, nurturing, and encouragement, dozens of people can play important leadership roles in a business organization. But, while improving their ability to lead, companies should remember that strong leadership with weak management is no better and sometimes worse. It is sometimes worse than the reverse.

The real challenge is to combine strong leadership and strong management and use each to balance the other.

Security supervisors and managers will be called on to make decisions every day. Some of these decisions will be easy, and others quite difficult. Every decision must be based on a foundation of education, training, and experience, supported by "street smarts." Decision-making ability may be introduced in a classroom or from a book, but it is perfected through experience. Being on the front line, being prepared, and being willing to make tough decisions are what being an effective security supervisor and manager is all about.

Chapter 127

Security Supervisors

What does it mean to be a supervisor? First, supervisors may be called upon to handle numerous conflicts. Second, they will be required to meet the expectations of management or their client in the daily routine of operational activities.

The supervisor is the backbone of the organization. His or her scope of responsibility is rather unique:

- The person who represents higher authority.
- The person who assesses situations and conditions to make on-the-spot judgments without favor, prejudice, or fear.
- The person who is a responder to any and all situations.
- The person who must galvanize the efforts of many to attain stated goals.
- The person who must assign tasks and ensure compliance and constant quality performance.
- The accountable person and, therefore, first in line to shoulder reaction, both good and bad.
- Finally, the person who must decide for management, based on his or her professional development.

New Supervisors

The most demanding problem for the supervisors within a security program will be transitioning from the position of security officer to that of supervisor. The supervisor's role should be to assist in enabling the manager to provide support within the organization. Supervisors must take responsibility for corporate regulations moral and ethical tone and provide the required level of security and customer service.

DOI: 10.4324/9781003402718-129

Chapter 128

Security Managers

- A manager designs and develops security, safety, and investigative programs.
- Managers work with budgets and other resources (equipment, uniforms, technology, software, etc.) to achieve the protective mission.
- Managers oversee processes (procedures) that accomplish organizational goals and objectives.
- Managers may perform staff functions without a supervisory span of control over line employees. Training, technical support, auditing, etc., are staff functions.
- A manager coordinates activities rather than supervising them.
- Turnover and job rotation can create overall improvement and a challenge.
- The manager should stay current on industry events by reviewing news, trade publications, and web sources.

As the job changes, so must the training and the level of skills within the department increase. Professionals develop a "discipline of training" and continuously seek to improve their knowledge and abilities.

Similarly, new managers have some adjusting to do. We feel it is important to advise readers that as a new manager, one has to learn how to develop and exercise (not abuse) their newly acquired authority, power, and influence effectively. This can be done by establishing one's credibility and earning a subordinate's commitment and support.

Management is an art and a science; it is, perhaps, more art than science. New managers are at a crossroads, looking to make the right turns. Consider the following: a new manager is the person in charge. His or her elevation to the status of manager through promotion has given him or her authority.

DOI: 10.4324/9781003402718-130

- A new manager is a person with a level of power and is a decision-maker.
- Security managers must also stay current with trends and issues such as cybercrime, terrorism, emergency management, fire safety issues, and new training initiatives, such as *Stop the Bleed*.[1]
- A new manager is knowledgeable in his or her field.
- A new manager uses his or her developed skills, ideas, education, and experience.
- A new manager supervises his or her subordinates and passes information down the line and up the chain of command.
- A new manager is responsible for being aware of employer policy as well as client requirements and the level of security required within the organization.
- As one develops on-the-job experience as a new manager, he or she starts to understand and accept the new responsibilities and further understand what it means to be a manager.
- Those who have been promoted to the rank of supervisor or manager should:
- Learn how to supervise and adjust to the new role.
- Develop leadership skills.
- Develop interpersonal skills.
- Develop knowledge of who they are.
- Learn how to cope and deal with stress and emotions associated with management concerns.

As one progresses in his or her security career, these learning points become ingrained. They become second nature.

Note

1 Stop the Bleed. Retrieved on October 29, 2023 from: https://www.dhs.gov/stopthebleed

Chapter 129

Recruiting, Hiring, and Orientation for Security Officers

It's a difficult job to find competent, professional security officers, and it's getting worse simply because there is a greater demand for private security.

Keep in mind that you're hiring not just for hard skills but also for soft skills. Taking your time during the hiring process will limit mistakes and turnover. It's important to know your cost per hire, the average time required to fill positions, your turnover rate (voluntary and involuntary), absenteeism rate and it's financial impact on the company, your total labor costs and your referral rate,

A 2021 US Bureau of Labor Statistics report predicts the employment of security guards and surveillance officers will grow 15% from 2020 to 2030, with an average of 165,000 openings for security officers projected each year over the decade.[1]

The security industry, as a whole, has a very high turnover rate, so it's important to maximize employee retention. Ensure that you are providing proper training, providing a company culture that is inclusive, offering a progressive career path, providing fair compensation, providing the equipment that is needed for the job, and recognizing security officers who do a good job.

Everyone wants to hire the right security officer for the job while at the same time spending less money and time on recruiting. Below are some ideas about where to find new hires:

- In-person at job fairs and recruitment events.
- Online through the company website, job boards online through the company website, job boards, and social media.

DOI: 10.4324/9781003402718-131

- Referrals from your current security officers who want to participate in the employee referral bonus program.
- Through networking with community groups.
- At security training institutions
- At local universities for criminal justice majors and offer tuition reimbursement incentives.
- Through partnerships with local military and law enforcement.

Orientation begins before the effective date of employment, before communicating the corporate benefits package, and before introducing your new hire to organizational staff members. "Orientation of New Employees" begins with posting a vacancy, the invitation to enter the employee screening process, and most importantly – the interview itself.

When conducting interviews for one or two open positions, your goal should be to interview at least ten applicants so you will have enough information to compare responses to the same questions. Look not only for education and professional certifications but also for previous job experience and years in the security industry or customer service field.

The key to successful personnel selection means taking the time to hire the right person by performing all the steps in the process. Security has changed dramatically over the years. There are now designated budgets for security similar to those for other management personnel. Security is now considered a crucial member of the management team. Because the image of security has truly changed and become more professional, we must continue to invest in future security personnel. This can only be accomplished by being dedicated to a thorough and well-defined hiring process supported by a comprehensive list of policies and procedures.

Background Checks/Investigations

Since security is synonymous with trust, ensuring a thorough background investigation is completed is a critical step in the hiring process.

Conducting a thorough background can involve:

- Criminal record check in a particular state or possibly nationwide.
- Social security number check.
- Motor vehicle record check.
- Employment verification.
- Credit check.
- Fingerprinting for criminal background check (some states require fingerprinting be done on individuals specifically in the security profession).
- Drug testing (post offer).

Technically speaking, the orientation of new employees begins when the applicant reports for their first day of employment. The mood should be light, the atmosphere comfortable, and the anticipation of beginning a new relationship (for both parties) be one of enthusiasm rather than anxiety, paranoia, or distress. Taking appropriate measures during the marketing and selection process will help to set the foundation for a marriage between your corporate objectives and your employees' desire for success.

What follows is a list of activities and/or topics that should help new staff become productive colleagues. Each organization should tailor this list to represent its unique business objectives and decide who will take responsibility for each item.

In this chapter, you will learn about measures that should be considered before the selection process as well as critical components that will help you plan for a seamless transition into your company. More importantly, you will learn about key review processes that must be taken as part of an ongoing business orientation program, and you will learn about performance measures that will help assess the effectiveness of your orientation program.

Pre-orientation

Interviewing 101 – "Make a good first impression." Your new employees will remember this cliché and their career path may be determined by how they present themselves throughout the interviewing process. They realize that all first impressions, especially the interview, are critical. While the applicants' first impressions establish a foundation for everything that follows during their interview process, the security supervisor must also consider that the candidate is also forming an impression of the supervisor and the institution. With this in mind, you must be cognizant of how you portray yourself and your organization. How you communicate, both verbally and nonverbally, leaves a lasting impression in the applicant's mind. You must recognize this fact when publishing position vacancies, position descriptions, scheduling interviews, and when meeting with the applicants for the first time. Your organization depends on you to represent the organization's interests and to portray a positive image at all times.

Personal Appearance and Uniform Maintenance

Security officers are issued "wash and wear" or "dry clean only" uniforms. They should be instructed on their uniforms' proper care and maintenance. Discuss items such as shoes, socks, hats, and belts, and what the security officer should do if their uniform needs repair, replacement, or alterations.

Explain the company policy regarding acceptable hairstyles, including length and color, visible piercings, and tattoos. Remember that reasonable accommodations may need to be made for religious beliefs or medical conditions.

Grooming and good personal hygiene are important aspects of projecting a professional image. Emphasize that appearance, attitude, and actions reflect on the organization as well as the individual security officer.

Within the First Week of Arrival

If not completed on the first day, within the first week of employment, the immediate supervisor will give each new employee a departmental orientation. The orientation will cover the department's functions, organization, and goals. Information given to the employee will also include job responsibilities, annual review, performance evaluation standards, and expectations, introduction to department members, a tour of the department, confidentiality, and emergency procedures.

Consider the following scenario: you have just hired a security officer who will be assigned either afternoon or night shift. It's important for an officer to be trained on the day shift because they need to see how things function and where their job responsibilities on their assigned shift fit into the overall operation of the site. All security officers need to be trained on the "front end" or the security desk/customer service desk. In this position, the security officer will learn how to respond to various situations and who to notify when there is a question or concern. When the recently hired security officer begins his/her on-the-job training with the site training officer, each step will be repeated and tours or "rounds" of the building will be completed. It is important that the new security officer be given a thorough orientation to the site. Field training officers (FTOs) are similar to mentors in that they help to socialize the new hire into the job they will be doing. FTOs differ from mentors in that they may also be responsible for evaluating the probationary employee's job performance and making recommendations to improve performance. FTOs must be trained in how to teach, train, and instruct, as well as how to evaluate and supervise security officers.

Training

Training topics, such as professionalism, ethics, confidentiality, limits of authority, use of force, drug and alcohol use, firearms and other weapons, workplace violence prevention, emergency response, harassment, and the company's social media policy may be addressed during orientation and then again at each customer location.

In addition to company information and site-specific guidelines contained in the post orders, if the site or company is a designated Department of Homeland Security (DHS) SAFETY Act-certified site, additional training, such as anti-terrorism awareness, weapons of mass destruction (WMD) and customs-trade partnership against terrorism (C-TPAT), may be required. This training may need to be completed by all security officers assigned to that particular site.

Additional training may be required by the Occupational Safety and Health Association (OSHA) or a state occupational safety and health program for security officers assigned to a specific location or industry. This training may include personal protective equipment (PPE), hazard communications (HazCom), global harmonization systems (GHS) training, fire extinguisher training, emergency response and preparedness, bloodborne pathogens, CPR/AED, and first aid training.

Depending upon the industry-specific requirements, training in verbal de-escalation techniques or non-violent physical crisis intervention (CPI) may also be required. It is important to know what industry-specific training is required.

If a security officer is assigned to a site where a firearm, handcuffs, mace or pepper spray, non-lethal weapons, etc., are required as a condition of assignment compliance, additional training will need to be conducted by a certified instructor to comply with local and state and federal laws.

Every security officer should receive training in human relations, providing excellent customer service, and effective communication techniques, including report writing, radio communications, and telephone etiquette.

Before New Staff Member Arrives

New employee orientation should begin with ease and transition for both the employee and the company. To make that connection, however, all facets of integration must be utilized. Concerning the embracing of a new employee, current staff and the prospective newcomer should be aware of their roles as well as those complementary to them.

The new employee should review and become familiar with their job description. This job description should specifically explain how the officers should perform. These job-specific instructions are called post orders. They should include control and planning tasks and system-wide obligations. The direct authority for the employees should also be identified to prevent conflicts arising from uncertainty as to who makes the decisions for particular issues. The job description should also reflect the organization's employees' expectations regarding self-management responsibilities and should include temporary job assignments that may happen during employment.

Recommended steps for you to take before the new employees' first day of employment include sending the new staff member:

- A welcome letter.
- A job description which you will go over again.
- Instructions for the first day and week, e.g., review of policy and procedures.
- When, how, and where to arrive.
- Who to ask for and a direct telephone number.
- Where to park and where not to park.

- Uniform attire.
- What to expect for the first few days.
- Orientation/introduction to people, job, office, department, and the organization.
- What to expect regarding meals, breaks, and time for personal business.
- Initial work responsibilities and how overtime is divided.
- Required or recommended reading, such as any publications created by your company or client.
- A description of the work setting.
- Other preparation is necessary for a smooth transition for the new security officer and the organization.

Consider the following before introducing the new security officer to staff members:

- Distribute an announcement to current staff.
- Schedule time for all staff to meet the new employee; block time for essential meetings with payroll, personnel, supervisor, etc.
- Communicate the new employee's role in the organization.
- List the experience/value the security officer will bring to the company or client.
- Disseminate a photograph if possible.
- Ask staff to make an effort to get them to know the new security officer.

Many organizations prefer to utilize an employee handbook and the security officer will sign acknowledging receipt of the handbook. This may be helpful because the new employee will have written material to review when questions arise.

The handbook may include the following information:

- The mission of the organization and company values.
- The environment in which they will be working will outline company policies on EEO, discrimination, ADA, harassment, drug and alcohol policies and testing, workplace violence, unsafe working conditions, and how to report issues in the workplace.
- Professional development, including training and recognition programs in addition to how to communicate effectively.
- Standards of conduct, which include ethics, guidelines, political activity, attendance, uniforms and appearance, post orders, equipment, communications, confidential information, conflicts of interest, nepotism, workplace relationships, dealing with the media, smoking, firearms policy, limits of authority, and use of force and vehicles.
- Company employment policies to include classification, probationary period, transfers and promotions, hours of work and overtime, meals, salary, leaves of absence, US Dept of Labor Family and Medical Leave Act (FMLA), medical-personal-military-bereavement leave, and jury duty.

- Benefits, including medical–dental–life–disability insurance programs, retirement, worker's compensation, and holidays–vacation–sick days.
- Discipline and termination policies, including voluntary/involuntary termination and layoffs, discipline and termination guidelines.

First Day of Work

At the start of the first day, each new employee shall have a payroll and personnel orientation. The orientation is designed to help new employees better understand personnel policies and procedures. The session may last up to one hour. It will review general payroll and personnel topics such as meeting the payroll/personnel team, pay rates and schedules, benefits, performance evaluation and standards, and holiday schedules.

Additional checkpoints for the first day should include:

- Issue an employee ID. Nothing says "Welcome to the Team" like a new badge with your employees' photo, name, and corporate logo.
- Meet with the employee's supervisor (and others as appropriate) for office orientation, goals, and objectives.
- Review primary activities.

Communicate policies, procedures, bulletins, pass-on logs, daily activity reports, and other governance documents such as working hours, telephone techniques and etiquette, customer service, correspondence styles, staff meetings, budget and accountability, service culture, confidentiality, ethics, working with supervisors, colleagues, assistants, and/or volunteers.

Mentoring

Mentoring is a formal process where mentors are trained and sometimes compensated for taking someone under their wing. Mentors are generally senior employees who can provide both an example to the new employee and address any concerns that they might have. Mentors are not supervisors. They perform no evaluative functions. They may represent management insofar as proper codes of conduct and performance are concerned, but they have no authority to discipline. A good mentor's objective is to see that his student advances within the profession.

Other Points to Consider

It is valuable to assign a "partner" to a new security officer, preferably a peer, to whom the new employee can ask any question without fear of reprisals. A colleague who is relatively new to the organization might be the best choice because they have a fresh perspective and are familiar with questions a new staff member might have. If a "partner" is not assigned, someone else should cover these topics with your new staff member.

Remember that overwhelming the employee can have the same effect as doing nothing at all.

The immediate supervisor should address and re-address all of the following key components during the first week:

- Ensure that the employee's' work area is set up.
- The supervisor should check in frequently to clarify expectations and answer the employee's questions.
- Colleagues should also check in to answer questions and offer support.
- A "partner," mentor, or field training officer (FTO) should check in daily to answer questions and offer support.

The new security officer should meet with the department business manager/payroll/personnel to cover, as appropriate, the following:

- Time cards.
- Vacation/sick/personal leave policies.
- Keys and/or access control credentials.
- Access to the office on nights and weekends.
- Telephone: access code, personal calls, and paying for personal long-distance calls.
- Email address and access to the system.
- Parking stamps and parking permits.
- Travel and reimbursement (if the security officer will be traveling).
- Company credit card (if issued).
- Telephone credit card use (if issued).
- Cellular phones, pagers, personal digital assistants and (PDAs).
- Company vehicle policies.
- Learn about and submit benefits applications (health and life insurance, retirement, etc.).
- Get company ID (highly recommended on the first day).
- Get a company parking permit (if appropriate).
- Meet with management information systems (MIS) personnel for computer assistance, network access, email, and policies. Assess knowledge of and comfort with computer hardware and software and schedule training if necessary.
- Overview of policies and procedures, including confidentiality and piracy.
- Hardware: turning on, backing up, printing, shutting down, etc.
- Software: word processing, data processing, email, etc. as needed.
- Tour the building and immediate area.

Within Six Months of Starting:

- Meet key people and offices within the company.
- Meet regularly with the supervisor to discuss issues and review the job description, expectations, and performance.
- "Partner/mentor" should continue to check in regularly to answer questions and offer support.
- Attend the company's new staff orientation (provides an overview of company people, departments, policies, and procedures and includes a tour of the company facilities).
- Have 90-day and 180-day performance review.
- Performance measures and program evaluation.

Orientation is a critical juncture in socializing the new employee. It "marries" recruitment, training, supervision, organizational attitudes, and personal characteristics into one consolidated impression. Due to the significant importance of first impressions, the "reality" of present-day security force training, and the critical element of understanding the organizational culture by protection officers, orientation must be carefully programmed and regularly evaluated for effectiveness.

Reviewing your success should be part of every professional's personal assessment. As all professionals should effectively pursue opportunities to improve continuously, so should the image of our organization. While self-evaluation is highly recommended, all recruiters, mentors, managers, and staff should regularly evaluate their orientation programs for both success and opportunities for improvement.

Note

1 Recruiting Ideas for Security: 5 Tips to Find New Guards. Retrieved on October 27, 2023 from: https://www.trackforcevaliant.com/blog/recruiting-ideas-for-security/

Chapter 130

Effective Security Officer Scheduling

The duty of a security officer is to protect a company's assets – property, employees, reputation, and visitors. Some of the typical daily scope of responsibilities of a security officer include the following:

- Providing excellent customer service.
- Patrolling and monitoring activities on the company's premises regularly to discourage criminals and ensure the environment is safe and secure.
- Evicting trespassers and violators and following legal protocols.
- Controlling the entry and exit of employees, visitors, and vehicles according to protocols.
- Monitoring surveillance cameras for suspicious or illegal activities.
- Providing detailed reports on daily activities and any incidents.
- Testing security systems and if needed, operating security equipment, such as magnetometers.
- Clear, concise, and effective communication using telephones and two-way radios.
- Performing CPR or first aid when needed.[1]

Because of the wide variety of job responsibilities, scheduling security officers can definitely be challenging when you are dealing with real people and unexpected emergencies that go along with the security profession. Nearly, all security supervisors, at some point in their careers, will be responsible for putting together a work schedule for their subordinate officers. Some security providers still develop and track security/protection officer schedules using paper and pencil, but new scheduling

DOI: 10.4324/9781003402718-132

software programs can make this task a little easier. Regardless, the process begins with the training level required for different posts or locations and any other special requirements. Although technology has simplified the scheduling process in many ways, supervisors must still understand not just *where* to place their officers but *when* to place them.

When determining a schedule, there are several factors involved, which include, but are not limited to how many officers are available; how many positions, locations, or posts must be staffed; the opening and closing hours of the locations; and whether overtime is authorized and how much. One factor that is itself complicating is identifying what skills are required at a particular post or location. For example, does a security officer need to be bilingual, certified in CPR/AED, or certified to operate special security equipment like a computer access control program or a magnetometer or do they need to be trained to conduct personal or vehicle searches, be proficient in crowd control or firearms?

Understanding scheduling is necessary, whether or not you have proprietary (in-house) security or contract security. Either way, you will want to understand the parameters for budgeting, training, retention, hours to staff, requirements, vacations, holidays, medical leave, and even union contracts that might affect the scheduling. You will also need to determine other factors like patrolling, offering escort services, how many officers a specific task might need, whether inspections are needed, physical demands, the number of entrances and exits that will be controlled, and special assignments. There are so many choices for scheduling, but knowing how many hours and types of shifts you want will help you determine what resource or programs you will use, and other resources. Any computer programs, webinars, books, websites, and other resources are designed to assist you. Preparing a schedule using a computer-generated software system is preferred for recording schedules, holidays, sick days, and vacations. Even with this, you must have an emergency contingency plan. Whether you use your security officers on a 24/7 basis or 7 am–7 pm, Monday–Friday, you will want to have enough staff to cover such things as overtime, overlapping shifts, training time, flexible scheduling, and supervision. Some shifts are rotating, where officers work in regular patterns of days on and days off. Sometimes, the shifts rotate, and other times, they do not. Whether you utilize eight-hour shifts or 12-hour shifts, both can easily be scheduled to rotate days off and/or to rotate shifts.

Some providers use 10-hour shifts because they can provide three days off each week, but since 24 cannot be divided evenly by 10, excessive shift overlap is required to fit three 10-hour shifts into a 24-hour day.

If your security officer coverage needs are for less than 24 hours a day, a combination of 10-hour shifts and 8- or 12-hour shifts can be used to adjust staffing levels to fit your needs. Some shifts may be longer than eight hours. It's not that a person can't work more than 8 hours at a stretch, but sometimes the costs outweigh the benefits. With 8-hour shifts, your security officers may experience less fatigue toward the end of their shifts and be more focused on their job duties. Shifts longer than 8 hours may increase job burnout but do give officers the flexibility to be able to work the occasional double shift, when necessary, without burning out. Sixteen hours is a long shift, but manageable if only worked occasionally.

Another approach to a four-day, 40-hour week uses two 12-hour and two eight-hour shifts a week. Saving resources, such as worker's compensation, vacation, health insurance, and other "per employee" expenses, would entail utilizing more part-time shifts than full-time shifts. The negative side to more part-time shifts may include problems with retention and security officer job satisfaction.

Security contracts are known as 108's (1 officer, 2 shifts, 7 days a week), 168s (1 officer, 3 shifts, 7 days a week), and 236's (2 officers, 3 shifts, 7 days a week) are fairly common. When only one security officer is scheduled at a time, remember he/she must have accessibility to a bathroom when needed or breaks while at the same time providing coverage for the site or post.

Careful examination is critical to client satisfaction and overall profitability. Security officers need to be alert and ready for anything. Shorter shifts help keep their energy levels engaged. Long shifts mean they are likely to become complacent toward the end of their shift. Teamwork is also important, so scheduling the same people at the same time may be beneficial if they work well together. A regular schedule often leads to happier employees and more job satisfaction. Consider having a policy that officers cannot work longer than a designated period of time or ensuring that the same officer works a particular shift, or making rotating shifts the norm. An advantage of rotating shifts is that the officer does not get complacent with the post or too familiar with the employees of the client or site. By conducting periodic evaluations of your security force and reviewing their effectiveness, you can determine which scheduling options are best suited for your company or site.

To begin the scheduling process, lay out each post and specify the hours it will be worked and the needed skills. For example, does the security officer need to be an Emergency Medical Technician (EMT) or qualified to run a magnetometer? Put that information into the post requirements. Setting up teams at specific sites or performing specific tasks may be helpful. Consider having one team properly operate the scanning area while another team patrols the perimeter of the property's perimeter.

Most security operations include "floater" or "rover" positions, filled by an individual who isn't assigned to one location, similar to a substitute teacher in schools – they work when and where they are needed. Floaters or rovers will be assigned work at a specific location or post to fill vacancies caused by call-offs, sick officers, leaves of absence, vacations, or open positions currently being recruited for. Floaters or rovers provide support to multiple sites, and it's imperative that the floater or rover can adapt to different work environments easily. They move to different sites for different periods of time and gain knowledge about each one. The number of hours floaters or rovers work per week varies depending on the needs of the company, and shifts are worked as needed.[2]

It doesn't matter whether the security officer works for a private or public business or individual, a government agency, an in-house operation, or a contract security company; the scheduling requirements are the same. To ensure the effective safety and security of people and assets, security officers must be assigned where and when they are needed and with the right skill set.

Notes

1 Security Guard Duties and Responsibilities. Retrieved on Feb 11, 2021 from: https://www.indeed.com/hire/job-description/security-guard?aceid=&gclid=CjwKCAiA65iBBhB-EiwAW253WxvvrwjJf0i9nAV2sRALK0Kqtv_MYUDKUJqp1SOoUgZCREISsZniNxoCt28QAvD_BwE

2 Security Guard Floater. Retrieved on February 8, 2021 from: https://jobs.garda.com/job/Montreal-Security-Guard%2C-Diplomatic-Contract-Queb/579807900/

Chapter 131

Developing a Security Budget

Security programs should be designed to protect people, property, information, and the operation's bottom line. Needs are identified by conducting a security assessment or vulnerability survey and should be evaluated at least annually so that all company assets are adequately protected and business continuity is ensured. When risks and vulnerabilities are identified, assets and available resources for mitigation should also be identified. After the completion of the security assessment or vulnerability survey, the security manager, along with other key management personnel, should identify exactly what is important to the business and outline the threats along with recommended mitigation strategies.

When presenting the proposed security budget to management decision-makers, it's important to "speak the language of money" and explain how security will help the organization meet business goals by protecting company assets. The security manager should develop key strategic allies with the organization, such as human resources, finance, and legal stakeholders. It's important that you can effectively articulate the value of your security program and it has its impact on overall business operations. Be prepared and do your homework!

When calculating security needs, gaps in the existing security program that allow vulnerabilities to exist should be identified. When a gap or a problem is presented, be prepared to discuss different techniques for dealing with the vulnerability and the cost and implications of implementing each. Be aware of what risks are affecting other organizations in your geographic area and risks that target your specific industry or group. Consider geopolitical risks and use incident monitoring programs as an example of available options. As a benchmark, be knowledgeable about the security

DOI: 10.4324/9781003402718-133

measures that similar organizations have in place and their monetary value. Be open to sharing information with other organizations and explain how security processes can help organizations achieve organizational goals and ensure business continuity. Represent the security department as a support function of the organization.

An example of calculating the cost of one manning one post by security officers who are paid $15 per hour, 24 hours per day is to multiply the total number of hours in a year by the hourly rate of the security officer. The calculation would be 24 hours per day, times 365 days, times the hourly rate. So, 24 × 365 × $15 = $131,400. Don't forget that there are some additional overhead expenses to consider – hiring and training costs, benefits, uniforms, etc. Administrative costs will vary by company or business entity. Find the cost of each of these through your relationship with legal and finance and keep in mind that hourly rate and labor costs may be as much as 70% of the total cost.

Keep in mind that when you discuss the return on investment (ROI) of a security program, it is hard to quantify prevention programs – such as lives that were saved because weapons were detected at screening points, monetary or product losses that were prevented, and security breaches that didn't happen. For example, you should know what the average active assailant incident costs a company (both tangible and intangible), the average theft losses for comparable businesses, and what the average security breach costs. The bottom line is what is the value of the security processes when compared to the potential losses?

Chapter 132

How to Design a Five-Year Plan

Let's start with the garage or parking areas needing updating or replacement. There may be emergency (blue light) phones in your parking lot or intercoms in your garage, the emergency lighting may be outdated or non-operational, the exterior fire extinguishers may be missing, and the fire detection and suppression system in your garage may need to be updated. Exterior lighting, garage lighting, and security surveillance systems upgrades aren't easy projects unless you have effectively budgeted for upgrades.

When we did our first five-year plan, this is how we started. Several cameras in the garage weren't working properly so we switched them to digital and replaced the units with high-definition, pan-tilt-zoom units as well as additional high-definition monitors. The intercoms except for two were not operating because of water damage. The lighting survey resulted in LED lights being installed in the parking lots and garage, which gave us a significant ROI.

Access control and badges were also a problem. At this particular company, there were 1,250 employees, but there were over 1,500 active badges. This was a complicated process because there were issues accessing activity reports for each badge. Finally, the badges of the inactive employees were deleted from the system. Luckily, the original badging machine broke (thank goodness), so we could do an upgrade out of necessity.

The fire alarm system was working except for 18 backup batteries with a lifespan of five years. All of the batteries were replaced, and we began tracking replacement dates.

DOI: 10.4324/9781003402718-134

It took five years to repair the components that needed fixing and complete the necessary upgrades to the security systems. It's understandable now because no one was effectively managing the physical security program.

Many times, people don't understand the shortcomings of technology and have a false sense of security.

Two examples:

1. The access control system worked about half of the time, and there were also terminated employees who had not been deleted from the system. It was not discovered because the system was never tested or audited.
2. The video surveillance system was over-rated and misunderstood. Yet, the company leaders demanded it as a deterrent, even though the system had nonoperational cameras and was not always actively monitored by security officers.

Chapter 133

Sexual Harassment: Additional Supervisor Responsibilities

Supervisors exercise authority on behalf of their employer as the employer's agent. This gives them important additional responsibilities regarding sexual harassment.

Any reports of harassment in the workplace *must be reported to your operations manager immediately*. Then, they must be reported to HR directly after that. This will ensure these matters can be handled in a confidential manner so as to not interfere with the workplace and to help accommodate immediate investigation and resolution. If necessary, HR may be contacted first.

Second, all supervisors must exercise their authority to ensure that their workplace is free of sexual harassment. They must take every complaint seriously and respond promptly to employees requesting help.

Third, supervisors who engage in unwelcome behavior toward others, including subordinates, take a very serious personal risk of career damage and financial loss.

All supervisors must be aware of their responsibilities. Anyone who ignores this responsibility and is found guilty of sexual harassment or fails to follow up on all claims properly may be held personally liable and may incur disciplinary action up to and including termination of employment.

DOI: 10.4324/9781003402718-135

Chapter 134

Managing a Multigenerational Workforce

People are at the very heart of the workplace, and generational differences between individuals may impact workplace culture. Generations typically span 15–25 years. Today, more generations are working together than at any other time in history. There may be up to five generations in a single workplace.[1] Managing a multigenerational workforce requires a special skill set from supervisors and managers because people of different generations respond differently to situations and actions because they are influenced by historical, political, and social events that occurred during their lifetime. These different values, experiences, and attitudes can create misunderstandings and frustration in the workplace if not handled appropriately.

The five generations in the workplace today are:

1. **Traditionalists or the silent generation (born between 1922 and 1945)** – This generation grew up before the age of modern technology. They grew up during the economic depression, and they value hard work and typically "play by the rules." Even though there are not many workers in this generation left in the workforce, they are valuable employees because they are loyal and disciplined.
2. **The Baby Boomers or Boomers (born between 1946 and 1964)** – Baby Boomers look for job security and familiar environments. They generally had limited familiarity with new technologies because there was no digital communication when they were growing up. Baby Boomers make up a large part of the workforce today, and they are waiting longer to retire. They are

DOI: 10.4324/9781003402718-136

hard-working and have expertise in their specific industry. Many Baby Boomers are asked to mentor younger employees.

3. **Generation X or Gen Xers (born between 1965 and 1980)** – Generation X is more educated than previous generations and values monetary rewards. They are responsible, competent, and independent. Generation X is the first generation to be computer literate.
4. **Millennials, Gen Y or Net (born between 1981 and 1990)** – Millennials are hyper-connected and more tech-savvy than any previous generation. They want to be evaluated on their results, not by how many hours they spend working. This is the fastest-growing generation and is team oriented.
5. **Generation Z or Zoomers (born between 1997 and 2012)** – Generation Z prefers purpose-driven work and a good work–life balance. They prefer "meaningful work" and desire flexible schedules. Their long-term career goals include making the world a better place.

When generations fail to communicate effectively, it may impact turnover rates, tangible costs (recruitment, hiring, training, and retention), intangible costs (morale), grievances and complaints, and perceptions of fairness and equity.

Generational Preferred Methods of Communication[2]

Traditionalists

- Memos, letters, personal notes, and individual interactions.
- Words and tone of voice should be respectful, with good grammar, clear diction, and no slang or profanity. Language should be formal and professional, and the message should relate to the organization's history and long-term goals.

Baby Boomers

- Face-to-face, phone calls, personal interaction, and structured networking.
- Conversations should be more informal, perhaps over coffee or lunch. Boomers tend to see relationships and business results as intertwined. Ask about mutual interests (e.g., "How is your son doing in college?"). Make the conversation participative by getting the other's input and linking the message to the team or individual vision, mission, and values.

Generation Xers

- Voice mail, email, casual, and direct and immediate.
- Don't waste the person's time. Be direct and straightforward. Avoid corporate-speak. Please send an email or leave a voice mail stating clearly what you want, how it will serve the Gen Xer, and when you want it.

Millennials

- Digital (instant messages, blogs, and text messages) and collaborative interaction.
- Be positive. Send a text message or meet face-to-face. Tie the message to the Millennial's personal goals or the goals the whole team is working toward. Don't be condescending. Avoid cynicism and sarcasm.

Generation Z

- Digitally savvy and well-connected, so engage them with interactive content.
- Used to constant online professional communication, in-person conversations, and prefer difficult conversations by text.

As the supervisor or manager, a good starting point is to ask your employees how they prefer to communicate. You can decide which form of communication is best for a particular issue. Sometimes, an in-person conversation is best, and in others, a memo may be sufficient.

All generations have strengths, so encourage cross-generational mentoring with your security team.

Keep the communication information listed above in mind, but avoid stereotypes when managing your security team. Speak in ways that motivate each generation, but treat everyone as an individual. Misunderstood comments can have lasting repercussions in the workplace and lead to disgruntled employees that undermine the effectiveness of your security program. Assess security officers by their skill level, their willingness to learn, their work ethic, how they interact with co-workers, and how well they provide customer service. Engaged security officers can help inspire other employees and lead to positive change within the organization. Each generation has something to add to the workplace, and when these experiences are combined, it leads to a positive company culture (and bottom line).

Notes

1 Multigenerational Workforce and How to Lead It. Retrieved on 02-24-23 from: https://www.thehumancapitalhub.com/articles/Multigenerational-Workforce-And-How-To-Lead-It
2 Practical Advice for Managing a Multi-Generational Workforce. Retrieved on October 27, 2023 from: https://www.businessofgovernment.org/sites/default/files/HannamYordi

Chapter 135

How to Engage and Empower Security Officers

A great way to engage and empower security officers is through education about security and how they can learn to do their jobs more effectively. We've all heard that knowledge is power, so apply it to security. Through this knowledge, the security officer will begin to look at things in his/her environment differently and, at the same time, provide more productive customer service. Teaching them about Crime Prevention Through Environmental Design or CPTED is a great starting point. CPTED is a multidisciplinary approach to deterring criminal behavior through environmental design.[1]

CPTED is about the proper design and effective use of the built environment to reduce the incidence and fear of crime and improve the quality of life. Emphasis is placed on the physical environment, productive use of space, and people's behavior to create environments that are absent of environmental cues that cause opportunities for crime. Much of CPTED is common sense.

Simple Steps for Crime Prevention using CPTED

Residential:

- Remove/trim decorative shrubs and trees that may obstruct anyone seeing if a burglar is at your home. Provide an unobstructed view of the area around your home.

DOI: 10.4324/9781003402718-137

- Install fencing with a secure lockable gate to clearly define your property and prevent easy access to the back of your home.
- Provide marked transitional zones that indicate movement from public to semiprivate to private space.
- Installing bright security lighting and using motion detectors are good considerations for conserving energy while providing security.
- Install solid-core doors on all exterior doors with deadbolt locks.
- Secure all sheds and outbuildings, sure ensuring they are visible from home.

Commercial:

- Installing bright security lighting and using motion detectors are good considerations for conserving energy while providing security. Ensure all doors and windows are illuminated after dark.
- Install solid-core doors on all exterior doors with deadbolt locks and peepholes if there is no window.
- Install fencing around the perimeter of your property with secure lockable gates. Making access to the back of buildings and hidden areas with tall, secure fencing will deter many criminals.
- Control access to and from your property with automatic doors and gates.
- Install crash-resistant bollards to protect entrances and large glass windows.
- Enclose and lock any points of access to your roof.

Taking a little time and effort to examine and apply simple CPTED principles can go a long way for security officers to help increase safety and security on the job and at home.

Activity Support

Another tool to engage and empower security officers is to educate them about activity support. The concept of activity support is to deliberately design formal and informal support for increasing the levels of human activity in particular spaces as a crime prevention strategy.[2]

How do we accomplish this strategy? First, review how the facility property is being used, then consider adding bus stops, community gardens, food trucks, children's playgrounds, a cement table, and two seats for playing chess or checkers. Using the grounds will bring the community together and for a positive purpose. Bringing people together, and getting to know one another, becomes an asset when you create a neighborhood watch or business watch program.

It is important that security officers learn the basics about security and what part they play in keeping people and property safe. Over the years, soft targets have become crime problems due to individuals simply reacting to issues instead of implementing a proactive approach to addressing the issues. The goal of these proactive plans is for soft targets to become hard targets to protect property from crime. This is partly achieved by implementing physical security countermeasures, such as alarms, access control, network video systems, fences, walls, and the presence of law enforcement or security officers.

Notes

1 Crime Prevention Through Environmental Design (CPTED). Retrieved on January 15, 2019 from: https://www.niagarapolice.ca/en/community/Crime-Prevention-Through-Environmental-Design--CPTED-.aspx#

2 Cozens, P.M. (2016), Think Crime! Using evidence, theory, and CPTED for planning safer cities.

Chapter 136

100 Things Security Supervisors and Managers Need to Know

With the definitions of a supervisor and a manager in mind, we have developed the following list of 100 things a supervisor or manager must know to do their job effectively.

1. Supervisors and managers should ensure proper employee conduct in the work environment and identify problematic and/or suspicious behavior.
2. Managers should regularly, at least monthly, check all physical security devices to ensure they are operating well. Consider having audit logs for key management, fire extinguishers, Automated External Defibrillator (AED) checks, emergency lighting, alarm systems, and video operations.
3. Video surveillance systems are sometimes used for employee surveillance, especially concerning employee performance. In many geographic locations, video surveillance in the workplace is closely regulated or controlled by either legislation or union contracts.
4. Always ensure that every light works properly and that no exterior lights are on during the daytime.
5. Ensure that the total number of employees aligns with the total number of access badges issued.
6. Ensure all fire extinguishers are accounted for and checked regularly and that designated employees are trained in fire extinguisher use.
7. Ensure all exterior intercoms/phones working for mass notification.
8. Ensure all keys are properly secured and turned in upon termination.

DOI: 10.4324/9781003402718-138

9. Determine if exterior lighting is cost-effective.
10. Determine if the signage on or about the property is adequate.
11. The physical security of technology is an important component of cybersecurity.
12. Don't over-rely on electronic security systems and technology solutions. Remember to balance electronic, mechanical, and human tools for risk mitigation.
13. Recognize the value of effective training, policies, business practices, and people as part of your overall risk management strategy.
14. Recognize that "IT Security" is NOT the same as "Security IT." Protecting IT assets is very different than using IT assets to support an organization's security systems/program. Keep the distinction clear in your mind when you communicate with people.
15. Always ensure that your security program/assets protection strategy is aligned with the strategic goals of the organization you support … and make it very apparent that your goals are aligned. It doesn't matter whether your organization is a business, a government agency, a nonprofit, or another type of entity – this is critical.
16. If you are a manager or supervisor of an School Resource Officer (SRO) or school security practitioners, ensure that you are involved in and are a part of the following: emergency operations planning, tabletop and functional exercises, hazard, risk, vulnerability assessments, athletics, and after-school activities safety & security, parent/student reunification, life safety, security, and communications systems.
17. When post orders, training material, and security manuals are issued, they should be signed for and documented.
18. All supervisors and managers should be properly trained for the job to properly discharge their duties effectively and according to policy.
19. The secret of obtaining and retaining great security personnel is properly conducting the pre-employment interview, with prepared questions to ask the candidate.
20. Unity of command, means that the security officer is under the direct control of his immediate supervisor.
21. Span of control is when a supervisor can effectively control only a limited number of people, which is usually 12 employees or less.
22. Discipline can be complicated depending on the issue. However, confer with your supervisor if unsure of what course of action to take.
23. Emergency management of any incident BEGINS before something happens and awareness of the facility is critical.
24. Span of control under the National Incident Management System (NIMS) is a key component of any security and response organization.
25. Security officers ARE first responders whose training needs to reflect it.
26. The officers MUST be trained and properly educated in all phases of the facility's emergency management CULTURE and operations.
27. Pre-planning must be integral to any officer's onboarding process.

28. What we train our protection officers to do in the first moments of an emergency is critical to a successful outcome.
29. The effective implementation of an emergency management plan requires that all involved have proper training and are given exercises to ensure the understanding of existing plans.[1]
30. The secret to success in many organizations is to hire and retain the right people. Reliable pre-employment screening is at the core of successful operations management. This is particularly the case for protection programs. Security personnel are selected the same way as other workers in an organization; however, there are higher standards for determining applicants' previous legal, moral, and ethical behavior to guide employment decisions.
31. Security officers should be familiar with and train with police, fire, and Emergency Medical Services (EMS) responders.
32. Reducing and mitigating risk is a primary responsibility of security officers.
33. Training and exercises conducted beforehand will impact the outcome of any event.
34. No checkbox training – focus on competency.
35. Security officers will benefit from completing NIMS 700 and 100 training.
36. Security officers should be trained in GHS and NFPA 704 systems.
37. To keep everyone safe, security officers are the primary eyes in ensuring housekeeping is maintained.
38. Security officers should be trained in how to respond to unknown substances, such as white powder, hazmat releases, as well as fire, and EMS.
39. Security officers should be informed anytime a sprinkler or alarm system is activated, and it should be documented.
40. Fire behavior should be a curriculum topic in security officer training.
41. Security managers (SMs) should realize their officers will be first on the scene of any incident. This means they need to have all-hazards training for the first 10+ minutes. An old saying in the fire service is that the first five minutes will influence the next five hours. Step up initially and be prepared for a long day. Security officers are professional and should be considered as such.
42. Managers should periodically conduct drills and tabletop exercises for security personnel to ensure proper delivery of procedures is known and followed.
43. IT and physical security are intrinsically connected; they are NOT separate disciplines. One cannot have one without the other. In today's world, there is no IT security without physical security, and there is no physical security without IT security. Organizations will remain unacceptably vulnerable until they approach security as one risk-reduction discipline.
44. Security problems can only be resolved by developing a cohesive culture focused on the overall welfare of everyone. Until virtually everyone in a culture shares the same general cultural values and goals (the overall welfare of everyone), and it becomes culturally unacceptable to harm others, crime will be a significant problem to the detriment of everyone. Crime thrives in an environment of, "I deserve, so I will take from others … or kill others

who do not agree with my beliefs." A homogeneous culture virtually eliminates this.

45. Due to the increasingly complex global environment many organizations operate in today, engaging in proactive crisis planning with relevant stakeholders is critical. This requires top leadership commitment and support at every step of the process to be successful. Top leadership is the catalyst for success in this important arena.
46. Emerging technologies, including robots, drones, and software that analyzes video footage for anomalies, could allow companies to expand surveillance without having to adopt intrusive inspections, experts said.[2]
47. Obtain security officer input for any policy and procedure implemented or significant changes to existing policies and procedures.
48. Conduct a comprehensive background investigation on all security officers prior to hiring and on a regular basis after employment.
49. Provide a means of confidential employee communication to security management via an anonymous "hotline."
50. Any security patrol scheme should be conducted in a varied and unpredictable manner. Occasionally, re-patrolling the area immediately after the initial patrol is an effective method to avoid predictability and keep a potential criminal from discerning a routine patrol pattern.
51. Review with and practice with the security staff the policies and procedures related to demonstrations and mass-gathering events that may impact your organization. Stress the importance of perimeter patrol and restraint.
52. Instill in the security staff that civil and/or criminal liability can arise from negligent performance of their duties and responsibilities. This applies to both the organization and the security staff.
53. Remind the security staff that the protection of life takes precedence over the protection of property in all cases. This is the top priority.
54. Develop a security awareness/crime prevention program and travel advisory program for the organization's personnel traveling abroad.
55. Develop data drive security metrics to demonstrate the effectiveness of the security program to top management.
56. Apply a business case approach when promoting new security projects to top management, utilizing the Return on Investment (ROI) and Total Cost of Ownership (TCO) concepts.
57. Push security out beyond the workplace by using concentric rings of security to identify and address threats well before they get to your front door.
58. Fight overreliance on security technology and keep humans involved in the process for a holistic view of your vulnerabilities and threats.
59. Don't assume serious insider threats are not in your organization; know which employees are struggling and the potential danger they may bring to the workplace.
60. Create a culture of safe reporting so employees will come forward with security concerns without fear of reprisal.

61. Don't assume that security rules are followed; have good policies and procedures, but also regularly assess compliance.
62. Build your crisis leadership skill set before bad things happen; practice how you and your staff will handle an emergency.
63. Focus your time and energy on preparing for a crisis, not predicting or calculating whether or not it will happen.
64. Craft the messages you will put on social media and give to the press in the event of a crisis in your organization.
65. In this unpredictable security landscape, your mitigation and response plans must be fluid and based on emerging threats.
66. People want to feel safe and will make their own assessment about whether to use your facilities or services; robust security will pull them in, not push them away!
67. Managers should have and/or develop an incident management system (IMS). An IMS provides the data required to effectively manage current or potential problems, issues, investigations, and planning for effective physical protection systems (PPSs). All incidents should be investigated by either a security officer or a manger. The findings of the investigation should be documented and logged into the IMS. All hazards or problematic behavior should be immediately reported to the SM or director.
68. Managers should have a notification system that clearly identifies who should be notified in case of an emergency, incident occurring, or any other noteworthy occurrence.
69. Managers should ensure their security officers have a patrol log to document patrol activities and observations during patrol, including life safety concerns. Managers should ensure policies and procedures for all employees are clearly written and defined to ensure proper enforcement of these rules by security. Managers should tailor their security applications to fit the environment they are protecting. Not all applications work in all environments.
70. Managers should be well-read and versed in managerial concepts and leadership.
71. Managers should lead by example; how managers expect their subordinates to act and comport themselves, they should do the same.
72. It is important that managers document the progress of their subordinates. Many managers fail to accurately document an employee's performance. Too often, they only document the negative and not the positive.
73. Communications

1. Names and cell phone contact info for immediate executive leadership, vice president (VP) – operations, human resources or on-call representative, corporate counsel, and corporate communications team should be accessible.

2. The SM should know the address, with cross streets and landmarks, for every facility under supervision or where business occurs, in the event an emergency call to 911/first responders is necessary.
3. The SM should be capable of using all communications platforms and trained to perform basic service or diagnostics on equipment to troubleshoot in case of crisis (when there is no time to call the help desk or the help desk is out of service.)
4. The SM should have names and contact info for fire and law enforcement, EMS, and other emergency response leaders with jurisdiction over the facility.
5. The SM should have names and contact info for all building systems contractors, including plumbing, HVAC, fire systems, overhead doors and access control equipment, and city water service/sewer service issues.
6. The SM should have names and contact info for all vehicles and transportation equipment maintenance providers in case of an accident, breakdown, or service need.
7. A good SM will have connections with professional organizations (IFPO, ASIS) for networking, mentoring, and advice on problem-solving.
8. A good SM should know how to communicate effectively with security officers, the public, executives, other employees, and all levels of constituents.
9. A good SM should have curiosity about current events locally, regionally, and globally, and the SM should be reading or checking the news for updated information on events locally relevant.
10. A good SM must know how to inspire, manage, reward, develop, support, and discipline employees within the company culture's expectations and within the law.

74. Training

1. Develop and implement a use-of-force policy and training credentials for all officers.
2. Conduct emergency medical training such as CPR/AED, stop bleeding, tactical emergency casualty care (TECC), and have a certified instructor or program to train new hires and update staff immediately.
3. Learn self-defense laws, such as protection of life vs. protection of private property.
4. Conduct training on verbal judo, de-escalation, conflict resolution, and management of aggressive behavior.
5. Conduct formal observation, surveillance, and counter-surveillance training
6. Ensure all security officers are physically fit and healthy. It would be best if you were an example to others.
7. Train all security officers in the use of all specialized security surveillance systems, access control, alarms, and monitoring equipment used by the department.

8. Educate yourself and have the basic ability to communicate in other languages that might be expected. This may also include access and knowledge on who to contact for interpreter services.
9. Know the incident command system that will be used when fire/EMS/police arrive for a significant event.
10. Ensure all training is documented and saved in each security officer's file.
11. Develop a security plan.

75. Ensure you understand the difference between ERM and ESRM. ERM is enterprise risk management and ESRM is enterprise security risk management. Both are built on risk practices and risk principles but ESRM is narrowly focused on security risks.

    ESRM is a security program management approach that links security activities to an enterprise's mission and business goals through risk management methods. The security leader's role in ESRM is to manage risks of harm to enterprise assets in partnership with the business leaders whose assets are exposed to those risks. ESRM involves educating business leaders on the realistic impacts of identified risks, presenting potential strategies to mitigate those impacts, and then enacting the option chosen by the business in line with the accepted levels of business risk tolerance.

(Petruzzi, 2017)

76. Understand the difference between integration and unification.
77. Strive toward having a seat at the C-Suite Table. Security directors should be at the C-Suite table to participate in planning and key decision-making. C-Suite gets its name from the titles of top senior executives, which tend to start with the letter C, for chief, as in chief executive officer (CEO), chief financial officer (CFO), chief operating officer (COO), and chief information officer (CIO). Also called "C-level executives" (Investopedia, 2018).
78. Ensure you are involved in business continuity planning.
79. Educate yourself about alternative revenue sources to fund security initiatives, such as grant writing.
80. Educate yourself about how to construct a formal request for proposal (RFP).
81. Educate yourself about how to write a formal after-action report.
82. Ensure you know how to conduct or plan exercises – tabletop, functional, and full-scale.
83. Ensure you know how to complete a security analysis.
84. Ensure that you have controls in place to meet all (local, county, state, and federal) requirements.
85. Develop an audit schedule, with controls in place for specific areas.
86. Educate yourself about NIMS and organize your security department around an incident command structure for emergency response. NIMS is the

National IMS, which provides a comprehensive, national approach to incident management.

> ICS is a widely applicable management system designed to enable effective, efficient incident management by integrating a combination of facilities, equipment, personnel, procedures, and communications operating within a common organizational structure. ICS is a fundamental form of management established in a standard format, with the purpose of enabling incident managers to identify the key concerns associated with the incident—often under urgent conditions—without sacrificing attention to any component of the command system. It represents organizational "best practices" and, as an element of the Command and Management Component of NIMS, has become the standard for emergency management across the country.

(Homeland Security, 2018)

87. An EOP is an emergency operations plan. The security director is a key stakeholder and should be familiar with the organization's plan and pass this information to SMs and supervisors. The security director should be an important part of the incident command system and on the incident command team to manage emergencies, which always include security components.
88. Ensure there is an EOP and know the essential elements of the plan.
89. Check the EOP and ensure there are procedures for special events, third-party rentals, etc.
90. Check to make sure third-party rentals include security standards and costs.
91. Familiarize yourself with how to use and monitor social media. The security director represents the "boots on the ground" perspective and provides valuable insight into many life safety, security, and communication systems. He/she should be a part of the process, not just an end user. Once the systems are selected, the security director and his/her team should be trained in these systems. Communications systems are the foundation for managing an incident, especially one that is time sensitive and/or presents a threat, so redundancy in communication tools is critical. Beyond landlines, radios, and email notifications, other communication tools may include the public address system, mass notification systems, and social media.
92. If you are an SM or supervisor in a school, ensure there are plans for parent/student reunification.
93. Ensure you are one of the decision-makers in the selection of life safety, security, and communication systems (fire, access control, phone, PA, mass notification, etc.)
94. Get involved in helping to formulate crisis communications plans and ensure you have established a working relationship with the local media.

95. Assess the physical property of your organization and ensure Crime Prevention Through Environmental Design (CPTED) concepts and principles are being used.
96. Ensure security officers are trained in mental health protocols.
97. Consider being a mentor for young or new security officers.
98. As a manager or supervisor, ensure you stay current with HR policies and procedures (interviewing, hiring, firing, harassment, etc.)? The HR director and security director should work hand in hand from the initial stages of interviewing a prospective employee (background checks) to the release of an employee and many practices in between. Some examples include drug testing, investigations (theft), clearances (access control), threat assessments (protective orders), employee conduct (harassment), cybersecurity policies (lack of adherence to company policies), and many others.
99. Reach out to your local first responders to establish a working relationship and invite them to become familiar with your facility.
100. Test all handheld radios and other communication devices and confirm that all are operational and that there are no "dead spots" on the property.

Notes

1 Security Management, April, 2018, p. 70, Dr. Marie-Helen Maras & Dr. Lauren R. Shapiro.

2 REUTERS News. Technology News April 4, 2018 / 9:12 PM / 8 days ago.

Chapter 137

Facility Security Plan

Section 5(a)(1) of the Occupational Safety and Health Act (the General Duty clause) states that organizations are required to provide employees with a safe workplace. Every employer must provide a secure workplace where employees can work without fear for their safety.[1]

Recommended security plan elements:

- Security policy and procedures.
- Personal security procedures.
- Equipment security.
- How to protect sensitive business information.
- How to help prevent workplace theft.

At a minimum, a facility security program should include:

- A physical security survey of each facility is needed to determine the security level of the facility and the minimum-security safeguards required for protecting personnel and assets.
- Periodic reassessments of facilities to determine whether a security program meets pertinent regulations and policies.
- Comprehensive and continuing awareness and education to employees, contractors, consultants, and visitors.
- Procedures for taking immediate, positive, and orderly action to safeguard life and property during an emergency.

DOI: 10.4324/9781003402718-139

The Facility Security Plan can be integrated with other environmental, health, and safety (EHS) plans adopted at your facility including:

- Emergency action plan
- Fire prevention plan
- Disaster recovery/business continuity plan
- Other environmental and workplace safety plans and programs

Businesses should adopt the following security practices:

- Monitor and control who enters your workplace: current employees, former employees, and commercial delivery and service personnel.
- Check identification and ask individuals to identify the purpose of their visit to your workplace.
- Report broken doors, windows, and locks to your organization's or building security staff as soon as possible.
- Make backups or copies of sensitive and critical information and databases.
- Store, lock, and inventory your organization's keys, access cards, uniforms, badges, and vehicles.
- Monitor and report suspicious activity in or near your facility's entry/exit points, loading docks, parking areas, garages, and immediate vicinity.
- Report suspicious-looking packages to your local police. DO NOT OPEN or TOUCH.
- Shred or destroy all documents no longer needed.
- Keep an inventory of your most critical equipment, hardware, and software.
- Store and lock your personal items such as wallets, purses, and identification when not in use.

Note

1 OSH Act of 1970. Retrieved on October 29, 2023 from: https://www.osha.gov/laws-regs/oshact/section5-duties

Chapter 138

Cross-Training

Chris Cancialosi, a former contributor to Forbes, uses this example about cross-training: You are part of a dangerous military combat mission. Suddenly, one of your team members with a mission-critical skill is injured or killed. Do you give up and leave? Of course, not! To the military, cross-training is an integral part of how operations are run. They understand that duplication in the human system is one of the best ways to mitigate risk and ensure success.[1]

For most of us, the mission of our facility is not life or death; businesses simply cannot risk failure. Cross-training your security officers can help mitigate risk so your company can respond to fluctuating workflows, such as unexpected vacancies or sick employees. Cross-training can also include training for different skill sets if someone leaves the company or may help employees prepare to move up within the organization.

Cross-training can be handled as on-the-job training (OJT) with a more experienced security officer or supervisor. OJT is much more effective than having a security officer watch hours of videos or presentations.

Regardless of post assignment, all security officers should be trained in emergency procedures, including CPR/AED and using a fire extinguisher. In addition to these basic life-saving skills, all security officers should know how to operate the technology located at the site. This includes cameras, alarm panels, access control, magnetometers (if utilized), and telephone systems. Technology is a part of the overall security process, so if security officers are not trained to operate all of the equipment at the site, there will be vulnerabilities in the process that may compromise the safety and security of assets.

Note

1 Cross-Training: Your Best Defense Against Indispensable Employees. Retrieved on October 29, 2023 from: https://www.forbes.com/sites/chriscancialosi/2014/09/15/cross-training-your-best-defense-against-indispensable-employees/?sh=1933f7c37d90

DOI: 10.4324/9781003402718-140

Chapter 139

Building an Effective Security Team

To have an effective security team, you must have the right "mix" of people (security officers, supervisors, and managers), appropriate technology, and policies and procedures that are followed.

Strong Leadership

A strong leader – either a security supervisor or manager – can help build trust throughout the team and communicate effectively. Strong relationships within the group will help the security officers to work together more efficiently to achieve the goals of the security program.

Clearly Defined Roles

Each security officer, supervisor, or manager needs to have clearly defined roles so that each is aware of their purpose and duties so the security operation will operate efficiently. Another important aspect of building an effective security guard team is to define everyone's role clearly so each individual knows where they "fit" within the operation. Duties and tasks should be delegated while keeping in mind each individual's strengths and talents, and the work distribution should be fair.

 DOI: 10.4324/9781003402718-141

Set Clear Objectives

Individual security officers need to understand how their job duties are a part of the overall goals of the security program. Each security team member has a role and is responsible for their job as it relates to the program's overall success.

Communication

Effective and clear communication will help prevent misunderstandings and ensure that the security team works together toward common goals. Information should flow from the top down, from the bottom up, and also from side to side. In other words, communication within the security department should flow in all directions.

To track the effectiveness of a security team, progress must be measured and the individual components of the security program must be evaluated to ensure they are all working in conjunction with one another. Changes may need to be made. For example, the policy may be that all vendors are checked into the facility, but the procedure may change from a scanned ID card to biometrics. The policy remained the same, but the procedure changed.

Chapter 140

Female Security Officers

Security is one of the fastest-growing professions in the world, but it is not one that, historically, women have considered. In the past, the security industry comprised of predominantly men with law enforcement or military backgrounds. Today that is not the case. To address evolving threats and security concerns, individuals from diverse backgrounds and capabilities are needed safeguard people, property, and assets.

Diversity may be overlooked as a significant change to improving security and culture. Still, female security officers have different life experiences than their male counterparts and this will many times allow them to see security from a different perspective.

There has been a push to improve gender diversity in ALL industries, but security is still one of those careers where it is a male-dominated industry. Only 28.0% of all security officers are women.[1]

For example, studies have shown that female security officers may have a different approach to resolving conflicts than male security officers. Women are less likely to respond initially with aggression than men and, many times, are skilled in problem-solving through more of a focus on communication. Additionally, having more female security officers can make the security staff more representative of the people they protect. A security officer staff that is male-only may be more intimidating, but may also affect how willing people are to report potential problems or suspicious behavior. People need to "feel" safe and know their concerns will be respected. Gender-based violence and harassment continue to be issues, and many times, because of their personal perspective and experience, female security officers may more quickly identify gender-based incidents, and females may be more comfortable reporting these incidents to a female security officer. Female security officers can also respond to "woman-only" spaces and perform physical searches, when necessary. This is especially true in the education sector and healthcare settings.

DOI: 10.4324/9781003402718-142

Research by the Chicago Police Department found that female law enforcement officers use force 28% less often than their male counterparts. They also make 7% fewer arrests. Although the research didn't include why these differences exist, we know that unnecessary arrests and use of force can damage the relationship with the community and lead to lawsuits.[2]

This indicates that the security industry could benefit from hiring more women. Women make up approximately 13% of full-time law enforcement officers in the United States, even though they make up 60% of the US workforce. For security in schools, universities, and hospitals, 44% of their security or campus police departments have 10% or fewer female employees, according to Campus Safety's 2018 Salary and Benefits Survey. More than four out of five say that women comprise less than 30% of their employees.[3]

Some male security officers may be resistant to change and will be unwilling to accept a woman on their team, and sexism at some level continues to be a problem in all male-dominated industries. Some still believe that men are better security officers than women simply because of physical characteristics such as size and strength. Still, the security industry should have certainly evolved past this outdated, sexist way of thinking. It's critical that the professional security officer of today be a good communicator, have in-depth knowledge of the industry, have integrity, be vigilant, be motivated, and provide excellent customer service – regardless of whether they are male or female. Unfortunately, many female officers still have to "prove" themselves to their male counterparts, management, and the public to be accepted in the security industry.

Ten reasons women choose not to pursue a career in security are[4]:

1. Security is a male-dominated industry.
2. Sexism is still prevalent in the sector.
3. Fears that gender will impede career progression.
4. The perception that security work is unsafe for women.
5. Lack of female role models, particularly in higher positions.
6. The belief is that typical "female" characteristics will be considered inferior.
7. The misconception that men are stronger and, therefore, more able.
8. The idea that security work is incompatible with family life.
9. Evidence that female security staff face high levels of discrimination, sexual harassment, and bullying.
10. Perceived lack of opportunities for women within the industry.

Everyone in the security industry should work toward promoting gender diversity by hiring, retaining, and promoting women. Successful organizations are diverse organizations.[5]

Notes

1 Security Guard Demographics and Statistics in the US. Retrieved on October 20, 2023 from: https://www.zippia.com/security-guard-jobs/demographics/
2 Recruiting and Retaining Female Employees in Campus Security and Law Enforcement. Retrieved on October 20, 2023 from: Recruiting and Retaining Female Employees in Campus Security and Law Enforcement - Campus Safety (campussafetymagazine.com).
3 Ibid.
4 Women in Security: Holding Your Own in a Male-Dominated Industry. Retrieved on October 20, 2023 from: https://www.churchillsupportservices.com/resources/news-insights/women-in-security/
5 Being a Woman is an Advantage in the Security Industry. Retrieved on October 20, 2023 from: https://www.securitymagazine.com/articles/89141-being-a-woman-is-an-advantage-in-the-security-industry

Chapter 141

What Does Employee Turnover Really Cost?

An employee may leave an organization for any number of reasons – either voluntary or involuntary. Voluntary turnover is when an employee chooses to leave for a better opportunity or retirement; involuntary turnover is when an employee is terminated.

According to the Bureau of Labor Statistics,[1] the number of US employees voluntarily leaving their jobs has increased since 2021 in a trend known as the Great Resignation. While the trend has slowed in recent months, many workers continue to leave their jobs voluntarily. According to the Bureau of Labor Statistics' January 2023 news release, 4.2 million people quit their jobs in November 2022.[1]

When an employee leaves, it affects the remaining employees because they may have lost a work friend. Seventy percent of employees say having a friend at work is the most crucial element to happiness. Fifty percent of employees with a best friend reported feeling a stronger connection to their organization.[2]

Frequent voluntary turnover rates may hurt your organization. The total effects of employee turnover include[3]:

- **Recruitment costs** – The direct costs of hiring a new employee, including advertising, interviewing, pre-employment screening, and hiring.
- **Onboarding costs** – Onboarding a new person, including training and management time.
- **Lost productivity** – It may take a new employee one to two years to reach the productivity of an existing person, resulting in indirect costs to your organization.

DOI: 10.4324/9781003402718-143

- **Lost engagement and impact on employee morale** – Other employees who see high turnover tend to disengage and lose productivity, affecting team morale.
- **Customer service and errors** – New employees take longer to complete their work and are often less adept at solving problems.
- **Training costs** – Over two to three years, a business likely invests 10–20% of an employee's salary or more in training.
- **Lost institutional knowledge** – When highly skilled or longtime employees leave, your organization loses some institutional knowledge or your business's combined skill set and experience.
- **Cultural impact** – Whenever someone leaves, others ask why.

There are different reasons why an employee may voluntarily leave an organization – a better opportunity and disagreements with co-workers or supervisors; they don't feel valued as an employee, lack of adequate compensation, or a lack of career progression opportunities. A 2021 Pew Research Center survey found that low pay, a lack of opportunities for advancement, and feeling disrespected at work were the reasons 63% of those surveyed quit their jobs.[4]

Remember that the "offboarding" process is just as important as your "onboarding" process because it is a part of your overall security program. You want to ensure that everything the employee has access to is secure. There are three critical steps to an effective offboarding process:

- Legal and formal steps
- Transfer of company materials
- Transfer of company knowledge

A well-documented offboarding process can help comply with employment laws, protect company assets, such as a laptop, and obtain any knowledge about the company and client processes that may cause a problem.

To increase employee retention, take your time when hiring security officers by hiring the best employee for the job and setting clear goals and expectations from day one. Offer growth and recognize when employees are doing a good job. Above all, keep the lines of communication open.

Notes

1 Employee retention: the real cost of losing an employee. Retrieved on October 27, 2023 from: https://www.peoplekeep.com/blog/employee-retention-the-real-cost-of-losing-an-employee
2 Ibid.
3 Ibid.

4 Majority of workers who quit a job in 2021 cite low pay, no opportunities for advancement, and feeling disrespected. Retrieved on October 27, 2023 from: https://www.pewresearch.org/short-reads/2022/03/09/majority-of-workers-who-quit-a-job-in-2021-cite-low-pay-no-opportunities-for-advancement-feeling-disrespected/

Chapter 142

Diversity, Equity, and Inclusion in the Security Industry

Everyone wants to feel like they "belong" and are a valued workplace team member and also that their employer is supportive of the differences in individuals, but what are diversity, equity, and inclusion?

Diversity, Equity, and Inclusion[1]

Diversity refers to who is represented in the workforce, such as gender diversity (men, women, and nonbinary), age diversity (mix of different age groups/generations), ethnic diversity (different backgrounds represented), and physical ability and neurodiversity (people with visible or not visible disabilities).

Equity refers to fair treatment for all people, so that the norms, practices, and policies in place ensure identity does not affect opportunities.

Inclusion refers to experiences in the workplace and how the employer allows them to make meaningful contributions and feel as though their voices are heard.

The following statistics taken from a McKinsey & Company survey help identify the problem of diversity, equity, and inclusion in the workplace[2]:

- Nearly 40% of respondents say they have turned down or chosen not to pursue a job because of a perceived lack of inclusion at the organization.

 DOI: 10.4324/9781003402718-144

- Over 30% of respondents say their organizations don't put enough effort into creating a diverse, inclusive environment (while only 6% say too much is being done).
- 84% of respondents say they have experienced microaggressions at work. More than one in four say they have needed to correct others' assumptions about their personal lives, for example. High levels of respondents have experienced everyday slights rooted in bias, such as not receiving credit for their ideas, being asked to speak as a representative for a group of people like themselves, or being coached to communicate in a way that feels inauthentic.
- Looking only at LGBTQ+ respondents, 37% say they have had an uncomfortable experience coming out to colleagues in the preceding month.
- Among respondents who identified as racial or ethnic minorities, 40% of those who indicated they have discussed identity-related issues at work in the preceding month say they have felt at least slightly uncomfortable in those situations.

The core values of an organization must include diversity, equity, and inclusion in the workplace. It is more than just making someone feel as though they belong. Each individual should feel free to be able to contribute their unique perspectives on issues in the workplace without fear of ridicule or embarrassment. Companies that make diversity, equity, and inclusion a priority will see increased employee retention and greater problem-solving skills. This will in turn lead to increased profitability and greater customer satisfaction.

Notes

1 What is diversity, equity, and inclusion? Retrieved on October 22, 2023 from: https://www.mckinsey.com/featured-insights/mckinsey-explainers/what-is-diversity-equity-and-inclusion
2 Ibid.

Chapter 143

Dealing with the Press or News Media after an On-Site Incident

After you have notified the police about an incident or a crime, the press or news media may contact you to attempt to get additional information. You must not jeopardize the investigation or place anyone in danger by providing unauthorized information.

A security officer who is valued in the workplace for their friendly and helpful demeanor can sometimes be too talkative with the press or news media and unwittingly provide background details and information for a story. Just as damaging, a security officer who "stonewalls" and comes across as uncooperative or defensive can irritate journalists and make his/her employer or customer appear unsympathetic.

To ensure that the situation is handled appropriately:

- There should be a designated spokesperson already in place.
- Act professionally. Be calm, polite, and helpful, offering to bring the journalist's questions to the attention of the spokesperson.
- Avoid speculation. Make it clear that you are not qualified to respond on the company's behalf. Stick to the media brief you have hopefully been given by management.
- Ensure you don't inadvertently provide information to the press or news media.
- Never release information about your employer, your customer, or facts about the incident.
- Ensure you do not release names or details about the crime or incident.

 DOI: 10.4324/9781003402718-145

- Information should only be released by the designated spokesperson.
- Do not allow press or news media members to enter the building or access the property because the scene may be compromised.

Some Basic Guidelines If You Are the Contact Person

1. Be sure to write down everything. Read the news release several times to ensure you're happy with it and are well aware of the content.
2. If it has been announced that the press conference will be at 3 pm, don't be late. Be prompt.
3. Be accurate. Double-check all of the facts in your speech – including the dates, time, names, and facts.
4. Be accurate. Be honest. Be Brief. Be business-like and Professional.

Don't

- Don't plead or request the reporters to cover the story.
- Don't push old news items that happened last week.
- Don't ever offer news media gifts of any kind.

Good vs. Bad Delivery

Characteristics of Good Delivery

1. Prompt start time.
2. Visual aids lined up and ready to use.
3. Be professional in appearance and behavior.
4. Show your ability to communicate clearly by delivering an informative message.
5. Take questions from the group to show you're a good listener on all issues.

Characteristics of a Bad Delivery

1. Not starting on time.
2. Being poorly introduced.
3. Poor appearance.
4. Lack of clarity and being vague on issues
5. Not making your point clear
6. Don't tell jokes

Chapter 144

Managing in the Age of Technology

Some managers may be intimidated by the word technology. During our careers, we have seen many changes. For example, we have gone from a simple doorbell to a smart doorbell that transmits to your cell phone a live video of who is at your door. Technology advances on an almost daily basis.

It is important that security officers be tech-savvy and comfortable with change. Manual processes are being replaced with technology to improve operations. Training needs to be conducted to ensure security officers can use devices to perform tasks that make them more efficient. In the past, there were very minimal requirements for security officers. Still, daily duties involve the use of mobile devices, cloud software, drones, cameras, and biometric access control systems. Research indicates that approximately 16% of security officers use drone technology and 60% plan to implement it in the future.[1] Smartphones are now used to perform key job duties such as scheduling and clocking in and out of shifts. Reports can be created on smartphones, and patrols can be verified. Managers can oversee operations in real time as reports are created, and patrols are conducted. Instead of paper files, reports are stored "in the cloud," and "pass-on" logs are virtual. Biometrics are becoming more common for access control, and security officers need to understand how facial recognition, hand geometry, retinal scans, and fingerprint technology work. Biometrics are unique physical characteristics that can be used for automated recognition.[2]

Consider the following:

1. Set a general policy that leads security officers to explore opportunities for organizational learning and change.

DOI: 10.4324/9781003402718-146

2. Develop online training and video call technologies followed up by open discussion and in-person exercises.
3. The world is becoming more turbulent than ever before. Physical security is changing with advanced technology capabilities. Foster organizational learning so responsibilities will be redefined to include specialist staffing.
4. Ensure that you understand the effect of technology on how you perform your job duties, such as interpreting security reports that include analytics and artificial intelligence.
5. And most importantly, educate yourself!

Technology will continue to improve the security officer industry, and the right technology can help improve job efficiency and safety.

Notes

1 Security Guard Industry and the Technology Evolution. Retrieved on 02-20-23 from: https://parkcommunity.com/personal/services/

2 Biometric. Retrieved on 02-20-23 from: https://www.dhs.gov/biometrics

Chapter 145

Leadership vs. Management

Leadership differs from management, but not for the reasons most people think. Leadership isn't mystical and mysterious. It has nothing to do with having charisma or other exotic personality traits. It is not the province of a chosen few. Nor is leadership necessarily better than management or a replacement for it. Rather, leadership and management are two distinctive and complementary systems of action. Each has its function and characteristic activities. Both are necessary for success in today's business environment.

Management is about coping with complexity. Its practices and procedures are largely in response to the emergence of large, complex organizations in the twentieth century. Leadership, by contrast, is about coping with change. Part of the reason it has become so important in recent years is that the business world has become more competitive and more volatile. More change always demands more leadership.

Our opinion is that most US corporations today are over-managed and underled. Organizations need to develop their capacity to exercise leadership. Successful corporations don't wait for leaders to come along. They actively seek out people with leadership potential and expose them to career experiences designed to develop that potential. Indeed, with careful selection, nurturing, and encouragement, dozens of people can play important leadership roles in a business organization. But while improving their ability to lead, companies should remember that strong leadership with weak management is no better, and is sometimes actually worse, than the reverse. The real challenge is to combine strong leadership and strong management and use each to balance the other.

DOI: 10.4324/9781003402718-147

Public Relations and the Art of Service

What is your favorite restaurant and why? Consider this – last week, we went to a restaurant in the neighborhood. We were greeted at the door by the owner. We introduced the people who were with us. The Italian meal was great, the service and drinks as well, and the owner stopped by the table to confirm we all were happy with the service and the meal. We know everyone has had bad experiences at restaurants, but, if it's a *bad experience* do you go back? "NO!"

Let's say, for example, that a security officer works at the front desk of a large office building. He/she answers the phone and talks with people in person, not realizing that they are being judged by everyone who overhears every conversation. Most people never comment on whether or not it was a good experience or a bad experience. Consider the following points:

1. **Command presence** – A security officer is an authority figure and if someone has a question or a problem, they will expect the security officer to have the solution. The question is, was the issue handled swiftly and appropriately?
2. **Communicating with angry people** – A security officer should reply in a clear but soft tone of voice. If an individual is upset or angry, the first objective should be not only to help them but also to calm them down.
3. **Communication** – A security officer should listen very closely to the requests being made, to pleas for help and assistance, and also listen closely to instructions.
4. **Dealing with mentally ill persons** – A security officer should remember to not always assume the worst of conditions. Instead, be protective, understanding, and helpful.
5. **Defusing conflict and crisis** – A security officer should ask questions if they don't understand something.
6. **Engaging the customer** – A security officer should always act in a professional manner.
7. **Lobby or reception area** – A security officer should always remember that many times they are working in a public space and their professionalism is always on display.
8. **Lost children** – A security officer should treat this as an emergency procedure that needs to be practiced and followed.
9. **Tactical communications** – A security officer should be professional and direct when transmitting on the radio or cell phone.
10. **Public relations** – A security officer should remember that professionalism is 100% of their job.

Chapter 146

How Secure Is Your Security Operation?[1]

A former surgical resident impersonated a physician and gained access to restricted areas to observe surgical procedures and participate in patient rounds at Brigham and Women's Hospital in Boston, MA. Cheryl Wang, who was previously dismissed from a residency program in New York City, wandered into operating rooms in official Brigham scrubs she was thought to have obtained from a previous visit. Although Brigham staff is required to scan their identification badges to enter operation rooms, Wang slipped into the surgical suites by walking in behind other employees who were holding the door open for each other. Following the security breach, the hospital has strengthened its policy for allowing observers into its operating rooms. Physicians are now required to verify that a doctor-in-training is in good standing with his or her educational institution. The hospital also plans to educate staff about the dangers of "tailgating," or letting people follow staff into restricted areas without scanning an ID card. Electronic card access and surveillance cameras are considered security best practices, but hospital security experts are considering other safeguards, including turnstiles, security officers, and biometric systems.

We have always felt that if someone looked professional, greeted others, and gave the impression that they "fit in," they could gain access practically anywhere. We frequently get to test our theory because some organizations want penetration testing conducted to determine whether or not their access control policies and procedures are effective. We were doing such an exercise at a country club in California at 3:00 pm on a Sunday. As we drove to the guard house, the security officer on duty waved as he let us in. Another time, while assessing a school, the facilities manager took us to the third floor of the administration building, pointed to different offices, and said, "This is the president's area, the VP's office is over there, the controller is there,

 DOI: 10.4324/9781003402718-148

and my office is at the other end. This is a secure area, so you don't have to worry about this part of the building." When we returned later that night, we took the elevator to the second floor, walked down the hall to the freight elevator, and pushed the third-floor button. We were not surprised when the elevator door opened, and we were in the "secure area." We entered the facility manager's unlocked office and left a note on his desk. **So, How Secure is Your Security Operation?**

Note

1 The Intruder in the Brigham OR - How Did She Get There? Retrieved on February 8, 2017 from: https://www.bostonglobe.com/metro/2017/02/04/dressed-scrubs-she-roamed-hospital-but-she-wasn-supposed-there/3OkuPYs4PklE3MGdeLirhM/story.html

Chapter 147

US Bureau of Labor Statistics: Security Guards (Aka: SECURITY OFFICERS)

Occupational Employment and Wage Statistics, May 2022[1]

33-9032 Security Guards

Guard, patrol, or monitor premises to prevent theft, violence, or infractions of rules. May operate X-ray and metal detector equipment. Excludes "Police Officers" (33-3050) and "Transportation Security Screeners" (33-9093).

Tables 147.1 and 147.2 are several statistics related to US national estimates for security guard roles and pay.

Tables 147.3–147.5 are industry profiles for security guards.

Table 147.1 Employment estimate and mean wage estimates for security guards.

Employment	*Employment RSE*	*Mean hourly wage*	*Mean annual wage*	*Wage RSE*
1,124,890	0.4 %	$ 17.64	$ 36,700	0.3 %

DOI: 10.4324/9781003402718-149

Table 147.2 Percentile wage estimates for security guards.

Percentile	*10%*	*25%*	*50% (Median)*	*75%*	*90%*
Hourly wage	$ 11.55	$ 13.88	$ 16.71	$ 18.96	$ 24.69
Annual wage	$ 24,020	$ 28,860	$ 34,750	$ 39,440	$ 51,350

Table 147.3 Industries with the highest levels of employment in security guards.

Industry	*Employment*	*Percent of industry employment*	*Hourly mean wage*	*Annual mean wage*
Investigation and security services	690,810	72.83	$ 16.67	$ 34,660
General medical and surgical hospitals	42,610	0.76	$ 19.83	$ 41,240
Elementary and secondary schools	40,190	0.48	$ 19.96	$ 41,520
Traveler accommodation	31,750	1.88	$ 18.16	$ 37,780
General merchandise retailers	26,730	0.83	$ 15.87	$ 33,020

Table 147.4 Industries with the highest concentration of employment in security guards.

Industry	*Employment*	*Percent of industry employment*	*Hourly mean wage*	*Annual mean wage*
Investigation and security services	690,810	72.83	$ 16.67	$ 34,660
Gambling industries	13,530	6.71	$ 16.45	$ 34,210

(Continued)

Table 147.4 (Continued)

Industry	*Employment*	*Percent of industry employment*	*Hourly mean wage*	*Annual mean wage*
Monetary authorities – Central Bank	1,180	5.62	$ 30.44	$ 63,310
Promoters of performing arts, sports, and similar events	7,490	5.38	$ 19.31	$ 40,160
Drinking places (alcoholic beverages)	15,460	3.92	$ 14.31	$ 29,760

Table 147.5 Top paying industries for security guards.

Industry	*Employment*	*Percent of industry employment*	*Hourly mean wage*	*Annual mean wage*
Other heavy and civil engineering construction	80	0.07	$ 42.95	$ 89,330
Jewelry, luggage, and leather goods retailers	580	0.47	$ 34.94	$ 72,680
Scientific research and development services	1,680	0.19	$ 31.26	$ 65,020
Monetary authorities – Central Bank	1,180	5.62	$ 30.44	$ 63,310
Electric power generation, transmission, and distribution	3,960	1.05	$ 29.97	$ 62,330

Note

1 Occupational Employment and Wage Statistics. Retrieved on October 27, 2023 from: https://www.bls.gov/oes/current/oes339032.htm

Chapter 148

Change and the Visionary

Some people hate change. If you move security officer Smith from the front desk to the shipping area and move security officer Jones from the shipping area to the front desk, you may have two unhappy security officers. Determine where your security officers will "fit" within the organization and assign them to areas that suit their talents and personalities. Work toward helping them succeed in the organization.

If you move investigators who have been on the first floor where they could come and go and move about the campus freely and place them on the fifth floor with administration where they are expected to be at their desks, you may have unhappy employees struggling to adjust to a different environment.

Similarly, rather than adjust to change, some police officers retire when a new commissioner or chief comes in and wants to run the department differently than to which they have become accustomed. They may use the old adage that they are "too old to change" when the real reason is that they fear the unknown or may be concerned that they will lose some "status" in the organization. It's the uncertainty of the changes that make them uncomfortable.

Retaining professional, quality security officers is cost-efficient and healthy for the organization rather than being in a constant hiring and training mode. It will help the security department run more efficiently and stabilize the organization. Trained, experienced security officers are valuable. Take care of them! The lives of employees and the assets of the organization depend on them.

It's still important to cross-train your security officers. Expose them to different assignments to determine where they excel. Acknowledge when a job is done well and explain why they must be trained to cover different areas. They need to learn to be flexible and that they are a critical part of the security program. Being a team player is an important attribute of a security officer. When someone is sick or on

DOI: 10.4324/9781003402718-150

vacation, the post will still need to be filled by an experienced security officer who has been trained for that position. When an untrained security officer "fills in" but has not been trained for the post, it jeopardizes everyone.

Embrace change and teach those within your organization to adapt to change and accept new responsibilities. The integrity of your security program depends on it.

Chapter 149

Raising the Bar for Security Officers

In the past, being a security officer was "just a job you did until something better came along." That is no longer the case. Being a security officer is now a career and opportunities are becoming more lucrative. Education, technology, and security certifications have increased the level of professionalism in the industry. Security "guards" are no longer needed or wanted. Organizations want knowledgeable, competent individuals who are working toward developing their careers in the changing security industry. Well-trained professional security officers are the next generation of the security industry.

The Future of a Career as a Security Officer

1. Security certifications through ASIS International and the International Foundation for Protection Officers (IFPO) are becoming a requirement, not an option, because security positions are becoming more specialized.
2. Virtual tours have replaced walking/vehicle patrol procedures in many locations.
3. Hiring processes are becoming more competitive with an emphasis on education, training, and experience and "fitting" the job candidate with the security program needs.
4. Post-high-school education/training is required and security officers must possess above-average computer skills and be proficient with different forms of technology.

DOI: 10.4324/9781003402718-151

5. Training is ongoing with the increased use of online and virtual training platforms.
6. Educational opportunities are available that enable a security officer to specialize in different aspects of security, such as becoming a subject matter expert in cybersecurity, physical security, electronic security, or Crime Prevention Through Environmental Design (CPTED).
7. Situational awareness, which is not a new concept, is necessary and is used throughout the security industry to increase individual and overall organizational security performance and improve crime prevention efforts.
8. A professional security officer must have the ability to understand that competency models are being used as a template for enterprise security which is a holistic approach to look at the "big picture" for security processes and integration.
9. A career in the security industry requires a working knowledge of NFPA 730, Guide for Premises Security.
10. Career-minded security officers should strive to be a part of working together as a team with public–private sector partnerships, including law enforcement, to increase workplace and community safety.
11. Remember that education is ongoing, and training and education together make for a much more robust security officer.
12. Crisis management begins with you; always keep your situational awareness at the forefront.

Times have changed in the security industry since the events of 9/11 and we must also change in order to stay in step with the changing needs of the security industry.

Chapter 150

There Is Hope for the Future of the Security Industry

The future looks strong worldwide for the private security industry.

According to US labor statistics, there are over 1.1 million private security officers in the United States compared to 666,000 police officers. *Globally*, there is still a trend of needing more private security firms than law enforcement officers. India has an estimated 7 million private security workers compared to just 1.4 million police officers. Likewise, in China, approximately 5 million people are employed in private security compared to a police force of 2.7 million.[1]

The events of 9/11, along with more recent acts of terrorism and civil unrest throughout the world have increased the need for security officers. Security officers represent the company, the property owner/manager or the client, and law enforcement officers represent a government agency. The days are gone when security officers were considered "guards" who were unprofessional, paid low wages, had little or no training, and provided poor customer service. Unfortunately, many times the appearance of the "guard" of the past perpetuated this perception. The security officer of today is better educated and better trained than at any other time. This evolution is because of the greater need for private security and companies' demand for a higher caliber, more professional individual to be the "face" of their organization.

The demand for competent, professional, and trained security officers is growing. This is in part because of the growing crime and terrorism threats throughout the world. There will always be a need for protection, but currently, law enforcement is stretched too thin. Law enforcement agencies throughout the United States are

DOI: 10.4324/9781003402718-152

understaffed. They simply cannot possibly provide the level of protection required for private companies and individuals. Security officers are willingly filling this void. People have come to rely on security officers to protect them and make them "feel" safe. Law enforcement agencies are primarily a "reactive" force meaning that they respond after something has occurred.A police presence may be somewhat of a deterrence to criminals, but professional, well-trained security officers can many times be a more "proactive" presence as well as a crime deterrent.

Professional security organizations like ASIS International and IFPO have changed their membership strategies to attract more members. The security profession has always had its ups and downs. Still, things are moving forward in the security industry, and jobs are being accepted as careers instead of "just a paycheck until something better comes along." The demand for experienced security officers with professional certifications from ASIS International and IFPO is increasing.

We must continue to be proactive in our thinking to move the security industry forward. The choice is yours – do nothing or make a change and become a true security professional.

Note

1 Law enforcement versus private security in the United States. Retrieved on October 29, 2023 from: https://www.securitymagazine.com/blogs/14-security-blog/post/96189-law-enforcement-versus-private-security-in-the-united-states#:~:text=According%20to%20U.S.%20labor%20statistics,firms%20than%20law%20enforcement%20officers

Index

Pages in *italics* refer to figures and pages in **bold** refer to tables.

D

E

F

G

H

Printed in the United States
by Baker & Taylor Publisher Services